A.S.A. MONOGRAPHS

General Editor: MICHAEL BANTON

3

Anthropological Approaches
to the Study of Religion

ANTHROPOLOGICAL
APPROACHES TO THE
STUDY OF RELIGION

Edited by Michael Banton

FREDERICK A. PRAEGER, *Publishers*

NEW YORK · WASHINGTON

Published in the United States of America in 1966
by Frederick A. Praeger, Inc., Publishers
111 Fourth Avenue, New York 3, N.Y.
First Published in 1966
© Association of Social Anthropologists of the
Commonwealth, 1966
Library of Congress Catalog Card Number: 65-16223
Printed in Great Britain by T. & A. Constable Ltd.
Edinburgh

This volume derives from material presented at a Conference on
'New Approaches in Social Anthropology' sponsored by the
Association of Social Anthropologists of the Commonwealth, held
at Jesus College, Cambridge, 24-30 June 1963.

IN MEMORIAM

A. R. RADCLIFFE-BROWN

FIRST CHAIRMAN AND LIFE PRESIDENT

OF THE ASSOCIATION OF SOCIAL ANTHROPOLOGISTS

OF THE COMMONWEALTH

Contents

MAX GLUCKMAN and FRED EGGAN
Introduction   *page* xi

CLIFFORD GEERTZ
Religion as a Cultural System   1
    I   1
    II   3
      1 *a system of symbols*   4
      2 *establishing powerful, pervasive, and longlasting
        moods and motivations*   8
      3 *formulating conceptions of a general order of
        existence*   12
      4 *clothing those conceptions with such an aura of
        factuality that*   24
      5 *the moods and motivations seem uniquely realistic*   35
    III   40
    Notes   42
    Acknowledgements   43
    References   44

VICTOR W. TURNER
Colour Classification in Ndembu Ritual   47
    Colour classification in African ritual   47
    Colour classification in Ndembu life-crisis ritual   49
    Colour classification in Ngonde life-crisis ritual   55
    Colour classification and the high god in Central Africa   57
    The Ndembu interpretation of the colour triad   58
      White   58
      Red   59
      Black   60
      Commentary on the black symbolism   61
    The white-black contrast   64
      The characteristics of the colours white and red   64
      (a) *Whiteness*   64
      (b) *Redness*   68

vii

Contents

White and red as a binary system — 70
Some comparative data — 72
  Africa — 72
  Malay Peninsula — 74
  Australia — 74
  North American Indian — 75
  The Ancient World — 75
  Commentary — 76
The three colours in archaeological literature — 77
The significance of the basic colour triad — 79
Notes — 83
References — 83

MELFORD E. SPIRO
Religion: Problems of Definition and Explanation — 85
  Introduction — 85
  The problem of definition in religion — 87
  A definition of 'religion' — 96
  Explanation in social anthropology — 98
  The 'truth' of religious beliefs — 101
  The practice of religious belief — 106
    Needs — 107
    Functions — 108
      Cognitive — 109
      Substantive — 112
      Expressive — 114
  Causal and functional explanations — 117
  Conclusion — 121
  Notes — 123
  Acknowledgement — 124
  References — 125

R. E. BRADBURY
Fathers, Elders, and Ghosts in *Ẹdo* Religion — 127
  The *Ẹdo* village — 129
  Categories of the dead — 130
  'Fathers' and 'elders' in the lineage context — 133
  'Elders' of the village — 139
  References — 153

Contents

EDWARD H. WINTER

Territorial Groupings and Religion among the Iraqw   155
    Introduction   155
    The Iraqw   157
    Conclusion   171
    References   174
Notes on Contributors   175

Max Gluckman and Fred Eggan

Introduction

The several disciplines of modern anthropology – prehistoric archaeology, physical anthropology, social or sociological anthropology, cultural anthropology, and psychological anthropology – have separated out of a general anthropology which in the second half of the nineteenth century and into the twentieth century aimed to study man both as a biological and as a social being. There are still many general anthropologists, mainly in the United States but also in Europe; and the various aspects of anthropology are still taught in many universities as a combined degree. Nevertheless, by the 1930s the different disciplines were beginning to separate from one another, though some scholars were still eminent in more than one discipline. As each anthropological discipline separated out, its practitioners turned to other subjects, whose techniques and modes of analysis were more appropriate to their problems than were those of their erstwhile colleagues. Physical anthropologists depended more on the biological sciences; psychological anthropologists (who studied the interaction of culture and personality) on psychology, especially depth psychology, and psychiatry; and social anthropologists on sociology, history, political science, law, and economics. Cultural anthropologists alone continued to draw on the biological, psychological, and sociological sciences.

Outwardly the common mark of social, cultural, and psychological anthropology was that they all continued to be comparative and cross-cultural in outlook, with an emphasis on the small-scale tribal societies of the world; and for many years the study of such a society was virtually the initiation ceremony which admitted a scholar into the ranks of anthropology. Hence all anthropologists felt they had something in common, besides their joint membership in such organizations as the

American Anthropological Association and the Royal Anthropological Institute of Great Britain and Ireland.

We believe they had something more in common, drawn from their traditional unity, besides their previous, almost unique, concentration on the tribal societies. This was a continuing focusing of interest on *customs*, as having an interrelated dependence on one another, whether in forming cultural patterns, or in operating within systems of social relations, or in the structuring of various types of personality in different groups. This focus on customs in interdependence has continued to distinguish the disciplines of anthropology from the other subjects with which each branch is increasingly associated. The analysis of custom remains one of the distinctive contributions of all anthropological studies to the human sciences.

The extent to which anthropologists specialized in one or other aspect of the general subject varied in different countries. In Great Britain, the trend has steadily moved more and more to distinctive specialization as an archaeologist, a physical anthropologist, or a sociological-social anthropologist. In Oxford and Cambridge, where anthropology has been longest taught, regulations provide for general anthropological qualifications, but it is possible for students to qualify entirely in social anthropology and other social sciences, or at most to have minimal tuition in other types of anthropology. Compulsory training on the biological side is perhaps strongest for social anthropological specialists at University College, London. At other London colleges, and at the other British universities where social anthropology has been established since the last war, the subject has usually been placed in social science faculties or departments, with sociology, economics, and political science. In a few universities only are links strong with geography or psychology within a combined Honours degree.

The British Honours degree necessarily leads, except for the Cambridge Tripos system, to a reduction in the types of other subjects that can be taken by undergraduates specializing in social anthropology. This process does not operate in the American undergraduate schools of anthropology, and hence at that level students who wish to become social anthropologists take a much greater variety of subjects, and the anthropology they are taught tends to continue to cover several branches of the subject. This naturally influences graduate schools of anthropology, since their products have to be able to teach in more than one branch of anthropology, if they are appointed to small colleges (see Mandelbaum, Lasker, and Albert, 1963).

Nevertheless, in the United States most anthropologists are becoming as specialized as they are in British universities, and are correspondingly associating with various cognate disciplines according to their type of specialization. Owing to the greater size of the country, and the far greater number of universities and of anthropologists, there is in the United States a greater variety of types of anthropologist than in the British Commonwealth. It is in the States that cultural and psychological anthropology flourish in addition to the social anthropology, physical anthropology, linguistics, and prehistoric archaeology that are represented in Britain. The flourishing of these several branches of anthropology in the States is probably fertilized, too, by the absence of the Honours degree system: there is a more varied interdisciplinary contact, which continues beyond the undergraduate level.

The increasing specialization of British social anthropologists with a decreasing interest on their part in prehistoric archaeology, physical anthropology, and cultural anthropology, in 1946 led the practitioners of the subject in Britain – then under a score – to form the Association of Social Anthropologists of the Commonwealth. Though they wished still to support the Royal Anthropological Institute, they considered that they had specific and limited interests, sufficiently distinct from those of general anthropology to require the support of a specific organization. This has meant, for example, that social anthropologists in Britain have had an organized means of giving evidence on their own problems to commissions advising the British Government on higher education and research, besides evidence given by the Royal Anthropological Institute for anthropology in general. The process of *partial* separation from general anthropology continued until, in 1960, the social anthropologists joined with sociologists and social psychologists to form a new Sociology Section of the British Association for the Advancement of Science. Two of the five presidents of the Section to date have been social anthropologists. Social anthropologists still participate in the older Anthropology and Archaeology Section, but they submit more papers to, and attend in greater numbers at, meetings of the new section.

Between 1946 and 1962 the Association of Social Anthropologists of the Commonwealth increased its membership from under a score to over one hundred and fifty, even though election to membership required normally both the holding of a teaching or research post in the Commonwealth and the attainment of either a post-graduate degree (usually a doctorate) or substantial publication. Meetings of the Association in Britain ceased to be small gatherings of perhaps a dozen people, and were attended by between thirty and sixty members.

In 1962 Professor Raymond Firth, then Chairman of the Association, proposed that it should try to raise the funds to invite a dozen American social anthropologists to one of its meetings. He suggested that since the milieux in which American social anthropologists worked were so much more varied than the milieu of British social anthropologists, it would be profitable to see what was common between us and where we differed, in a series of papers on 'New Approaches in Social Anthropology'. He pointed out that though there were many individual contacts between some members of the Association and American colleagues, many British and Americans had not met one another: moreover, we had never had a joint, organized stocktaking. He further suggested that papers should be read only by scholars who had entered the subject since the war: so the phrase 'new approaches' signifies that the papers collected in these four volumes present the problems and views of a younger generation of anthropologists.

When the Association enthusiastically adopted Firth's proposal, there was no corresponding organization of social anthropologists in the U.S.A. with whom there could be discussions and arrangements. The Association therefore more or less thrust on Professor Fred Eggan of the University of Chicago the task of representing American social anthropologists. It did so for several reasons, besides his own standing as a social anthropologist. The late Professor A. R. Radcliffe-Brown, who had been for the first years of the Association's existence its Life President, and to whose memory this series of A.S.A. Monographs is dedicated, had taught at Chicago from 1931 to 1937. Eggan had succeeded, so to speak, to Radcliffe-Brown's position, and under the Roman rule of universal succession might be regarded as representing him. Above all, under Radcliffe-Brown's influence there had developed in Chicago perhaps the strongest single group of *social* anthropologists in the U.S.A. Eggan agreed to help organize the meeting, but insisted, of course, that his British colleagues should select the dozen American scholars whom they wished to hear. With great difficulty, the British, eventually by vote, chose a dozen from the large number they would have liked to invite. If there seems a bias to Chicago, or Chicago-trained Americans (as one or two of the others rather ironically suggested), the British are responsible, and not Eggan. The American Anthropological Association agreed to sponsor a request for support, and the National Science Foundation generously financed the Americans' journey to Britain.

The programme, to which twice as many British as Americans contributed papers, was divided into four main sections. Two to three papers were presented in a group, and discussion was then opened by either an American or a British anthropologist – again, those opening the discussions were selected from the post-war generation, though more senior anthropologists were allowed to join in the general discussion. But these Monographs are not a report on the proceedings of the Conference. They embody theoretical papers by twenty younger anthropologists, who have amended their arguments, where they felt it necessary, after listening to the comments of their colleagues. Effectively the papers present, therefore, growing-points in social anthropology as seen by a new generation of practitioners.

Two years passed between the time when Firth, as Chairman of the Association, made his original proposal, and the meeting itself, which was held in Jesus College, Cambridge, in June 1963. By that time Gluckman had succeeded Firth as Chairman, and on him, and the yet-again conscribed Eggan, has fallen the task of introducing the Monographs. It has been a difficult task: the papers cover a range of ethnographic areas and of problems which they cannot themselves compass competently.

Hence this Introduction makes no attempt to assess the substantive problems and solutions suggested in the papers. Instead, it tries to pull together the kinds of issue which crop up as interesting the contributors in several of the papers.

There was also a major technical difficulty. The papers are published in four separate volumes, covering, respectively:

1. The relevance of models for social anthropology;
2. Political systems and the distribution of power;
3. Anthropological approaches to the study of religion;
4. The social anthropology of complex societies.

Since the Introduction was planned to cut across all four volumes, we decided to write a single text and print it in each volume. Various readers may approach the series through any of the four. The arabic figures 1, 2, 3, and 4 indicate in which of the monographs is located an essay referred to in the Introduction.

SPECIALIZATION AND SPREAD: LINKS WITH THE SOCIAL SCIENCES

The specialization of social anthropologists in a separate discipline, and the extent to which they have turned to sociology and political science, are particularly marked in these monographs. This is not surprising in the volumes on political problems (2) and on complex societies, including both peasantries and urban areas (4), where the problems dealt with are common to the three disciplines. As it happens, the other disciplines that are commonly grouped in the social sciences – economics and law – are not cited.

This is partly a matter of chance. We could provide for only a limited number of papers, and arrangements had been made to have a paper on the use of economic models in social anthropology by Mrs Lorraine Baric; but at the crucial time she went to Yugoslavia to do field-research.

Two papers do deal with 'economic problems', in the widest but not the technical sense of 'economics'. The first is by Marshall Sahlins, 'On The Sociology of Primitive Exchange', in Monograph 1. Though by its title this might be thought to deal with economic problems, its actual emphasis is on 'sociology'. It considers types of exchange in terms of degrees of reciprocity as these alter along a scale of contexts of tribal social relations, from the most personal to the least personal – if we reduce a complex analysis to a single sentence. Sahlins makes no reference to economic theorizing as such, and indeed part of the discussion of his paper turned on this point.

Eric Wolf carries out a somewhat similar analysis of morphological changes in 'Kinship, Friendship, and Patron-Client Relations in Complex Societies' (4). In this essay, Wolf examines the kinds of situation in terms of ecological and economic situations in which kinship, friendship, and patron-client relationships respectively are dominant outside the nuclear family. No more than with Sahlins, would one expect this problem to lead Wolf into the use of economic theory as such. Save for one citation from Schumpeter, he does not rely on the economists.

The absence of reference to economic theory in the papers hence means that one approach, whether it be new or old, is not covered in these four monographs. We think it is true to say that technical economics has had less influence on social anthropological research than other social sciences have had, possibly because of its highly abstract nature. In the Register of the Association of Social Anthropologists less than 3 in a 100 members list 'economics' among their special interests, and there are also few specialists in the U.S.A. Yet before the war, among other senior anthropologists, Firth, originally trained as an economist, had used the technical concepts of economics to good effect for a tribal society in his *Primitive Polynesian Economy* (1939) and, after the War, for a peasant society in his *Malay Fishermen* (1946). More recently, a number of younger anthropologists, some with training in economics, have used this training impressively. But this is perhaps more marked among those who have studied peasant societies than among those who have studied tribes, as is shown, perhaps, in *Capital, Saving and Credit in Peasant Societies* (Firth & Yamey (eds.), 1964), a symposium containing essays by nine younger British social anthropologists, by four Americans, and by one Norwegian who was trained partly in Britain.

The Association of Social Anthropologists hopes in the near future to publish a monograph in which the use of theoretical economics in recent work by British scholars will be considered.

When these symposia were planned, arrangements had also been made to have at least one paper on problems in the field of law. Illness prevented P. J. Bohannan from preparing this. The absence of any treatment of tribal law, and more generally of processes of social control, does not reflect the extent to which these problems have interested social anthropologists in recent decades, particularly since the publication of Llewellyn and Hoebel's *The Cheyenne Way: Conflict and Case Law in Primitive Jurisprudence* (1941). That book, and Hoebel's earlier work, inspired a number of studies on jurisprudential problems, particularly on juristic method in the judicial or arbitral process, among both American and British social anthropologists. This work has drawn largely, if sometimes indirectly, on American sociological jurisprudence. This field of research is therefore not covered in the Monographs.

Here, then, are two social sciences not drawn on for this symposium.

References outside those to the work of social anthropologists are clearly most numerous to sociologists – for example, to sociometric work and to the work of the sociologists Ginsberg, Homans and W. F. Whyte, by Adrian Mayer in his treatment of 'The Significance of Quasi-Groups in the Study of Complex Societies' (4). J. Clyde Mitchell in the same volume discusses 'Theoretical Orientations in African Urban Studies' and he begins by stating that 'differences in behaviour as between people in the town and in the country have for long been the topic of study of sociologists and other social scientists in Europe and America . . .'. Though Mitchell cites only a few of these sociologists, their work clearly has influenced not only Mitchell, but also the numerous other anthropologists who have studied urban areas in Africa and who are cited by Mitchell.

But it would seem that, leaving aside Durkheim, whose school's influence on social anthropology has always been marked, the influence of Weber on younger social anthropologists in recent years has been considerable. If anything, that influence is under-represented in these essays: it has been very marked in a number of monographs, as in L. A. Fallers's *Bantu Bureaucracy* (no date: about 1956). With the influence of Weber – and partly inspired by his writings – goes the influence of Talcott Parsons among modern sociologists.

Perhaps the most cited and influential of modern sociologists in these monographs is R. K. Merton. His discussions of levels of theory, and of the distinction between manifest and latent functions, have always been exploited by anthropologists; and Melford Spiro uses them in his essay on religion in Monograph 3. But generally it is the increasing interest in the more meticulous analysis of social roles (referred to below) which inspired the writers to draw on Merton's treatment of role-sets – Ward Goodenough in 'Rethinking "Status" and "Role"' (1), Aidan Southall on roles in different political systems (2), and Ronald Frankenberg in an essay on the changing structure of roles in different types of British communities (3), use Merton, appreciatively and critically.

Parsons too has influenced anthropologists' thinking about this key concept. There are also indications of a growing importance here of the work of Erving Goffman – himself influenced by the work of social anthropologists – on how people operate their roles. Goodenough has drawn markedly on Goffman's books on *The Presentation of Self in Everyday Life* (1959) and *Encounters* (1961). Frankenberg argues that there is a convergence between the ideas of Goffman and those developed in British social anthropology, especially by Barnes, Gluckman, and Turner.

These references must be sufficient to show how much social anthropologists are now drawing on the cognate subject of sociology. The essays thus reflect, in research and analysis, the tendency in both countries for social anthropology and sociology to be taught either in one department or in closely linked departments.

The references above are to certain types of sociology. No essay makes use of demographic analysis – but Mitchell's and a couple of other essays refer to the importance of demographic analysis, which in general has been inadequately used by social anthropologists in their reports on communities. However, it is worth noting here that anthropologists such as Mitchell and

J. A. Barnes have, in their treatment of suitable problems, been contributing to theory in demographic studies.

In their Introduction to *African Political Systems* (1940), Fortes and Evans-Pritchard wrote that: 'We have not found that the theories of political *philosophers* [italics added] have helped us to understand the societies we have studied and we consider them of little scientific value . . .' (at p. 5). At least one reviewer asked why they did not draw on the work of political *scientists*. Since Fortes and Evans-Pritchard, with *African Political Systems*, virtually established 'political anthropology', their successors have turned increasingly to political scientists for assistance in their analysis. We have already cited Fallers's use of Weber's hypotheses in his study of Soga bureaucracy, and many other monographs on political problems have used Weberian ideas as well as works by those who are more specifically political scientists or constitutional historians. Every essay in Monograph 2 refers to works in political science. The most-cited work is Easton's study of *The Political System* (1953), and his article on 'Political Anthropology' in *Biennial Review of Anthropology* (1959). Easton, in Lloyd's words (4), 'took time from his studies of modern societies to examine the progress made by social anthropologists. [Easton] castigates the failure of the anthropologists to develop any broad theoretical orientation to politics, ascribing this to their preoccupation with general problems of social control, conflict, and integration and their reluctance to define the respective limits of political and other – social, religious, economic – systems. Easton offers a classification of African political systems which is based upon the differentiation in political roles. . . .'

We are tempted to point out that in the kinds of societies traditionally studied by social anthropologists political, economic, religious, and social systems are in fact often not differentiated, and to reply that political scientists have not themselves made so clear a definition of political systems. But, reviewing the essays under consideration, Easton's own suggestion about the classification of political systems in terms of differentiation in roles fits in with a main concern of recent anthropology – marked in Aidan Southall's essay on 'A Critique of the Typology of States and Political Systems' (2).

Introduction

For the rest, the social anthropologist in his analysis of political problems seems to turn to whatever source, outside of anthropology, he feels can assist his specific analysis. Thus when F. G. Bailey considers 'Decisions by Consensus in Councils and Committees: with special reference to village and local government in India' (2), he uses work by Morris-Jones, a political scientist, on India; Wheare's now classic survey of *Government by Committee* (1955); a study of contemporary parties and politics in Japan; and F. M. Cornford's witty analysis of Cambridge University politics, *Microcosmographia Academica* (1908). Nicholas, in a comparative analysis of 'Factions' (2), equally uses a small number of political science studies. We are not suggesting that these writers use all – or even the most important – relevant sources from political science: indeed, we ourselves know of others they might have used. We indicate here only that there is a readiness to turn to political science, and Bailey's essay has more references to works by political scientists than to works by other anthropologists. Political anthropology, at least, is linking up with its cognate discipline: and this clearly is not difficult, since the concepts and analytic framework of political science are not too diverse from those of social anthropology. No new techniques have to be learned to master them.

SPECIALIZATION AND SPREAD:
LINKS WITH BIOLOGY, PSYCHOLOGY, AND
CULTURAL ANTHROPOLOGY

In contrast to this turn towards sociology of various kinds and to at least some fields of political science, plus the under-represented use of economics and law, we note relatively few references to cultural anthropology, psychological anthropology, psychology, and the biological sciences. In the volume on religion (3) there are references to the work of Margaret Mead, partly in the particular ethnographic context of Bali in which she worked with Gregory Bateson. This is in Clifford Geertz's essay on 'Religion as a Cultural System'. He begins by stating that the detailed studies of religion in particular societies which have characterized social anthropology are in 'a state of general stagnation', suffering under what 'Janowitz has called the dead hand of competence'. Geertz summarizes the achievements of anthropological study of religion as: 'Yet one more meticulous case-in-point for such well-established propositions as that ancestor worship supports the jural authority of elders, that initiation rites are means for the establishment of sexual identity and adult status, that ritual groupings reflect political oppositions, or that myths provide charters for social institutions and rationalizations of social privilege may well finally convince a great many people, both inside the profession and out, that anthropologists are, like theologians, firmly dedicated to proving the indubitable.'

We do not believe that these summary statements at the opening of Geertz's essay are quite fair assessments of the acute and complicated analyses actually made by social anthropologists of ancestor cults, initiation ceremonies, political rituals, and the social context of myths, exemplified in the three essays on religion in specific societies in the same volume – by V. W. Turner on 'Colour Classification in Ndembu Ritual', by R. Bradbury on 'Fathers, Elders, and Ghosts in Ẹdo Religion', and by E. Winter on 'Territorial Groupings and Religion among the Iraqw'. Geertz has himself written a notable analysis (1960) of a single society's religions.

Geertz is clearly being critical of his own, as well as of his colleagues', work, in order to plead for a much wider treatment of the general 'cultural dimension of religious analysis'. And he is not unique among younger anthropologists in feeling that the social anthropological analysis of religion by itself is inadequate. We take it that this mode of analysis is restricted to examining the role of religion, with emphasis on custom, rite, and belief, in social relations; and we believe that those who follow this procedure realize that they are not explaining 'the whole of religion'. They accept that they are analysing religion in only one of its dimensions, and that other dimensions have to be analysed by other types of discipline, using different techniques and perhaps examining other types of data. Clearly any set of phenomena as complicated as religion – indeed any social complex – for total understanding has to be subjected to investigation by several disciplines.

Introduction

We believe that most social anthropologists would accept
this. Melford Spiro in his essay on 'Religion: Problems of
Definition and Explanation' (3) states in his 'Conclusion' to his
argument 'that an adequate explanation for the persistence of
religion requires both psychological (in this instance, psycho-
analytical) and sociological variables'. Religion, or family
structure, or motivations, can be taken variously as independent
or dependent variables. Spiro continues: 'But many studies of
religion, however, are concerned not with the explanation
of religion, but with the role of religion in the explanation of
society. Here, the explanatory task is to discover the contributions which religion, taken as the independent variable,
makes to societal integration, by its satisfaction of sociological
wants. This is an important task, central to the main concern
of anthropology, as the science of social systems. We seriously
err, however, in mistaking an explanation of society for an
explanation of religion which, in effect, means confusing the
sociological functions of religion with the bases for its performance.' In his introductory paragraphs to his essay on Iraqw
ritual (3) Winter makes the same clarification.

We have cited Spiro at length because it is in the study of
religion that some social anthropologists have manifested a
reluctance to accept that a specifically social anthropological
analysis, giving an admittedly limited explanation, provides
anything like an adequate explanation. The essays by Geertz
and Spiro exhibit some of this feeling, which has appeared also
in work published elsewhere, by Britons as well as Americans.
Where they invoke psychology, not all of them follow Spiro in
calling for some form of depth-psychology. The psychic framework employed may be an intellectualist one, in which the explanatory value for the observers is emphasized, as in the claim
that the difference between tribal and universalistic rituals stems
from the way people in tribal societies construct their model of
the universe on the model they abstract from their own
social relations (Horton, 1964).

Spiro and Winter clarify the issues involved. To understand
religion, in a commonsense use of 'understand', [at least] both
sociological and psychological explanations are required. The
sociological – that is, the social anthropological – analysis alone

is an explanation of the role of religion in social relations; and a psychological analysis alone is an explanation of the role of religion in the functioning of the personality. Nevertheless, we note that there is this dissatisfaction with the limited extent of social anthropological analysis in this field, which does not show in the treatment of political and a number of other problems.

Spiro's remains a general, abstract essay. Geertz's interestingly enough after his castigatory opening, is largely taken up with a penetrating analysis of a specific situation in Java. With all respect, we believe that there is not 'a state of general stagnation' in the subject: the evidence of several monographs shows that social anthropological understanding of religion and ritual in specific societies continues to advance. Geertz calls for a study of symbols: we consider this is illuminatingly achieved in Turner's essay on colour symbolism among the Ndembu. Geertz 'slights' such well-established propositions as that 'ancestor worship supports the jural authority of elders': we consider that Bradbury's essay on the role of ghosts and spirits among the Ẹdo, in a comparative background, and Winter's similar attempt to illuminate the specific variants of spirit-cult organization among the Iraqw, show by contrast how steady, deep, and wide is the penetration of the subject's understanding here.

Moreover, a discipline may advance by the working out logically of basic theoretical propositions, some of which are perhaps based on observation. This applies to theoretical economics and to some aspects of Parsons's theory of action in sociology. Social anthropology has not shown a corresponding development, save perhaps in some of Lévi-Strauss's analyses. Advance may also be achieved by the formulation of a series of propositions, based on observation. In the natural sciences, a number of these propositions have been cumulatively brought under a hierarchy of increasingly embracing laws. Social anthropology, like sociology and political science, has numerous propositions at the first level. It may lack widely embracing laws to cover many of these, but, like sociology and political science, it does have some theories of the middle range, as Merton (1958), with others, has phrased the situation. These middle-range theories are applied within a 'general orientation towards substantive materials' (ibid, pp. 87-88).

The kind of general approach to their data which social anthropologists have developed is illustrated throughout these essays: an insistence by most that there are interdependencies between both social relations and customs, and further associations between these interdependencies. Analysis of these interdependencies is often set in an evolutionary framework, even if it be a morphological rather than a temporal one, as the essays by Sahlins on primitive exchange (1), Wolf on kinship, friendship, and patron-client relations (4), and Mitchell and Frankenberg on the rural to non-rural continuum (4) well illustrate. The same framework is used by Lloyd and Southall, to some extent, in their essays on the typology of political systems (2). Yet social anthropology, judging by these essays, still lacks the kind of fundamental orientation found, for example, in Marxist sociology.

Individual propositions, stated baldly out of the context of this orientation, and of both field situation and corpus of allied propositions, may appear to be truistic – and hence banal. But the skill of anthropologists, like that of practitioners of the cognate disciplines, lies to a large extent still in their ability to apply, and weigh the application of, selected propositions to specific situations. This may be done within a single situation, with comparative checking implicit, or it may be done with occasional explicit comparison, or it may be done outright as a comparative study. On the whole, these procedures, and attempts to develop them with refinement of the basic propositions, appear to us to dominate these essays on 'new approaches' in the subject. The striving is after clarification; elimination of muddles; clearing away of concepts that, though once useful, now appear to be too gross and to block analysis; and the formulation of better theories of the middle range. These tendencies are marked in the essays by Geertz and Spiro, though these are also the only essays which press for, and aim at, much higher-level theories.

One attempt to formulate further theories of the middle range is appropriately referred to in this section on links with psychology and cultural anthropology. Wolf's analysis of the contexts in which kinship, friendship, and patron-client relations are respectively dominant in complex societies (4), is in some respects complementary to Sahlin's essay on the changing contexts of exchange in tribal societies (1): basically, it is *social* anthropological in tackling its problems, with the emphasis on making a living, handling relations with authorities, etc. But at the end of the essay, Wolf suggests that the varying texture of relations with kin, friends, and patrons or clients may have 'a point of encounter with what has sometimes been called the national character approach'. Examining works in this field, he is struck by the fact that 'they have utilized – in the main – data on the interpersonal sets discussed in [his] paper, and on the etiquettes and social idioms governing them'. Wolf cites three instances, and concludes: 'It is obvious that such descriptions and analyses do not cope with the institutional features of national structure. Yet it is equally possible that complex societies in the modern world differ less in the formal organization of their economic or legal or political systems than in the character of their supplementary interpersonal sets. Using the strategy of social anthropology, moreover, we would say that information about these sets is less meaningful when organized in terms of a construct of homogeneous national character, than when referred to the particular body of social relations and its function, partial or general, within the supplementary or parallel structure underlying the formal institutional framework. . . . The integration of the great society requires the knitting of these interstitial relations.'

We have cited Wolf at length because he appears to us explicitly to map in outline common ground between several of the essays which deal with what can be the social anthropological contribution to the study of complex societies. It is clearly accepted that a study of large-scale institutional frameworks such as the economic, or the administrative and political, falls to the lot of economists, political scientists, and sociologists. With this acceptance, goes the assumption, to quote Wolf again, of a possibility 'that complex societies of the modern world differ less in the formal organization of their economic or legal or political system than in the character of their supplementary interpersonal sets'. Anthropologists of all kinds have always been fascinated by the variety of human behaviour, even when they have sought uniformity and generality in that variety. So that aside from their interest in the small-scale, which fits with their techniques of observation, they tend to concentrate on those features of complex – as of tribal – societies where there are some distinctive sets of customs which require to be explained. We think this tendency shows in Bailey's treatment of committees and Nicholas's of factions in modern India (2).

This tendency is particularly marked in Monograph 4, specifically devoted to complex societies. In his essay on 'Theoretical Orientations in African Urban Studies' Mitchell begins by stating that 'in Africa, as elsewhere, urban studies raise the same questions'. He continues by stating that 'the focus of sociological interest in African urban studies must be on the way in which the behaviour of town-dwellers fits into, and is adjusted to, the social matrix created by the commercial, industrial, and administrative framework of a modern metropolis – having regard to the fact that most African town-dwellers have been born and brought up in the rural hinterland of the city, in which the cultural background is markedly dissimilar from that of the city'. After discussing social surveys and intensive studies, he distinguishes between 'historical' or 'processive' change to cover overall changes in the social system, and 'situational change', which covers changes in behaviour 'following participation in different social systems'. In dealing with both these types of change, Mitchell emphasizes the importance of relations of kinship and friendship – thus he faces the same problems as Wolf. He is then concerned to distinguish structural from categorical relationships, before passing to emphasize the importance of studying 'the network of personal links which individuals have built around themselves in towns'. Seeing problems very similar to those seen by Wolf, he suggests that the study of networks may show 'the way in which norms and values are diffused in a community, and how the process of "feedback" takes place.' In these studies, gossip, joking relations, historical antecedents, can all be taken into account.

In Monograph 4 Adrian Mayer treats, with technical detail, a similar set of problems, in an essay on 'The Significance of

Quasi-Groups in the Study of Complex Societies'. He too emphasizes the importance of networks and action-sets of relations, as against groups, and tries to clarify and refine those concepts. He applies them to an Indian electoral struggle. He concludes: 'It may well be that, as social anthropologists become more interested in complex societies and as the simpler societies themselves become more complex, an increasing amount of work will be based on ego-centred entities such as action-sets and quasi-groups, rather than on groups and sub-groups' – the latter being, presumably, what Wolf calls 'the formal organization' of complex societies.

Burton Benedict, in the same monograph, considers 'Sociological Characteristics of Small Territories' such as Mauritius. He sets his task as an assessment of the relation between the scale of society and: the number, kinds, and duration of social roles; types of values and alternatives; magico-religious practices; jural relations; political structure; and economic development. The first three are traditionally in the field of social anthropology. What is more significant is that in handling the last two sets of problems, Benedict emphasizes that the elites involved are small, and, though not explicitly, we are back with the problems of quasi-groups, networks, and action-sets.

Frankenberg's discussion (also in 4) of changes in the structure of social roles and role-sets in a range of British 'communities', from the truly rural to the housing-estate, hinges again on changes, in both groups and quasi-groups, which determine the structure of individuals' varied roles; but he illustrates too the urgent need to study custom, belief, and ceremonial as our specific contribution.

We see here, then, a common orientation, and a drive towards a common set of concepts, as social anthropologists tackle the problems of urban societies and of changing tribal and peasant communities. Some of them argue explicitly that these concepts developed to handle 'complex' situations, would also illuminate studies of tribal societies. These studies deal with problems which social anthropologists share with sociologists and political scientists, rather than with other types of anthropologists, and it may be that the *social* part of the title 'social anthropology' will begin to outweigh the *anthropology*. Yet there remain specific interests derived from the common tradition of *anthropology*.

Only in the study of religion do any of the contributors argue for the essential place of some psychological treatment. As it happens, the studies of kinship relations included occur only in the volume on 'the relevance of models': the whole fruitful field of study in psychological anthropology, represented by Lewinson, Linton, Mead, Whiting, and many others, is not referred to. This may be partly a reflection of who was asked to contribute, and what those invited decided to write on. Yet these essays show that there is a whole dimension of marital and parental relations which, it is accepted, can be studied without reference to psychological concomitants.

Strikingly, the feeling that it is justifiable for social anthropologists to work without reference to studies in psychology, is shown in Joe Loudon's essay on 'Religious Order and Mental Disorder' in a South Wales community (4). Loudon is a qualified medical, who later turned to anthropology. He has been trained in psychiatry, and has worked for the British Medical Research Council on the position of the mentally ill in a community, and the community's reaction to such people. His research is into attitudes, yet he works with the same basic concepts as his colleagues: he analyses social roles in terms of class and social status, religious affiliation, length of residence in the district, etc., in relation to conscious attitudes, involving the allocation of culpability, assumption that mental disorder is illness, and so forth. So too in studying the religious order he is concerned with statements about the role of crises in personal relations, in so far as these affect reactions to mental disorder. He looks also at patterns of social mobility, and at the effect of these on individuals' social networks. His general mode of analysis 'fits' with the analyses we have just discussed: significantly, to handle social attitudes, he does not turn to work in social psychology.

GENERAL ORIENTATIONS

In this background of realignment with cognate disciplines, the essays show two main trends. The first is an insistence that certain concepts that were acceptable in preceding decades are now too gross to be useful, and have to be refined, or that they may even block further analysis. The second is the feeling that more work should be done to pull together, in a comparative framework, observations that are discrete in terms of subject-matter or of ethnographic milieu. Obviously, these are the two possibilities that offer themselves, aside from carrying out studies that repeat what has been done before – and we do not regard such studies as useless. One can either penetrate more deeply into an area of problems, or pull together what has already been done.

There are many new ideas in these essays, but no author has tried to put forward an altogether new theoretical approach – or even to recast the basic orientations of the subject. In making the statement, we do so with full allowance for Spiro's insistence (3) that to study religion, as against studying society, a psychological approach is as essential as a social anthropological one. Geertz pleads (3) for a new look – via philosophy, history, law, literature, or the 'harder' sciences – at religion, but he nevertheless considers that 'the way to do this is not abandon the established traditions of social anthropology in this field, but to widen them'. He still looks to Durkheim, Weber, Freud, and Malinowski as 'inevitable starting-points for any useful anthropological theory of religion'. The specific problems he deals with – suffering, evil, chance, the bizarre, ethics – are not in themselves new fields of problems, though his preferred solutions to the problems may be new.

The basic orientation in these essays is therefore still the acceptance that the events which comprise human behaviour exhibit regularities whose forms are mutually interdependent, over and above their interdependence, in the personality-behaviour systems of each individual actor. As Radcliffe-Brown put it, there are social systems whose structures can be analysed. An interdependence of cultural institutions, each of which has an elaborate structure, would perhaps be the parallel Malinowskian formulation. Given this general orientation, it seems to us that these social anthropologists have a much looser idea of a social system, or of a complex of institutions, than Radcliffe-Brown or Malinowski had. A social system is not seen in analogy with an organic system, whose structure is maintained by some customary procedure, as it was by Radcliffe-

Brown. Nor is there acceptance of Malinowski's ideas of the function of institutions in relation to a hierarchy of needs: Spiro (3) specifically criticizes this approach.

These 'tight' models of social systems or cultures were abandoned by the inter-war generation of social anthropologists (see Redfield, 1955). But those anthropologists continued to worry about the nature of social systems and cultures, or the structure of social fields. On the evidence of these essays, the younger anthropologists no longer consider this worry justified: at least none of them has dealt with that kind of problem at length, or as basic to his analysis. Geertz (3) goes to some pains to discuss 'culture'. Spiro (3) has some discussion of what a system is. David Schneider, in an essay on 'Some Muddles in the Models: or, How the System Really Works' (1) considers the competing, and hotly argued, opposed views of two sets of anthropologists on descent and affinity: and he states that one cause of their disputation is that they need to be clearer about whether the theory is advanced to cover the structure of a social system, or whether it is about how the individual finds his way in that system. He feels that the argument will get nowhere, unless this point is clarified. That is, he asks for clarity on problems set, and he is not concerned with the epistemology of the subject. We hope that our younger colleagues feel that earlier disputation on the nature of social systems and social fields, or on the nature of culture, clarified the issues, if only through the substantive work done; and that the disputation was not always meaningless.

When we say there seems to be no new general orientation shown, but a determination to get on with the job with established orientations, we must mention the 'new' evolutionary school of Leslie White, represented here by Sahlins's essay on primitive exchange in Monograph 1. The evolutionary argument is not marked in this particular essay, and on the whole Sahlins's analysis is similar in structure to the arguments of Wolf about kinship, friendship, and patron-client relations (4), of Frankenberg about the association of role types with forms of British community (4), of Benedict about the characteristics of small-scale territories (4), and of Lloyd and Southall about the typology of African political systems (2). The type of argument is shown in the cautious hypothesis about primitive money which, among others, is advanced by Sahlins: 'it [primitive money] occurs in conjunction with unusual incidence of balanced reciprocity in peripheral social sectors. Presumably it facilitates the heavy balanced traffic'. This is precisely the sort of hypothesis about an association between social variables which is commonly sought by anthropologists, and is well illustrated in the four other essays just cited. But Sahlins continues: 'The conditions that encourage primitive money are most likely to occur in the range of primitive societies called tribal and are unlikely to be served by band or chiefdom development . . . Not all tribes provide circumstances for monetary development and certainly not all enjoy primitive money, as that term is here understood. For the potentiality of peripheral exchange is maximized only by some tribes. Others remain relatively inner-directed.'

We consider that, despite the turning against the simple evolutionary theories of the nineteenth century, some kind of evolutionary, or morphological, framework has been implicit in most comparative work in social anthropology. We say, 'or morphological', because many scholars have avoided an outright evolutionary statement in order to evade temporal implications. Radcliffe-Brown did this, but he believed strongly in social evolution. The result is that, aside from their important theses on the relation between use of energy and social forms, the new evolutionists, as Sahlins's essay shows, are trying to handle associations of concomitant variations, rather than items of culture, in somewhat similar ways to their colleagues. Nevertheless, we note that this new evolutionary theorizing is here represented only in the interstices, rather than in the central part, of Sahlins's essay.

REFINEMENT OF CONCEPTS

We have said that one main line of approach in these monographs, represented in several essays, is the refinement of standard concepts, in hopes of penetrating more deeply into the structure of social life. This tendency is marked in the several discussions of social roles. Even before Linton in 1936 advanced his definitions of 'status' and 'role', the handling of these phenomena was important in social anthropology: one has only to think of Radcliffe-Brown's concern with social personality and persona. But Linton's formulation, with the increasing interest of social anthropologists in sociological studies, focused attention more sharply on social structures as systems of roles (see, for example, Nadel, 1957). The work on social roles of Merton and Parsons, and later Goffman, as already cited, became influential. Some of the essays accept that, for certain purposes, 'role' can be used in analysis, as a general concept: but it is also subjected to a closer reexamination than almost anything else in the monographs.

This tone is set by the very first essay, Goodenough's 'Rethinking "Status" and "Role": Toward a General Model of the Cultural Organization of Social Relationships' (1). Goodenough is dissatisfied with the impasse into which we have run through the use of status and role as, to use our own shorthand, 'global' concepts, covering types of facts which need to be clearly differentiated. At the same time, he is dissatisfied with the present tendency to look at structural relationships apart from their cultural content. Drawing analogies from structural linguistics, he therefore attempts to construct a means of establishing both vocabularies and a syntax of the rules of 'roles.' To do this, he aims at a clearer specification of terms to describe the attributes of individuals and the relationships between them. He suggests, therefore, that status should not be, as he says Linton treated it, a means of reference to categories or kinds of persons, but that it should be confined to combinations of right and duty only. Social 'positions' in a categorical sense he calls 'social identities'. Each person has several social identities, and in specific situations one is selected as appropriate: this Goodenough terms 'the selector's *social persona* in the interaction'.

We are not, in this Introduction, summarizing any of the essays, and the preceding sketch is intended only to indicate the drive for the refinement of concepts which in the past have been illuminatingly employed, in order to secure more penetrating analysis. Having specified his terms, Goodenough proceeds to outline different types of situation in which these clarify relations between various egos and alters. On the cultural content side, he distinguishes the ranges of rights and duties, as against privileges and immunities – following here the terminology of the jurist, Hohfeld, which Hoebel has tried to get anthropologists to adopt. Goodenough thereupon proposes a technique by use of scalograms, to work out whether there are right-duty/ privilege-immunity clusters in particular identity relationships as seen *by single informants*. Varied cultural demands – such as 'sleeping in the same house', 'joking sexually in public' – are taken, and the informant is asked whether each demand applies in a particular identity relationship. These combine to give specific composite pictures of duty-scales. Goodenough argues that owing to limitations on the cognitive power of individuals – here is another example of an author citing psychological research – the demands, each forming a 'status dimension', must be limited in number to seven or less. He suggests that these duty-scales can be powerful instruments of social analysis, since (as he demonstrates by examples) they will allow objective measurement of anger, insult, flattery, and the gravity of offences. The last point is illustrated by a situation where breach of norm on the part of one identity justifies severe breach of duty by another. This will lead to precision in the study of single societies, and in the comparison of different societies.

This summary does not set out all the intricacies of the argument; but we have discussed this essay in order to illustrate what we mean when we say several authors see one line of advance in an increasing refinement of established concepts, and specification of others, to replace single concepts which, in their traditional global form, have outlived their usefulness. Goodenough's essay is the most explicit treatment of 'status' and 'role' in this way; but it seems to us that similar procedures are at least implicit in those parts of Lloyd's and Southall's essays on political systems (2) which aim to relate changes in role patterns with changes in macroscopic political structures. The explicit reformulation of the ideas involved in social roles emerges again in Frankenberg's essay (4) on changes in roles with 'movement' from British rural areas, through villages and small towns, into cities. Like Goodenough, he concerns himself with patterns of interaction – and he turns to cybernetics for ideas to handle these patterns. Both of them find in Goffman's searching study of *The Presentation of Self in Everyday Life* (1959) and *Encounters* (1961) stimulus in handling the nuances involved in the complexity of daily social interaction, as against the more formal earlier analysis of roles in structural frameworks.

The same drive towards the breaking up of established concepts in order to examine more meticulously both the framework of social relations and the interaction between individuals shows in other fields. It is present in Sahlins's essay on types of primitive exchange (1) and Wolf's treatment of relations of kinship, friendship, and patronage *vis-à-vis* clientship (4), which have been considered by us in other contexts. It occurs as explicitly as in Goodenough's essay on status and role, in Mayer's article on 'The Significance of Quasi-Groups in the Study of Complex Societies' (4). Goodenough discusses the history of the concepts 'status' and 'role' and the ambiguities in their use, with difficulties that have arisen in applying them. Mayer looks equally closely at the way in which J. A. Barnes (1954) and E. Bott (1957) used the idea of 'the social network' – an idea which Barnes advanced in its present general form, and whose importance was stressed by Redfield (1955, p. 28) in a Huxley Memorial Lecture delivered shortly afterwards.

Mayer is concerned to clarify the different kinds of networks and action-sets that have to be distinguished, and also procedures for measuring their form and ramifications. As stated above, the same theme is present in essays by Mitchell, Benedict, and Loudon in Monograph 4 on the study of complex societies, and in Bailey's essay on committees and Nicholas's on factions in Monograph 2. These scholars are finding that theories based on concepts of groups, groupings and associations, and dyadic relationships, are inadequate for their problems: the network, and other forms of quasi-groups, which are ego-centred, are becoming more significant in bridging the gap between structural framework and individual action. There is clearly a close fit here with attempts to improve on the concepts of status and role. We note here too Mitchell's (4) distinction between structural and categorical relationships (i.e. between relationships set in associations and institutions, and relationships based on common attributes, such as race, tribe, and class).

The urge to clarify and refine appears also in a different context in Barbara Ward's essay 'Varieties of the Conscious Model' (1), where she considers the situation of a group of boat-dwelling fishermen in Hong Kong. These people consider themselves to be Chinese; and, Ward asks, by what model can their Chinese identity be assessed? Her starting-point is Lévi-Strauss's distinction 'between culturally produced models and observer's models. The former, constructs of the people under study themselves, he calls conscious models; the latter, unconscious, models'. Ward argues that to understand her field situation, she had to take into account several conscious models – that of Chinese society held by Chinese literati, that of the group under study held by themselves, those of this group held by other groups of Chinese – as well as the unconscious, the anthropologist's, model. She examines the relationship between these models, as set in the context of different areas of Chinese society, to assess where 'the uniformity and continuity of the traditional Chinese social system' lay; and she finds it in family structures.

The demand for rethinking, clarification, and refinement runs through all the essays in Monograph 1, that on 'models'. We have cited it from the essays by Goodenough, Sahlins, and Ward. It appears as strikingly in the other essays: by Ioan Lewis on 'Problems in the Comparative Study of Unilineal Descent' and David Schneider on 'Some Muddles in the Models'. Lewis argues that if correlations are to be established in comparative work, it is necessary to measure the intensity of such a principle as unilineal descent. He attempts to do this by applying various criteria to four patrilineal societies. He comes to the conclusion after his survey that by these principles involved in unilineal descent, various societies scale differently, and hence he suggests that this kind of classification is difficult and probably unfruitful. He argues that the functional significance of descent varies too much, hence canons of descent may not be fruitful criteria. 'The lumping together of societies on the basis of patriliny or matriliny alone can only lead to confusion. The functional implications of descent are much more significant than whether descent is traced in the patri – or matri-line' – an argument advanced by Leach in *Rethinking Anthropology* (1961).

Since Lewis does not suggest alternative criteria, we take his essay to be an example of that important class of work which aims to prove that a particular line of research is fruitless. The implications of the final sentence are clear: more refined, multiple variables must be sought.

Schneider's essay is much more difficult to delineate. It deals with a heated controversy between anthropologists about relationships of descent, and relationships of marriage or alliance. The argument is complex, and difficult to follow without detailed knowledge of the background literature which is discussed – and at least one of us, a political anthropologist, frankly confesses his difficulties here. Nevertheless, for present purposes it is clear that Schneider is trying to clarify the terminological and other muddles that he considers obstruct agreement: he points out to the contestants where they are talking in fact about different things, when they appear to be talking about the same thing. For, he says, there are two categories of anthropologists involved, and though there may be differences between the members of each category, they are distinctive from the others. There are the descent theory anthropologists (Fortes, Gluckman, Goody), who look for actual groups of people who intermarry with one another, and alliance theory anthropologists (Lévi-Strauss, Leach, Needham), who are primarily interested in 'that construct or model which is fabricated by the anthropologist and which is presumed to have, as its concrete expression, the norms for social relations and the rules governing the constitution of social groups and their interrelations'. Schneider argues that aside from weaknesses in each theory, they both contain contradictions and obscurities in their formulations. Most of the disputants are not clear in their arguments with one another on how far they are erecting conceptual models, which do not refer to real segments of the society, and how far they are referring to actual segments, based mainly on ownership of property and other jural rights. He suggests that this is because each of the theories is elaborated for a different type of society. The alliance theory is formulated for systems (which Schneider calls segmental) in which marriages of women proceed always from one segment to another; the descent theory for systems (which Schneider calls segmentary) in which men in one segment can marry into a number of other segments.

Schneider feels that each protagonist is driven by the pole-mical situation to defend 'his type', and that leads to the 'propagation of whole-system, over-simple typologies'. His own plea is for the use of typologies for specific problems, 'not for sorting of concrete societies into unchangeable, inherent, inalienable categories'. Selection of various elements, rigorously defined, and examination of combinations, permutations, and recombinations of these elements in many constellations, will prove more profitable.

SPECIFICATION OF CONTEXT

Schneider's essay contains also a plea for the clearer specification of more limited and varying contexts of relations, in order to assess the association of variables. Similar demands are present in a number of other essays on various subjects. They appear in every essay of the Monograph 2 on political problems. Bailey, in examining the alleged value, or rather 'the mystique', of 'consensus' in committees, distinguishes what he calls elite and arena councils, the size of councils, forms of external relation-ships. Nicholas places factional disputes in various types of situation. Lloyd looks at a limited political problem, by classify-ing three polities in terms of modes of recruitment of the elite and analysing their association with four other important variables. Southall argues for 'partial analysis of partial systems', and takes as his criterion for classifying political systems the differentiation of political roles. In Monograph 3, Bradbury looks at the contexts in which Edo cults of the dead, as against ancestral cults, may be significant; while Winter, in analysing Iraqw religion, stresses, much as Schneider does, that there are with reference to this problem at least two types of society in Africa.

THE SEARCH FOR THE BROAD HYPOTHESIS OR THEORY

It seems, then, that most of the contributors to this volume favour clarification, the breaking down, and the refinement, of standard concepts, together with closer specification of narrower social contexts, as likely to be a more fruitful line of advance than the search for sweeping generalizations. This is explicitly stated in a few essays, and is implicit in others. Since contributors were asked to write papers indicating where they thought new approaches would be fruitful, we believe we may assume that the essays in this series reflect the feeling of our younger colleagues, and that they did not merely submit to us essays on a problem on which they happened to be working. There was, of course, in the discussion on the papers, argument on this point: as there was plenty of abstract argument about scientific method. But it must be significant that perhaps only two out of a score of papers can be seen as arguing for a much wider treatment of a specific problem – and we are not sure that this is a correct interpretation of Geertz's paper (3) when taken in its entirety, or of Spiro's essay at clarifying the various dimensions involved in the study or religion. Both of them emphasize the close and meticulous analyses of facts in restricted contexts: their plea is rather for an increase in the disciplines whose techniques and concepts should be employed in analysis by social anthropologists.

All the essays in fact show that social anthropologists are ready to turn where they feel they can get help to solve a specific problem. But the one difference we find between British and American contributors is that the British on the whole confine themselves to a narrower range of other disciplines – those commonly grouped as the social sciences. As stated above, Loudon's essay on 'Religious Order and Mental Disorder' (4) illustrates this restriction. Turner, in his analysis of Ndembu colour classification (3), is aware of how closely his problems raise issues treated by the psycho-analysts, but he eschews involvement in psycho-analytic interpretations. The American anthropologists are readier to move outside the restricted range of the social sciences to draw on disciplines which employ quite different techniques and concepts.

CONCLUSION

Overall, then, these essays, whether they consider a single society or make surveys over several societies, show the continuing balancing of detailed, meticulous analysis of limited social fields with comparative checking that has long characterized the subject. The meticulous analysis of a single situation dominates in Turner's essay on colour classification, as it does in Bradbury's on Edo and Winter's on Iraqw religion. It forms too a core to Geertz's paper (all in Monograph 3). The comparative survey dominates Sahlins's analysis of exchange (1) and Wolf's of kinship, friendship, and patronage. Both types of analysis are strongly present in all the essays.

We have not attempted in this Introduction to discuss the argument of each essay or to assess its merits. The field covered by the essays shows that, even setting aside ethnographic specialization, a social anthropologist now will find it difficult to be competent on political problems, economic problems, domestic life, religious action, etc. – particularly as more and more is drawn from cognate disciplines. Therefore we are not competent to assess more than a few of the essays, and to do that would have been invidious. Instead, we have tried to delineate what we see as common in these new approaches, spread over a variety of problems and printed in four Monographs. Our own essay may be at least a guide to where readers can find the new leads that are being pursued by a younger generation of social anthropologists.

ACKNOWLEDGEMENTS

Finally, we have to thank, for our colleagues and ourselves, a number of people on whom this symposium has depended. Professor Raymond Firth conceived the plan and pushed through the preliminary arrangements, with Professor Fred Eggan. The Executive Board of the American Anthropological Association was kind enough to sponsor a request to the National Science Foundation which provided the financial support to enable the Americans to travel to Britain. Dr Michael Banton, as Honorary Secretary of the Association, organized the conference, and has acted as editor of the Monographs. The Fellows and domestic staff of Jesus College, Cambridge, provided a setting in which we met in great comfort amidst pleasant surroundings; and this side of our foregathering was admirably handled by Mr G. I. Jones, Lecturer in Social Anthropology in Cambridge University and Fellow of Jesus College. Mr John Harvard-Watts and Miss Diana Burfield of Tavistock Publications have been invaluable and generous in help over publication.

A number of anthropologists worked hard in preparing openings to the discussion of each section. Some of the Americans who presented papers undertook this double duty. The following British anthropologists filled the role: Dr M. Banton, Dr P. Cohen, Dr J. Goody, and Professor P. M. Worsley. We had also the pleasure of the company of Professor G. C. Homans of Harvard, a sociologist who has worked with social anthropologists, and who effectively prevented us from developing too great ethnocentricity. He travelled especially from America to attend the meeting.

Finally, Gluckman insists, on behalf of the Association of Social Anthropologists of the British Commonwealth, on thanking Fred Eggan. As Firth inspired the meeting, Eggan, though acting as an individual, made it possible. In many ways, including his own presence as an American elder, supported only by the happy chance of Professor Sol Tax being in Britain, he contributed to what was a memorable occasion in the history of social anthropology – which is permanently encapsulated in these four volumes. And Eggan wishes, on behalf of the American group, to express their appreciation of the fine hospitality of their hosts which went beyond the strict requirements of the occasion, and to thank Max Gluckman for the excellence of his chairmanship and for assuming the task of drafting this introduction. To the authors of the essays, our joint thanks are due.

REFERENCES

BARNES, J. A. 1954. Class and Committees in a Norwegian Island Parish. *Human Relations* 7: 39-58.

BOTT, E. 1957. *Family and Social Network*. London: Tavistock Publications.

CORNFORD, F. M. 1908. *Microcosmographia Academica: Being a Guide for the Young Academic Politician*. Cambridge: Heffer (reprinted 1953).

EASTON, D. 1953. *The Political System*. New York: Knopf.
—— 1959. Political Anthropology. In B. J. Siegel (ed.), *Biennial Review of Anthropology*. Stanford: Stanford University Press.

FALLERS, L. A. No date: about 1956. *Bantu Bureaucracy: A Study of Integration and Conflict in the Politics of an East African People*. Cambridge: Heffer, for the East African Institute of Social Research.

FIRTH R. 1939. *Primitive Polynesian Economy*. London: Routledge.
—— 1946. *Malay Fishermen: Their Peasant Economy*. London: Kegan Paul, Trench, Trubner.

FIRTH, R. & YAMEY, B. S. 1964. *Capital, Saving and Credit in Peasant Societies*. London: Allen & Unwin.

FORTES, M. & EVANS-PRITCHARD, E. E. (eds.). 1940. *African Political Systems*. London: Oxford University Press, for the International African Institute.

GEERTZ, C. 1960. *The Religion of Java*. Glencoe, Ill.: The Free Press.

GOFFMAN, E. 1959. *The Presentation of Self in Everyday Life*. New York: Doubleday Anchor Books.
—— 1961. *Encounters: Two Studies in the Sociology of Interaction*. Indianopolis: Bobbs-Merrill.

HORTON, R. 1964. Ritual Man in Africa. *Africa* **34**.

LEACH, E. R. 1961. *Rethinking Anthropology*. London: Athlone Press.

LINTON, R. 1936. *The Study of Man*. New York: Appleton-Century.

LLEWELLYN, K. & HOEBEL, E. A. 1941. *The Cheyenne Way: Conflict and Case Law in Primitive Jurisprudence*. Norman: University of Oklahoma Press; London: Allen & Unwin.

MANDELBAUM, D., LASKER, G. W. & ALBERT, E. M. 1963. *The Teaching of Anthropology*. American Anthropological Association, Memoir 94.

MERTON, R. K. *Social Theory and Social Structure*. 1957 (revised and enlarged edition). Glencoe, Ill.: The Free Press.

NADEL, S. F. 1957. *The Theory of Social Structure*. London: Cohen & West; Glencoe, Ill.: The Free Press.

REDFIELD, R. 1955. Societies and Cultures as Natural Systems. *Journal of the Royal Anthropological Institute* **85**: 19-32.

WHEARE, K. C. 1955. *Government by Committee*. Oxford: Clarendon Press.

Clifford Geertz

Religion as a Cultural System

'Any attempt to speak without speaking any particular language
is not more hopeless than the attempt to have a religion that
shall be no religion in particular . . . Thus every living and
healthy religion has a marked idiosyncrasy. Its power consists
in its special and surprising message and in the bias which that
revelation gives to life. The vistas it opens and the mysteries it
propounds are another world to live in; and another world to live
in – whether we expect ever to pass wholly over into it or no – is
what we mean by having a religion.'

SANTAYANA: *Reason in Religion* (1905-6)

I

Two characteristics of anthropological work on religion accomplished since the second world war strike me as curious when
such work is placed against that carried out just before and just
after the first. One is that it has made no theoretical advances of
major importance. It is living off the conceptual capital of its
ancestors, adding very little, save a certain empirical enrich-
ment, to it. The second is that it draws what concepts it does use
from a very narrowly defined intellectual tradition. There is
Durkheim, Weber, Freud, or Malinowski, and in any particular
work the approach of one or two of these transcendent figures is
followed, with but a few marginal corrections necessitated by
the natural tendency to excess of seminal minds or by the
expanded body of reliable descriptive data. But virtually no one
even thinks of looking elsewhere – to philosophy, history, law,
literature, or the 'harder' sciences – as these men themselves
looked, for analytical ideas. And it occurs to me, also, that these
two curious characteristics are not unrelated.

If the anthropological study of religion is in fact in a state of
general stagnation, I doubt it will be set going again by producing more minor variations on classical theoretical themes.
Yet one more meticulous case in point for such well-established
propositions as that ancestor worship supports the jural

1

authority of elders, that initiation rites are means for the establishment of sexual identity and adult status, that ritual groupings reflect political oppositions, or that myths provide charters for social institutions and rationalizations of social privilege, may well finally convince a great many people, both inside the profession and out, that anthropologists are, like theologians, firmly dedicated to proving the indubitable. In art, this solemn reduplication of the achievements of accepted masters is called academicism; and I think this is the proper name for our malady also. Only if we abandon, in a phrase of Leo Steinberg's (1953), that sweet sense of accomplishment which comes from parading habitual skills and address ourselves to problems sufficiently unclarified as to make discovery possible, can we hope to achieve work which will not just reincarnate that of the great men of the first quarter of this century, but match it.

The way to do this is not to abandon the established traditions of social anthropology in this field, but to widen them. At least four of the contributions of the men who, as I say, dominate our thought to the point of parochializing it – Durkheim's discussion of the nature of the sacred, Weber's *Verstehenden* methodology, Freud's parallel between personal rituals and collective ones, and Malinowski's exploration of the distinction between religion and common sense – seem to me inevitable starting-points for any useful anthropological theory of religion. But they are starting-points only. To move beyond them we must place them in a much broader context of contemporary thought than they, in and of themselves, encompass. The dangers of such a procedure are obvious: arbitrary eclecticism, superficial theory-mongering, and sheer intellectual confusion. But I, at least, can see no other road of escape from what, referring to anthropology more generally, Janowitz (1963, p. 151) has called the dead hand of competence.

In working toward such an expansion of the conceptual envelope in which our studies take place, one can, of course, move in a great number of directions; and perhaps the most important initial problem is to avoid setting out, like Stephen Leacock's mounted policeman, in all of them at once. For my part, I shall confine my effort to developing what, following

Parsons and Shils (1951), I refer to as the cultural dimension of religious analysis. The term 'culture' has by now acquired a certain aura of ill-repute in social anthropological circles because of the multiplicity of its referents and the studied vagueness with which it has all too often been invoked. (Though why it should suffer more for these reasons than 'social structure' or 'personality' is something I do not entirely understand.) In any case, the culture concept to which I adhere has neither multiple referents nor, so far as I can see, any unusual ambiguity: it denotes an historically transmitted pattern of meanings embodied in symbols, a system of inherited conceptions expressed in symbolic forms by means of which men communicate, perpetuate, and develop their knowledge about and attitudes toward life. Of course, terms such as 'meaning', 'symbol', and 'conception' cry out for explication. But that is precisely where the widening, the broadening, and the expanding come in. If Langer (1962, p. 55) is right that 'the concept of meaning, in all its varieties, is the dominant philosophical concept of our time', that 'sign, symbol, denotation, signification, communication . . . are our [intellectual] stock in trade', it is perhaps time that social anthropology, and particularly that part of it concerned with the study of religion, became aware of the fact.

II

As we are to deal with meaning, let us begin with a paradigm: viz. that sacred symbols function to synthesize a people's ethos – the tone, character, and quality of their life, its moral and aesthetic style and mood – and their world-view – the picture they have of the way things in sheer actuality are, their most comprehensive ideas of order (Geertz, 1958). In religious belief and practice a group's ethos is rendered intellectually reasonable by being shown to represent a way of life ideally adapted to the actual state of affairs the world-view describes, while the world-view is rendered emotionally convincing by being presented as an image of an actual state of affairs peculiarly well arranged to accommodate such a way of life. This confrontation and mutual confirmation has two fundamental effects. On the one hand, it objectivizes moral and aesthetic preferences by

3

depicting them as the imposed conditions of life implicit in a world with a particular structure, as mere common sense given the unalterable shape of reality. On the other, it supports these received beliefs about the world's body by invoking deeply felt moral and aesthetic sentiments as experiential evidence for their truth. Religious symbols formulate a basic congruence between a particular style of life and a specific (if, most often, implicit) metaphysic, and in so doing sustain each with the borrowed authority of the other.

Phrasing aside, this much may perhaps be granted. The notion that religion tunes human actions to an envisaged cosmic order and projects images of cosmic order onto the plane of human experience is hardly novel. But it is hardly investigated either, so that we have very little idea of how, in empirical terms, this particular miracle is accomplished. We just know that it is done, annually, weekly, daily, for some people almost hourly; and we have an enormous ethnographic literature to demonstrate it. But the theoretical framework which would enable us to provide an analytic account of it, an account of the sort we can provide for lineage segmentation, political succession, labor exchange, or the socialization of the child, does not exist.

Let us, therefore, reduce our paradigm to a definition, for, although it is notorious that definitions establish nothing, in themselves they do, if they are carefully enough constructed, provide a useful orientation, or reorientation, of thought, such that an extended unpacking of them can be an effective way of developing and controlling a novel line of inquiry. They have the useful virtue of explicitness: they commit themselves in a way discursive prose, which, in this field especially, is always liable to substitute rhetoric for argument, does not. Without further ado, then, a *religion* is:

(1) a system of symbols which acts to (2) establish powerful, pervasive, and long-lasting moods and motivations in men by (3) formulating conceptions of a general order of existence and (4) clothing these conceptions with such an aura of factuality that (5) the moods and motivations seem uniquely realistic.

1. *a system of symbols which acts to . . .*

Such a tremendous weight is being put on the term 'symbol' here that our first move must be to decide with some precision what we are going to mean by it. This is no easy task, for, rather like 'culture', 'symbol' has been used to refer to a great variety of things, often a number of them at the same time. In some hands it is used for anything which signifies something else to someone: dark clouds are the symbolic precursors of an on-coming rain. In others it is used only for explicitly conventional signs of one sort or another: a red flag is a symbol of danger, a white of surrender. In others it is confined to something which expresses in an oblique and figurative manner that which cannot be stated in a direct and literal one, so that there are symbols in poetry but not in science, and symbolic logic is misnamed. In yet others, however (Langer, 1953, 1960, 1962), it is used for any object, act, event, quality, or relation which serves as a vehicle for a conception – the conception is the symbol's 'meaning' – and that is the approach I shall follow here. The number 6, written, imagined, laid out as a row of stones, or even punched into the program tapes of a computer is a symbol. But so also is the Cross, talked about, visualized, shaped worriedly in air or fondly fingered at the neck, the expanse of painted canvas called 'Guernica' or the bit of painted stone called a churinga, the word 'reality', or even the morpheme '-ing.' They are all symbols, or at least symbolic elements, because they are tangible formulations of notions, abstractions from experience fixed in perceptible forms, concrete embodiments of ideas, attitudes, judgements, longings, or beliefs. To undertake the study of cultural activity – activity in which symbolism forms the positive content – is thus not to abandon social analysis for a Platonic cave of shadows, to enter into a mentalistic world of introspective psychology or, worse, speculative philosophy, and wander there forever in a haze of 'Cognitions', 'Affections', 'Conations', and other elusive entities. Cultural acts, the construction, apprehension, and utilization of symbolic forms, are social events like any other; they are as public as marriage and as observable as agriculture.

They are not, however, exactly the same thing; or, more precisely, the symbolic dimension of social events is, like the psychological, itself theoretically abstractable from those events as empirical totalities. There is still, to paraphrase a remark of Kenneth Burke's (1941, p. 9), a difference between building a house and drawing up a plan for building a house, and reading a poem about having children by marriage is not quite the same thing as having children by marriage. Even though the building of the house may proceed under the guidance of the plan or – a less likely occurrence – the having of children may be motivated by a reading of the poem, there is something to be said for not confusing our traffic with symbols with our traffic with objects or human beings, for these latter are not in themselves symbols, however often they may function as such.[1] No matter how deeply interfused the cultural, the social, and the psychological may be in the everyday life of houses, farms, poems, and marriages, it is useful to distinguish them in analysis, and, so doing, to isolate the generic traits of each against the normalized background of the other two (Parsons & Shils, 1951).

So far as culture patterns, i.e. systems or complexes of symbols, are concerned, the generic trait which is of first importance for us here is that they are extrinsic sources of information (Geertz, 1964a). By 'extrinsic', I mean only that – unlike genes, for example – they lie outside the boundaries of the individual organism as such in that intersubjective world of common understandings into which all human individuals are born, in which they pursue their separate careers, and which they leave persisting behind them after they die (Schutz, 1962). By 'sources of information', I mean only that – like genes – they provide a blueprint or template in terms of which processes external to themselves can be given a definite form (Horowitz, 1956). As the order of bases in a strand of DNA forms a coded program, a set of instructions, or a recipe, for the synthesization of the structurally complex proteins which shape organic functioning, so culture patterns provide such programs for the institution of the social and psychological processes which shape public behavior. Though the sort of information and the mode of its transmission are vastly different in the two cases, this comparison of gene and symbol is more than a strained analogy of the familiar 'social heredity' sort. It is actually a substantial relationship, for it is precisely the fact that genetically programmed processes are so highly generalized in men, as com-

pared with lower animals, that culturally programmed ones
are so important, only because human behavior is so loosely
determined by intrinsic sources of information that extrinsic
sources are so vital (Geertz, 1962). To build a dam a beaver
needs only an appropriate site and the proper materials – his
mode of procedure is shaped by his physiology. But man, whose
genes are silent on the building trades, needs also a conception
of what it is to build a dam, a conception he can get only from
some symbolic source – a blueprint, a textbook, or a string of
speech by someone who already knows how dams are built, or,
of course, from manipulating graphic or linguistic elements in
such a way as to attain for himself a conception of what dams
are and how they are built.

This point is sometimes put in the form of an argument that
cultural patterns are 'models', that they are sets of symbols
whose relations to one another 'model' relations among entities,
processes or what-have-you in physical, organic, social, or
psychological systems by 'paralleling', 'imitating', or 'simulat-
ing' them (Craik, 1952). The term 'model' has, however, two
senses – an 'of' sense and a 'for' sense – and though these are but
aspects of the same basic concept they are very much worth
distinguishing for analytic purposes. In the first, what is stressed
is the manipulation of symbol structures so as to bring them,
more or less closely, into parallel with the pre-established non-
symbolic system, as when we grasp how dams work by developing a theory of hydraulics or constructing a flow chart. The
theory or chart models physical relationships in such a way –
i.e. by expressing their structure in synoptic form – as to render
them apprehensible: it is a model *of* 'reality'. In the second, what
is stressed is the manipulation of the non-symbolic systems in
terms of the relationships expressed in the symbolic, as when we
construct a dam according to the specifications implied in an
hydraulic theory or the conclusions drawn from a flow chart.
Here, the theory is a model under whose guidance physical
relationships are organized: it is a model *for* 'reality'. For
psychological and social systems, and for cultural models that
we would not ordinarily refer to as 'theories', but rather as
'doctrines', 'melodies', or 'rites', the case is in no way different.
Unlike genes, and other non-symbolic information sources,

which are only models *for*, not models *of*, culture patterns have an intrinsic double aspect: they give meaning, i.e. objective conceptual form, to social and psychological reality both by shaping themselves to it and by shaping it to themselves.

It is, in fact, this double aspect which sets true symbols off from other sorts of significative forms. Models *for* are found, as the gene example suggests, through the whole order of nature, for wherever there is a communication of pattern such programs are, in simple logic, required. Among animals, imprint learning is perhaps the most striking example, because what such learning involves is the automatic presentation of an appropriate sequence of behavior by a model animal in the presence of a learning animal which serves, equally automatically, to call out and stabilize a certain set of responses genetically built into the learning animal (Lorenz, 1952). The communicative dance of two bees, one of which has found nectar and the other of which seeks it, is another, somewhat different, more complexly coded, example (von Frisch, 1962). Craik (1952) has even suggested that the thin trickle of water which first finds its way down from a mountain spring to the sea and smooths a little channel for the greater volume of water that follows after it plays a sort of model *for* function. But models *of* – linguistic, graphic, mechanical, natural, etc. processes which function not to provide sources of information in terms of which other processes can be patterned, but to represent those patterned processes as such, to express their structure in an alternative medium – are much rarer and may perhaps be confined, among living animals, to man. The perception of the structural congruence between one set of processes, activities, relations, entities, etc. and another set for which it acts as a program, so that the program can be taken as a representation, or conception – a symbol – of the programmed, is the essence of human thought. The inter-transposability of models *for* and models *of* which symbolic formulation makes possible is the distinctive characteristic of our mentality.

2. . . . *to establish powerful, pervasive, and long-lasting moods and motivations in men by* . . .

So far as religious symbols and symbol systems are concerned this inter-transposability is clear. The endurance, courage, independence, perseverance, and passionate willfulness in which the vision quest practices the Plains Indian are the same flamboyant virtues by which he attempts to live: while achieving a sense of revelation he stabilizes a sense of direction (Lowie, 1924). The consciousness of defaulted obligation, secreted guilt, and, when a confession is obtained, public shame in which Manus' seance rehearses him are the same sentiments that underlie the sort of duty ethic by which his property-conscious society is maintained: the gaining of an absolution involves the forging of a conscience (Fortune, 1935). And the same self-discipline which rewards a Javanese mystic staring fixedly into the flame of a lamp with what he takes to be an intimation of divinity drills him in that rigorous control of emotional expression which is necessary to a man who would follow a quietistic style of life (Geertz, 1960). Whether one sees the conception of a personal guardian spirit, a family tutelary or an immanent God as synoptic formulations of the character of reality or as templates for producing reality with such a character seems largely arbitrary, a matter of which aspect, the model *of* or model *for*, one wants for the moment to bring into focus. The concrete symbols involved – one or another mythological figure materializing in the wilderness, the skull of the deceased household head hanging censoriously in the rafters, or a disembodied 'voice in the stillness' soundlessly chanting enigmatic classical poetry – point in either direction. They both express the world's climate and shape it.

They shape it by inducing in the worshipper a certain distinctive set of dispositions (tendencies, capacities, propensities, skills, habits, liabilities, pronenesses) which lend a chronic character to the flow of his activity and the quality of his experience. A disposition describes not an activity or an occurrence but a probability of an activity being performed or an occurrence occurring in certain circumstances: 'When a cow is said to be a ruminant, or a man is said to be a cigarette-smoker, it is not being said that the cow is ruminating now or that the man is smoking a cigarette now. To be a ruminant is to tend to ruminate from time to time, and to be a cigarette-smoker is to be in the habit of smoking cigarettes' (Ryle, 1949, p. 117).

Similarly, to be pious is not to be performing something we would call an act of piety, but to be liable to perform such acts. So, too, with the Plains Indian's bravura, the Manus' compunctiousness, or the Javanese's quietism which, in their contexts, form the substance of piety. The virtue of this sort of view of what are usually called 'mental traits' or, if the Cartesianism is unavowed, 'psychological forces' (both unobjectionable enough terms in themselves) is that it gets them out of any dim and inaccessible realm of private sensation into that same well-lit world of observables in which reside the brittleness of glass, the inflammability of paper, and, to return to the metaphor, the dampness of England.

So far as religious activities are concerned (and learning a myth by heart is as much a religious activity as detaching one's finger at the knuckle), two somewhat different sorts of disposition are induced by them: moods and motivations.

A motivation is a persisting tendency, a chronic inclination to perform certain sorts of act and experience certain sorts of feeling in certain sorts of situation, the 'sorts' being commonly very heterogenous and rather ill-defined classes in all three cases:

'. . . on hearing that a man is vain [i.e. motivated by vanity] we expect him to behave in certain ways, namely to talk a lot about himself, to cleave to the society of the eminent, to reject criticisms, to seek the footlights and to disengage himself from conversations about the merits of others. We expect him to indulge in roseate daydreams about his own successes, to avoid recalling past failures and to plan for his own advancement. To be vain is to tend to act in these and innumerable other kindred ways. Certainly we also expect the vain man to feel certain pangs and flutters in certain situations; we expect him to have an acute sinking feeling when an eminent person forgets his name, and to feel buoyant of heart and light of toe on hearing of the misfortunes of his rivals. But feelings of pique and buoyancy are not more directly indicative of vanity than are public acts of boasting or private acts of daydreaming . . .' (Ryle, 1949, p. 86).

Similarly for any motivations. As a motive, 'flamboyant courage' consists in such enduring propensities as to fast in the

10

wilderness, to conduct solitary raids on enemy camps, and to thrill to the thought of counting coup. 'Moral circumspection' consists in such ingrained tendencies as to honor onerous promises, to confess secret sins in the face of severe public disapproval, and to feel guilty when vague and generalized accusations are made at seances. And 'dispassionate tranquility' consists in such persistent inclinations as to maintain one's poise come hell or high water, to experience distaste in the presence of even moderate emotional displays, and to indulge in contentless contemplations of featureless objects. Motives are thus neither acts (i.e. intentional behaviors) nor feelings, but liabilities to perform particular classes of act or have particular classes of feeling. And when we say that a man is religious, i.e. motivated by religion, this is at least part – though only part – of what we mean.

Another part of what we mean is that he has, when properly stimulated, a susceptibility to fall into certain moods, moods we sometimes lump together under such covering terms as 'reverential', 'solemn', or 'worshipful'. Such generalized rubrics actually conceal, however, the enormous empirical variousness of the dispositions involved, and, in fact, tend to assimilate them to the unusually grave tone of most of our own religious life. The moods that sacred symbols induce, at different times and in different places, range from exultation to melancholy, from self-confidence to self-pity, from an incorrigible playfulness to a bland listlessness – to say nothing of the erogenous power of so many of the world's myths and rituals. No more than there is a single sort of motivation one can call piety is there a single sort of mood one can call worshipful.

The major difference between moods and motivations is that where the latter are, so to speak, vectorial qualities, the former are merely scalar. Motives have a directional cast, they describe a certain overall course, gravitate toward certain, usually temporary, consummations. But moods vary only as to intensity: they go nowhere. They spring from certain circumstances but they are responsive to no ends. Like fogs, they just settle and lift; like scents, suffuse and evaporate. When present they are totalistic: if one is sad everything and everybody seems dreary; if one is gay, everything and everybody seems splendid.

11

Thus, though a man can be vain, brave, willful and independent at the same time, he can't very well be playful and listless, or exultant and melancholy, at the same time (Ryle, 1949, p. 99). Further, where motives persist for more or less extended periods of time, moods merely recur with greater or lesser frequency, coming and going for what are often quite unfathomable reasons. But perhaps the most important difference, so far as we are concerned, between moods and motivations is that motivations are 'made meaningful' with reference to the ends toward which they are conceived to conduce, whereas moods are 'made meaningful' with reference to the conditions from which they are conceived to spring. We interpret motives in terms of their consummations, but we interpret moods in terms of their sources. We say that a person is industrious because he wishes to succeed, we say that a person is worried because he is conscious of the hanging threat of nuclear holocaust. And this is no less the case when the interpretations invoked are ultimate. Charity becomes Christian charity when it is enclosed in a conception of God's purposes; optimism is Christian optimism when it is grounded in a particular conception of God's nature. The assiduity of the Navaho finds its rationale in a belief that, since 'reality' operates mechanically, it is coercible; their chronic fearfulness finds its rationale in a conviction that, however 'reality' operates, it is both enormously powerful and terribly dangerous (Kluckhohn, 1949).

3. . . . *by formulating conceptions of a general order of existence and* . . .

That the symbols or symbol systems which induce and define dispositions we set off as religious and those which place those dispositions in a cosmic framework are the same symbols ought to occasion no surprise. For what else do we mean by saying that a particular mood of awe is religious and not secular except that it springs from entertaining a conception of all-pervading vitality like mana and not from a visit to the Grand Canyon? Or that a particular case of asceticism is an example of a religious motivation except that it is directed toward the achievement of an unconditioned end like nirvana and not a conditioned one like weight-reduction? If sacred symbols did not at one and the same time induce dispositions in human beings and formulate, however obliquely, inarticulately, or unsystematically, general ideas of order, then the empirical differentia of religious activity or religious experience would not exist. A man can indeed be said to be 'religious' about golf, but not merely if he pursues it with passion and plays it on Sundays: he must also see it as symbolic of some transcendent truths. And the pubescent boy gazing soulfully into the eyes of the pubescent girl in a William Steig cartoon and murmuring, 'There is something about you, Ethel, which gives me a sort of religious feeling', is, like most adolescents, confused. What any particular religion affirms about the fundamental nature of reality may be obscure, shallow, or, all too often, perverse, but it must, if it is not to consist of the mere collection of received practices and conventional sentiments we usually refer to as moralism, affirm something. If one were to essay a minimal definition of religion today it would perhaps not be Tylor's famous 'belief in spiritual beings', to which Goody (1961), wearied of theoretical subtleties, has lately urged us to return, but rather what Salvador de Madariaga has called 'the relatively modest dogma that God is not mad'.

Usually, of course, religions affirm very much more than this: we believe, as James (1904, Vol. 2, p. 299) remarked, all that we can and would believe everything if we only could. The thing we seem least able to tolerate is a threat to our powers of conception, a suggestion that our ability to create, grasp, and use symbols may fail us, for were this to happen we would be more helpless, as I have already pointed out, than the beavers. The extreme generality, diffuseness, and variability of man's innate (i.e. genetically programmed) response capacities means that without the assistance of cultural patterns he would be functionally incomplete, not merely a talented ape who had, like some under-privileged child, unfortunately been prevented from realizing his full potentialities, but a kind of formless monster with neither sense of direction nor power of self-control, a chaos of spasmodic impulses and vague emotions (Geertz, 1962). Man depends upon symbols and symbol systems with a dependence so great as to be decisive for his creatural viability and, as a result, his sensitivity to even the remotest indication that they may prove unable to cope with one or another aspect of experience raises within him the gravest sort of anxiety:

'[Man] can adapt himself somehow to anything his imagination can cope with; but he cannot deal with Chaos. Because his characteristic function and highest asset is conception, his greatest fright is to meet what he cannot construe – the "uncanny", as it is popularly called. It need not be a new object; we do meet new things, and "understand" them promptly, if tentatively, by the nearest analogy, when our minds are functioning freely; but under mental stress even perfectly familiar things may become suddenly disorganized and give us the horrors. Therefore our most important assets are always the symbols of our general *orientation* in nature, on the earth, in society, and in what we are doing: the symbols of our *Weltanschauung* and *Lebensanschauung*. Consequently, in a primitive society, a daily ritual is incorporated in common activities, in eating, washing, fire-making, etc., as well as in pure ceremonial; because the need of reasserting the tribal morale and recognizing its cosmic conditions is constantly felt. In Christian Europe the Church brought men daily (in some orders even hourly) to their knees, to enact if not to contemplate their assent to the ultimate concepts' (Langer, 1960, p. 287, italics original).

There are at least three points where chaos – a tumult of events which lack not just interpretations but *interpretability* – threatens to break in upon man: at the limits of his analytic capacities, at the limits of his powers of endurance, and at the limits of his moral insight. Bafflement, suffering, and a sense of intractable ethical paradox are all, if they become intense enough or are sustained long enough, radical challenges to the proposition that life is comprehensible and that we can, by taking thought, orient ourselves effectively within it – challenges with which any religion, however 'primitive', which hopes to persist must attempt somehow to cope.

Of the three issues, it is the first which has been least investigated by modern social anthropologists (though Evans-Pritchard's (1937) classic discussion of why granaries fall on some Azande and not on others, is a notable exception). Even to consider people's religious beliefs as attempts to bring anomalous events or experiences – death, dreams, mental fugues, volcanic eruptions, or marital infidelity – within the circle of the at least potentially explicable seems to smack of Tyloreanism or worse. But it does appear to be a fact that at least some men – in all probability, most men – are unable to leave unclarified problems of analysis merely unclarified, just to look at the stranger features of the world's landscape in dumb astonishment or bland apathy without trying to develop, however fantastic, inconsistent, or simple-minded, some notions as to how such features might be reconciled with the more ordinary deliverances of experience. Any chronic failure of one's explanatory apparatus, the complex of received culture patterns (common sense, science, philosophical speculation, myth) one has for mapping the empirical world, to explain things which cry out for explanation tends to lead to a deep disquiet – a tendency rather more widespread and a disquiet rather deeper than we have sometimes supposed since the pseudo-science view of religious belief was, quite rightfully, deposed. After all, even that high priest of heroic atheism, Lord Russell, once remarked that although the problem of the existence of God had never bothered him, the ambiguity of certain mathematical axioms had threatened to unhinge his mind. And Einstein's profound dissatisfaction with quantum mechanics was based on a – surely religious – inability to believe that, as he put it, God plays dice with the universe.

But this quest for lucidity and the rush of metaphysical anxiety that occurs when empirical phenomena threaten to remain intransigently opaque is found on much humbler intellectual levels. Certainly, I was struck in my own work, much more than I had at all expected to be, by the degree to which my more animistically inclined informants behaved like true Tyloreans. They seemed to be constantly using their beliefs to 'explain' phenomena: or, more accurately, to convince themselves that the phenomena were explainable within the accepted scheme of things, for they commonly had only a minimal attachment to the particular soul possession, emotional disequilibrium, taboo infringement, or bewitchment hypothesis they advanced and were all too ready to abandon it for some other, in the same genre, which struck them as more plausible given the facts of the case. What they were *not* ready to do was abandon it for no other hypothesis at all; to leave events to themselves.

And what is more, they adopted this nervous cognitive stance with respect to phenomena which had no immediate practical bearing on their own lives, or for that matter on anyone's. When a peculiarly shaped, rather large toadstool grew up in a carpenter's house in the short space of a few days (or, some said, a few hours), people came from miles around to see it, and everyone had some sort of explanation – some animist, some animatist, some not quite either – for it. Yet it would be hard to argue that the toadstool had any social value in Radcliffe-Brown's (1952) sense, or was connected in any way with anything which did and for which it could have been standing proxy, like the Andaman cicada. Toadstools play about the same role in Javanese life as they do in ours and in the ordinary course of things Javanese have about as much interest in them as we do. It was just that this one was 'odd', 'strange', 'uncanny' – *aneh*. And the odd, strange, and uncanny simply must be accounted for – or, again, the conviction that it *could be accounted for* sustained. One does not shrug off a toadstool which grows five times as fast as a toadstool has any right to grow. In the broadest sense the 'strange' toadstool did have implications, and critical ones, for those who heard about it. It threatened their most general ability to understand the world, raised the uncomfortable question of whether the beliefs which they held about nature were workable, the standards of truth they used valid.

Nor is this to argue that it is only, or even mainly, sudden eruptions of extraordinary events which engender in man the disquieting sense that his cognitive resources may prove un-availing or that this intuition appears only in its acute form. More commonly it is a persistent, constantly re-experienced difficulty in grasping certain aspects of nature, self, and society, in bringing certain elusive phenomena within the sphere of culturally formulatable fact, which renders man chronically uneasy and toward which a more equable flow of diagnostic symbols is consequently directed. It is what lies beyond a relatively fixed frontier of accredited knowledge that, looming as a constant background to the daily round of practical life, sets ordinary human experience in a permanent context of metaphysical concern and raises the dim, back-of-the-mind suspicion that one may be adrift in an absurd world:

'Another subject which is matter for this characteristic intellectual enquiry [among the Iatmul] is the nature of ripples and waves on the surface of water. It is said secretly that men, pigs, trees, grass – all the objects in the world – are only patterns of waves. Indeed there seems to be some agreement about this, although it perhaps conflicts with the theory of reincarnation, according to which the ghost of the dead is blown as a mist by the East Wind up the river and into the womb of the deceased's son's wife. Be that as it may – there is still the question of how ripples and waves are caused. The clan which claims the East Wind as a totem is clear enough about this: the Wind with her mosquito fan causes the waves. But other clans have personified the waves and say that they are a person (Kontum-mali) independent of the wind. Other clans, again, have other theories. On one occasion I took some Iatmul natives down to the coast and found one of them sitting by himself gazing with rapt attention at the sea. It was a windless day, but a slow swell was breaking on the beach. Among the totemic ancestors of his clan he counted a personified slit gong who had floated down the river to the sea and who was believed to cause the waves. He was gazing at the waves which were heaving and breaking when no wind was blowing, demonstrating the truth of his clan myth' (Bateson, 1958, pp. 130-131).[2]

The second experiential challenge in whose face the meaningfulness of a particular pattern of life threatens to dissolve into a chaos of thingless names and nameless things – the problem of suffering – has been rather more investigated, or at least described, mainly because of the great amount of attention given in works on tribal religion to what are perhaps its two main loci: illness and mourning. Yet for all the fascinated interest in the emotional aura that surrounds these extreme situations, there has been, with a few exceptions such as

Lienhardt's recent (1961, pp. 151ff) discussion of Dinka divining, little conceptual advance over the sort of crude confidence-type theory set forth by Malinowski: viz. that religion helps one to endure 'situations of emotional stress' by 'open[ing] up escapes from such situations and such impasses as offer no empirical way out except by ritual and belief into the domain of the supernatural' (1948, p. 67). The inadequacy of this 'theology of optimism', as Nadel (1957) rather drily called it, is, of course, radical. Over its career religion has probably disturbed men as much as it has cheered them; forced them into a head-on, unblinking confrontation of the fact that they are born to trouble as often as it has enabled them to avoid such a confrontation by projecting them into sort of infantile fairy-tale world where – Malinowski again (1948, p. 67) – 'hope cannot fail nor desire deceive'. With the possible exception of Christian Science, there are few if any religious traditions, 'great' or 'little', in which the proposition that life hurts is not strenuously affirmed and in some it is virtually glorified:

'She was an old [Ba-Ila] woman of a family with a long genealogy. Leza, "the Besetting-One", stretched out his hand against the family. He slew her mother and father while she was yet a child, and in the course of years all connected with her perished. She said to herself, "Surely I shall keep those who sit on my thighs." But no, even they, the children of her children, were taken from her. . . . Then came into her heart a desperate resolution to find God and to ask the meaning of it all. . . . So she began to travel, going through country after country, always with the thought in her mind: "I shall come to where the earth ends and there I shall find a road to God and I shall ask him: "What have I done to thee that thou afflictist me in this manner?" She never found where the earth ends, but though disappointed she did not give up her search, and as she passed through the different countries they asked her, "What have you come for, old woman?" And the answer would be, "I am seeking Leza." "Seeking Leza! For what?" "My brothers, you ask me! Here in the nations is there one who suffers as I have suffered?" And they would ask again, "How have you suffered?" "In this way. I am

18

alone. As you see me, a solitary old woman; that is how I am!"
And they answered, "Yes, we see. That is how you are!
Bereaved of friends and husband? In what do you differ from
others? The Besetting-One sits on the back of every one of
us and we cannot shake him off." She never obtained her
desire: she died of a broken heart' (Smith & Dale, 1920, II,
pp. 197ff; quoted in Radin, 1957, pp. 100-101).

As a religious problem, the problem of suffering is, paradoxi-
cally, not how to avoid suffering but how to suffer, how to make
of physical pain, personal loss, worldly defeat, or the helpless
contemplation of others' agony something bearable, supportable
– something, as we say, sufferable. It was in this effort that the
Ba-Ila woman – perhaps necessarily, perhaps not – failed and,
literally not knowing how to feel about what had happened to
her, how to suffer, perished in confusion and despair. Where the
more intellective aspects of what Weber called the Problem of
Meaning are a matter affirming the ultimate explicability of
experience, the more affective aspects are a matter of affirming
its ultimate sufferableness. As religion on one side anchors the
power of our symbolic resources for formulating analytic ideas
in an authoritative conception of the overall shape of reality, so
on another side it anchors the power of our, also symbolic,
resources for expressing emotions – moods, sentiments, passions,
affections, feelings – in a similar conception of its pervasive
tenor, its inherent tone and temper. For those able to embrace
them, and for so long as they are able to embrace them,
religious symbols provide a cosmic guarantee not only for their
ability to comprehend the world, but also, comprehending it,
to give a precision to their feeling, a definition to their emotions
which enables them, morosely or joyfully, grimly or cavalierly,
to endure it.

Consider in this light the well-known Navaho curing rites
usually referred to as 'sings' (Kluckhohn & Leighton, 1946;
Reichard, 1950). A sing – the Navaho have about sixty different
ones for different purposes, but virtually all of them are dedicated to removing some sort of physical or mental illness – is a
kind of religious psychodrama in which there are three main
actors: the 'singer' or curer, the patient, and, as a kind of

antiphonal chorus, the patient's family and friends. The structure of all the sings, the drama's plot, is quite similar. There are three main acts: a purification of the patient and audience; a statement, by means of repetitive chants and ritual manipulations, of the wish to restore well-being ('harmony') in the patient; an identification of the patient with the Holy People and his consequent 'cure'. The purification rites involved forced sweating, induced vomiting, etc. to expel the sickness from the patient physically. The chants, which are numberless, consist mainly of simple optative phrases ('may the patient be well', 'I am getting better all over', etc.). And, finally, the identification of the patient with the Holy People, and thus with cosmic order generally, is accomplished through the agency of a sand painting depicting the Holy People in one or another appropriate mythic setting. The singer places the patient on the painting, touching the feet, hands, knees, shoulders, breast, back, and head of the divine figures and then the corresponding parts of the patient, performing thus what is essentially a communion rite between the patient and the Holy People, a bodily identification of the human and the divine (Reichard, 1950). This is the climax of the sing: the whole curing process may be likened, Reichard says, to a spiritual osmosis in which the illness in man and the power of the deity penetrate the ceremonial membrane in both directions, the former being neutralized by the latter. Sickness seeps out in the sweat, vomit, and other purification rites; health seeps in as the Navaho patient touches, through the medium of the singer, the sacred sand painting. Clearly, the symbolism of the sing focuses upon the problem of human suffering and attempts to cope with it by placing it in a meaningful context, providing a mode of action through which it can be expressed, being expressed understood, and being understood, endured. The sustaining effect of the sing (and since the commonest disease is tuberculosis, it can in most cases be only sustaining), rests ultimately on its ability to give the stricken person a vocabulary in terms of which to grasp the nature of his distress and relate it to the wider world. Like a calvary, a recitation of Buddha's emergence from his father's palace or a performance of *Oedipus Tyrannos* in other religious traditions, a sing is mainly concerned with the presentation of a specific and concrete image of truly human, and so endurable, suffering powerful enough to resist the challenge of emotional meaninglessness raised by the existence of intense and unremovable brute pain.

The problem of suffering passes easily into the problem of evil, for if suffering is severe enough it usually, though not always, seems morally undeserved as well, at least to the sufferer. But they are not, however, exactly the same thing – a fact I think Weber, too influenced by the biases of a monotheistic tradition in which, as the various aspects of human experience must be conceived to proceed from a single, voluntaristic source, man's pain reflects directly on God's goodness, did not fully recognize in his generalization of the dilemmas of Christian theodicy Eastward. For where the problem of suffering is concerned with threats to our ability to put our 'undisciplined squads of emotion' into some sort of soldierly order, the problem of evil is concerned with threats to our ability to make sound moral judgements. What is involved in the problem of evil is not the adequacy of our symbolic resources to govern our affective life, but the adequacy of those resources to provide a workable set of ethical criteria, normative guides to govern our action. The vexation here is the gap between things as they are and as they ought to be if our conceptions of right and wrong make sense, the gap between what we deem various individuals deserve and what we see that they get – a phenomenon summed up in that profound quatrain:

> The rain falls on the just
> And on the unjust fella;
> But mainly upon the just,
> Because the unjust has the just's umbrella.

Or if this seems too flippant an expression of an issue that, in somewhat different form, animates the Book of Job and the *Baghavad Gita*, the following classical Javanese poem, known, sung, and repeatedly quoted in Java by virtually everyone over the age of six, puts the point – the discrepancy between moral prescriptions and material rewards, the seeming inconsistency of 'is' and 'ought' – rather more elegantly:

21

We have lived to see a time without order
In which everyone is confused in his mind.
One cannot bear to join in the madness,
But if he does not do so
He will not share in the spoils,
And will starve as a result.
Yes, God; wrong is wrong:
Happy are those who forget,
Happier yet those who remember and have deep insight.

Nor is it necessary to be theologically self-conscious to be religiously sophisticated. The concern with intractable ethical paradox, the disquieting sense that one's moral insight is inadequate to one's moral experience, is as alive on the level of so-called 'primitive' religion as it is on that of the so-called 'civilized'. The set of notions about 'division in the world' that Lienhardt describes (1961, pp. 28-55) for the Dinka is a useful case in point. Like so many peoples, the Dinka believe that the sky, where 'Divinity' is located, and earth, where man dwells, were at one time contiguous, the sky lying just above the earth and being connected to it by a rope, so that men could move at will between the two realms. There was no death and the first man and woman were permitted but a single grain of millet a day, which was all that they at that time required. One day, the woman – of course – decided, out of greed, to plant more than the permitted grain of millet and in her avid haste and industry accidently struck Divinity with the handle of the hoe. Offended, he severed the rope, withdrew into the distant sky of today, and left man to labor for his food, to suffer sickness and death, and to experience separation from the source of his being, his Creator. Yet the meaning of this strangely familiar story to the Dinka is, as indeed is Genesis to Jews and Christians, not homiletic but descriptive:

'Those [Dinka] who have commented on these stories have sometimes made it clear that their sympathies lie with Man in his plight, and draw attention to the smallness of the fault for which Divinity withdrew the benefits of his closeness. The image of striking Divinity with a hoe . . . often evokes a certain amusement, almost as though the story were indul-

gently being treated as too childish to explain the consequences attributed to the event. But it is clear that the point
of the story of Divinity's withdrawal from men is not to
suggest an improving moral judgement on human behaviour.
It is to represent a total situation known to the Dinka today.
Men now are – as the first man and woman then became –
active, self-assertive, inquiring, acquisitive. Yet they are also
subject to suffering and death, ineffective, ignorant and poor.
Life is insecure; human calculations often prove erroneous,
and men must often learn by experience that the consequences
of their acts are quite other than they may have anticipated
or consider equitable. Divinity's withdrawal from Man as the
result of a comparatively trifling offence, by human standards,
presents the contrast between equitable human judgements
and the action of the Power which are held ultimately to
control what happens in Dinka life. . . . To the Dinka, the
moral order is ultimately constituted according to principles
which often elude men, which experience and tradition in part
reveal, and which human action cannot change . . . The myth
of Divinity's withdrawal then reflects the facts of existence
as they are known. The Dinka are in a universe which is
largely beyond their control, and where events may contra-
dict the most reasonable human expectations' (Lienhardt,
1961, p. 53-54).

Thus the problem of evil, or perhaps one should say the
problem *about* evil, is in essence the same sort of problem of or
about bafflement and the problem of or about suffering. The
strange opacity of certain empirical events, the dumb senseless-
ness of intense or inexorable pain, and the enigmatic unaccounta-
bility of gross iniquity all raise the uncomfortable suspicion
that perhaps the world, and hence man's life in the world, has
no genuine order at all – no empirical regularity, no emotional
form, no moral coherence. And the religious response to this
suspicion is in each case the same: the formulation, by means of
symbols, of an image of such a genuine order of the world which
will account for, and even celebrate, the perceived ambiguities,
puzzles, and paradoxes in human experience. The effort is not
to deny the undeniable – that there are unexplained events,

E   23

that life hurts, or that rain falls upon the just – but to deny that there are inexplicable events, that life is unendurable, and that justice is a mirage. The principles which constitute the moral order may indeed often elude men, as Lienhardt puts it, in the same way as fully satisfactory explanations of anomalous events or effective forms for the expression of feeling often elude them. What is important, to a religious man at least, is that this elusiveness be accounted for, that it be not the result of the fact that there are no such principles, explanations, or forms, that life is absurd and the attempt to make moral, intellectual or emotional sense out of experience is bootless. The Dinka can admit, in fact insist upon, the moral ambiguities and contradictions of life as they live it because these ambiguities and contradictions are seen not as ultimate, but as the 'rational', 'natural', 'logical' (one may choose one's own adjective here, for none of them is truly adequate) outcome of the moral structure of reality which the myth of the withdrawn 'Divinity' depicts, or as Lienhardt says, 'images'.

The Problem of Meaning in each of its intergrading aspects (how these aspects in fact intergrade in each particular case, what sort of interplay there is between the sense of analytic, emotional, and moral impotence, seems to me one of the outstanding, and except for Weber untouched, problems for comparative research in this whole field) is a matter of affirming, or at least recognizing, the inescapability of ignorance, pain, and injustice on the human plane while simultaneously denying that these irrationalities are characteristic of the world as a whole. And it is in terms of religious symbolism, a symbolism relating man's sphere of existence to a wider sphere within which it is conceived to rest, that both the affirmation and the denial are made.[3]

4. ... *and clothing those conceptions with such an aura of factuality that ...*

There arises here, however, a profounder question: how is it that this denial comes to be believed? how is it that the religious man moves from a troubled perception of experienced disorder to a more or less settled conviction of fundamental order? just what does 'belief' mean in a religious context? Of all the problems surrounding attempts to conduct anthropological analysis of religion this is the one that has perhaps been most troublesome and therefore the most often avoided, usually by relegating it to psychology, that raffish outcast discipline to which social anthropologists are forever consigning phenomena they are unable to deal with within the framework of a denatured Durkheimianism. But the problem will not go away, it is not 'merely' psychological (nothing social is), and no anthropological theory of religion which fails to attack it is worthy of the name. We have been trying to stage Hamlet without the Prince quite long enough.

It seems to me that it is best to begin any approach to this issue with frank recognition that religious belief involves not a Baconian induction from everyday experience – for then we should all be agnostics – but rather a prior acceptance of authority which transforms that experience. The existence of bafflement, pain, and moral paradox – of The Problem of Meaning – is one of the things that drive men toward belief in gods, devils, spirits, totemic principles, or the spiritual efficacy of cannibalism (an enfolding sense of beauty or a dazzling perception of power are others), but it is not the basis upon which those beliefs rest, but rather their most important field of application:

'We point to the state of the world as illustrative of doctrine, but never as evidence for it. So Belsen illustrates a world of original sin, but original sin is not an hypothesis to account for happenings like Belsen. We justify a particular religious belief by showing its place in the total religious conception; we justify a religious belief as a whole by referring to authority. We accept authority because we discover it at some point in the world at which we worship, at which we accept the lordship of something not ourselves. We do not worship authority, but we accept authority as defining the worshipful. So someone may discover the possibility of worship in the life of the Reformed Churches and accept the Bible as authoritative; or in the Roman Church and accept papal authority' (MacIntyre, 1957, pp. 201-202).

This is, of course, a Christian statement of the matter; but it is not to be despised on that account. In tribal religions authority lies in the persuasive power of traditional imagery; in mystical ones in the apodictic force of supersensible experience; in charismatic ones in the hypnotic attraction of an extraordinary personality. But the priority of the acceptance of an authoritative criterion in religious matters over the revelation which is conceived to flow from that acceptance is not less complete than in scriptural or hieratic ones. The basic axiom underlying what we may perhaps call 'the religious perspective' is everywhere the same: he who would know must first believe.

But to speak of 'the religious perspective' is, by implication, to speak of one perspective among others. A perspective is a mode of seeing, in that extended sense of 'see' in which it means 'discern', 'apprehend', 'understand', or 'grasp'. It is a particular way of looking at life, a particular manner of construing the world, as when we speak of an historical perspective, a scientific perspective, an aesthetic perspective, a common-sense perspective, or even the bizarre perspective embodied in dreams and in hallucinations.[4] The question then comes down to, first, what is 'the religious perspective' generically considered, as differentiated from other perspectives; and second, how do men come to adopt it.

If we place the religious perspective against the background of three of the other major perspectives in terms of which men construe the world – the common-sensical, the scientific, and the aesthetic – its special character emerges more sharply. What distinguishes common sense as a mode of 'seeing' is, as Schutz (1962) has pointed out, a simple acceptance of the world, its objects, and its processes as being just what they seem to be – what is sometimes called naïve realism – and the pragmatic motive, the wish to act upon that world so as to bend it to one's practical purposes, to master it, or so far as that proves impossible, to adjust to it. The world of everyday life, itself, of course, a cultural product, for it is framed in terms of the symbolic conceptions of 'stubborn fact' handed down from generation to generation, is the established scene and given object of our actions. Like Mt. Everest it is just there and the thing to do with it, if one feels the need to do anything with it at all, is to climb it. In the scientific perspective it is precisely

this givenness which disappears (Schutz, 1962). Deliberate
doubt and systematic inquiry, the suspension of the pragmatic
motive in favor of disinterested observation, the attempt to
analyze the world in terms of formal concepts whose relationship to the informal conceptions of common sense become
increasingly problematic – there are the hallmarks of the
attempt to grasp the world scientifically. And as for the aesthetic
perspective, which under the rubric of 'the aesthetic attitude'
has been perhaps most exquisitely examined, it involves a
different sort of suspension of naïve realism and practical
interest, in that instead of questioning the credentials of everyday experience that experience is merely ignored in favor of an
eager dwelling upon appearances, an engrossment in surfaces,
an absorption in things, as we say, 'in themselves': 'The function
of artistic illusion is not "make-believe" . . . but the very
opposite, disengagement from belief – the contemplation of
sensory qualities without their usual meanings of "here's that
chair", "That's my telephone" . . . etc. The knowledge that
what is before us has no practical significance in the world is
what enables us to give attention to its appearance as such'
(Langer, 1957, p. 49). And like the common-sensical and the
scientific (or the historical, the philosophical, and the autistic),
this perspective, this 'way of seeing' is not the product of some
mysterious Cartesian chemistry, but is induced, mediated, and
in fact created by means of symbols. It is the artist's skill which
can produce those curious quasi-objects – poems, dramas,
sculptures, symphonies – which, dissociating themselves from
the solid world of common sense, take on the special sort of
eloquence only sheer appearances can achieve.

The religious perspective differs from the common-sensical
in that, as already pointed out, it moves beyond the realities of
everyday life to wider ones which correct and complete them,
and its defining concern is not action upon those wider realities
but acceptance of them, faith in them. It differs from the
scientific perspective in that it questions the realities of everyday life not out of an institutionalized scepticism which
dissolves the world's givenness into a swirl of probabilistic
hypotheses, but in terms of what it takes to be wider, non-
hypothetical truths. Rather than detachment, its watchword is

27

commitment; rather than analysis, encounter. And it differs from art in that instead of effecting a disengagement from the whole question of factuality, deliberately manufacturing an air of semblance and illusion, it deepens the concern with fact and seeks to create an aura of utter actuality. It is this sense of the 'really real' upon which the religious perspective rests and which the symbolic activities of religion as a cultural system are devoted to producing, intensifying, and, so far as possible, rendering inviolable by the discordant revelations of secular experience. It is, again, the imbuing of a certain specific complex of symbols – of the metaphysic they formulate and the style of life they recommend – with a persuasive authority which, from an analytic point of view is the essence of religious action.

Which brings us, at length, to ritual. For it is in ritual – i.e. consecrated behavior – that this conviction that religious conceptions are veridical and that religious directives are sound is somehow generated. It is in some sort of ceremonial form – even if that form be hardly more than the recitation of a myth, the consultation of an oracle, or the decoration of a grave – that the moods and motivations which sacred symbols induce in men and the general conceptions of the order of existence which they formulate for men meet and reinforce one another. In a ritual, the world as lived and the world as imagined, fused under the agency of a single set of symbolic forms, turn out to be the same world, producing thus that idiosyncratic transformation in one's sense of reality to which Santayana refers in my epigraph. Whatever role divine intervention may or may not play in the creation of faith – and it is not the business of the scientist to pronounce upon such matters one way or the other – it is, primarily at least, out of the context of concrete acts of religious observance that religious conviction emerges on the human plane.

However, though any religious ritual, no matter how apparently automatic or conventional (if it is truly automatic or merely conventional it is not religious), involves this symbolic fusion of ethos and world-view, it is mainly certain more elaborate and usually more public ones, ones in which a broad range of moods and motivations on the one hand and of metaphysical conceptions on the other are caught up, which shape the spiritual consciousness of a people. Employing a useful term introduced by Singer (1955), we may call these full-blown ceremonies 'cultural performances' and note that they represent not only the point at which the dispositional and conceptual aspects of religious life converge for the believer, but also the point at which the interaction between them can be most readily examined by the detached observer:

> 'Whenever Madrasi Brahmans (and non-Brahmans, too, for that matter) wished to exhibit to me some feature of Hinduism, they always referred to, or invited me to see, a particular rite or ceremony in the life cycle, in a temple festival, or in the general sphere of religious and cultural performances. Reflecting on this in the course of my interviews and observations I found that the more abstract generalizations about Hinduism (my own as well as those I heard) could generally be checked, directly or indirectly, against these observable performances' (Singer, 1958).

Of course, all cultural performances are not religious performances, and the line between those that are and artistic, or even political ones is often not so easy to draw in practice, for, like social forms, symbolic forms can serve multiple purposes. But the point is that, paraphrasing slightly, Indians – 'and perhaps all peoples' – seem to think of their religion 'as encapsulated in these discrete performances which they [can] exhibit to visitors and to themselves' (Singer, 1955). The mode of exhibition is however radically different for the two sorts of witness, a fact seemingly overlooked by those who would argue that 'religion is a form of human art' (Firth, 1951, p. 250). Where for 'visitors' religious performances can, in the nature of the case, only be presentations of a particular religious perspective, and thus aesthetically appreciated or scientifically dissected, for participants they are in addition enactments, materializations, realizations of it – not only models *of* what they believe, but also models *for* the believing of it. In these plastic dramas men attain their faith as they portray it.

As a case in point, let me take a spectacularly theatrical cultural performance from Bali – that in which a terrible witch called Rangda engages in a ritual combat with an endearing monster called Barong.[5] Usually, but not inevitably presented on the occasion of a death temple celebration, the drama consists of a masked dance in which the witch – depicted as a wasted old widow, prostitute, and eater of infants – comes to spread plague and death upon the land and is opposed by the monster – depicted as a kind of cross between a clumsy bear, a silly puppy, and a strutting Chinese dragon. Rangda, danced by a single male, is a hideous figure. Her eyes bulge from her forehead like swollen boils. Her teeth become tusks curving up over her cheeks and fangs protruding down over her chin. Her yellowed hair falls down around her in a matted tangle. Her breasts are dry and pendulous dugs edged with hair, between which hang, like so many sausages, strings of colored entrails. Her long red tongue is a stream of fire. And as she dances she splays her dead-white hands, from which protrude ten-inch claw-like fingernails, out in front of her and utters unnerving shrieks of metallic laughter. Barong, danced by two men fore-and-aft in vaudeville horse fashion, is another matter. His shaggy sheepdog coat is hung with gold and mica ornaments that glitter in the half-light. He is adorned with flowers, sashes, feathers, mirrors, and a comical beard made from human hair. And though, a demon too, his eyes also pop and he snaps his fanged jaws with seemly fierceness when faced with Rangda or other affronts to his dignity, the cluster of tinkling bells which hang from his absurdly arching tail somehow contrives to take most of the edge off his fearfulness. If Rangda is a satanic image, Barong is a farcical one, and their clash is a clash (an inconclusive one) between the malignant and the ludicrous.

This odd counterpoint of implacable malice and low comedy pervades the whole performance. Rangda, clutching her magical white cloth, moves around in a slow stagger, now pausing immobile in thought or uncertainty, now lurching suddenly forward. The moment of her entry (one sees those terrible long-nailed hands first as she emerges through the split gateway at the top of a short flight of stone stairs) is one of terrific tension when it seems, to a 'visitor' at least, that everyone is about to break and run in panic. She herself seems insane with fear and hated as she screams deprecations at Barong amid the wild clanging of the gamelan. She may in fact go amok. I have myself seen Rangdas hurl themselves headlong into the gamelan

or run frantically about in total confusion, being subdued and
reoriented only by the combined force of a half-dozen spectators; and one hears many tales of amok Rangdas holding a whole
village in terror for hours and of impersonators becoming
permanently deranged by their experiences. But Barong, though
he is charged with the same mana-like sacred power (*sakti* in
Balinese) as Rangda, and his impersonators are also entranced,
seems to have very great difficulty in being serious. He frolics
with his retinue of demons (who add to the gaiety by indelicate
pranks of their own), lies down on a metallaphone while it is
being played or beats on a drum with his legs, moves in one
direction in his front half and another in his rear or bends his
segmented body into foolish contortions, brushes flies from his
body or sniffs aromas in the air, and generally prances about in
paroxysms of narcissistic vanity. The contrast is not absolute,
for Rangda is sometimes momentarily comic as when she
pretends to polish the mirrors on Barong's coat, and Barong
becomes rather more serious after Rangda appears, nervously
clacking his jaws at her and ultimately attacking her directly.
Nor are the humorous and the horrible always kept rigidly
separated, as in that strange scene in one section of the cycle in
which several minor witches (disciples of Rangda) toss the
corpse of a stillborn child around to the wild amusement of the
audience; or another, no less strange, in which the sight of a
pregnant woman alternating hysterically between tears and
laughter while being knocked about by a group of grave-diggers,
seems for some reason excruciatingly funny. The twin themes of
horror and hilarity find their purest expression in the two
protagonists and their endless, indecisive struggle for dominance, but they are woven with deliberate intricacy through the
whole texture of the drama. They – or rather the relations
between them – are what it is about.

It is unnecessary to attempt a thoroughgoing description of a
Rangda-Barong performance here. Such performances vary
widely in detail, consist of several not too closely integrated
parts, and in any case are so complex in structure as to defy
easy summary. For our purposes, the main point to be stressed
is that the drama is, for the Balinese, not merely a spectacle to
be watched but a ritual to be enacted. There is no aesthetic

distance here separating actors from audience and placing the depicted events in an unenterable world of illusion, and by the time a full-scale Rangda-Barong encounter has been concluded a majority, often nearly all, of the members of the group sponsoring it will have become caught up in it not just imaginatively but bodily. In one of Belo's examples (1960, pp. 159-168) I count upwards of seventy-five people – men, women, and children – taking part in the activity at some point or other, and thirty to forty participants is in no way unusual. As a performance, the drama is like a high mass not like a presentation of *Murder in the Cathedral*: it is a drawing near, not a standing back.

In part, this entry into the body of the ritual takes place through the agency of the various supporting roles contained in it – minor witches, demons, various sorts of legendary and mythical figures – which selected villagers enact. But mostly it takes place through the agency of an extraordinarily developed capacity for psychological dissociation on the part of a very large segment of the population. A Rangda-Barong struggle is inevitably marked by anywhere from three or four to several dozen spectators becoming possessed by one or another demon, falling into violent trances 'like firecrackers going off one after the other' (Belo, 1960), and, snatching up krisses, rushing to join the fray. Mass trance, spreading like a panic, projects the individual Balinese out of the commonplace world in which he usually lives into that most uncommonplace one in which Rangda and Barong live. To become entranced is, for the Balinese, to cross a threshold into another order of existence – the word for trance is *nadi*, from *dadi*, often translated 'to become' but which might be even more simply rendered as 'to be'. And even those who, for whatever reasons, do not make this spiritual crossing are caught up in the proceedings, for it is they who must keep the frenzied activities of the entranced from getting out of hand by the application of physical restraint if they are ordinary men, by the sprinkling of holy water and the chanting of spells if they are priests. At its height a Rangda-Barong rite hovers, or at least seems to hover, on the brink of mass amok with the diminishing band of the unentranced striving desperately (and, it seems almost always successfully) to control the growing band of the entranced.

In its standard form – if it can be said to have a standard form – the performance begins with an appearance of Barong, prancing and preening, as a general prophylactic against what is to follow. Then may come various mythic scenes relating the story – not always precisely the same one – upon which the performance is based – until finally Barong and then Rangda appear. Their battle begins. Barong drives Rangda back toward the gate of the death temple. But he has not the power to expel her completely and he is in turn driven back toward the village. At length, when it seems as though Rangda will finally prevail, a number of entranced men rise, krisses in hand, and rush to support Barong. But as they approach Rangda (who has turned her back in meditation), she wheels upon them and, waving her *sakti* white cloth, leaves them comatose on the ground. Rangda then hastily retires (or is carried) to the temple, where she herself collapses, hidden from the aroused crowd which, my informants said, would kill her were it to see her in a helpless state. The Barong moves among the kris dancers and wakens them by snapping his jaws at them or nuzzling them with his beard. As they return, still entranced, to 'consciousness', they are enraged by the disappearance of Rangda, and unable to attack her they turn their krisses (harmlessly because they are entranced) against their own chests in frustration. Usually sheer pandemonium breaks out at this point with members of the crowd, of both sexes, falling into trance all around the courtyard and rushing out to stab themselves, wrestle with one another, devour live chicks or excrement, wallow convulsively in the mud, and so on, while the non-entranced attempt to relieve them of their krisses and keep them at least minimally in order. In time, the trancers sink, one by one, into coma from which they are aroused by the priests' holy water and the great battle is over – once more a complete stand-off. Rangda has not been conquered, but neither has she conquered.

One place to search for the meaning of this ritual is in the collection of myths, tales, and explicit beliefs which it supposedly enacts. However, not only are these various and variable – for some people Rangda is an incarnation of Durga, Siva's malignant consort, for others she is Queen Mahendradatta, a figure from a court legend set in eleventh-century Java, for yet

others, the spiritual leader of witches as the Brahmana Priest
is the spiritual leader of men; and notions of who (or 'what')
Barong is are equally diverse and even vaguer – but they seem
to play only a secondary role in the Balinese' preception of the
drama. It is in the direct encounter with the two figures in the
context of the actual performance that the villager comes to
know them as, so far as he is concerned, genuine realities. They
are, then, not representations of anything, but presences.
And when the villagers go into trance they become – *nadi* –
themselves part of the realm in which those presences exist.
To ask, as I once did, a man who has *been* Rangda whether
he thinks she is real is to leave oneself open to the suspicion of
idiocy.

The acceptance of authority that underlies the religious
perspective that the ritual embodies thus flows from the
enactment of the ritual itself. By inducing a set of moods and
motivations – an ethos – and defining an image of cosmic order –
a world-view – by means of a single set of symbols, the performance makes the model *for* and model *of* aspects of religious
belief mere transpositions of one another. Rangda evokes fear
(as well as hatred, disgust, cruelty, horror, and, though I have
not been able to treat the sexual aspects of the performance
here, lust); but she also depicts it:

'The fascination which the figure of the Witch holds for the
Balinese imagination can only be explained when it is
recognized that the Witch is not only a fear inspiring figure,
but that she is Fear. Her hands with their long menacing
finger-nails do not clutch and claw at her victims, although
children who play at being witches do curl their hands in such
gestures. But the Witch herself spreads her arms with palms
out and her finger flexed backward, in the gesture the
Balinese call *kapar*, a term which they apply to the sudden
startled reaction of a man who falls from a tree. . . . Only
when we see the Witch as herself afraid, as well as frightening,
is it possible to explain her appeal, and the pathos which
surrounds her as she dances, hairy, forbidding, tusked and
alone, giving her occasional high eerie laugh' (Bateson & Mead,
1942, p. 36).

And on his side Barong not only induces laughter, he incarnates the Balinese version of the comic spirit – a distinctive combination of playfulness, exhibitionism, and extravagant love of elegance which, along with fear, is perhaps the dominant motive in their life. The constantly recurring struggle of Rangda and Barong to an inevitable draw is thus – for the believing Balinese – both the formulation of a general religious conception and the authoritative experience which justifies, even compels, its acceptance.

5. . . . *that the moods and motivations seem uniquely realistic*
But no one, not even a saint, lives in the world religious symbols formulate all of the time, and the majority of men live in it only at moments. The everyday world of common-sense objects and practical acts is, as Schutz (1962, pp. 226ff.) says, the paramount reality in human experience – paramount in the sense that it is the world in which we are most solidly rooted, whose inherent actuality we can hardly question (however much we may question certain portions of it), and from whose pressures and requirements we can least escape. A man, even large groups of men, may be aesthetically insensitive, religiously unconcerned, and unequipped to pursue formal scientific analysis, but he cannot be completely lacking in common sense and survive. The dispositions which religious rituals induce thus have their most important impact – from a human point of view – outside the boundaries of the ritual itself as they reflect back to color the individual's conception of the established world of bare fact. The peculiar tone that marks the Plains vision quest, the Manus confession, or the Javanese mystical exercise pervades areas of the life of these peoples far beyond the immediately religious, impressing upon them a distinctive style in the sense both of a dominant mood and a characteristic movement. The interweaving of the malignant and the comic, which the Rangda-Barong combat depicts, animates a very wide range of everyday Balinese behavior, much of which, like the ritual itself, has an air of candid fear narrowly contained by obsessive playfulness. Religion is sociologically interesting not because, as vulgar positivism would have it (Leach, 1954, pp. 10ff.), it describes the social order (which, in so far as it does,

it does not only very obliquely but very incompletely), but because, like environment, political power, wealth, jural obligation, personal affection, and a sense of beauty, it shapes it.

The movement back and forth between the religious perspective and the common-sense perspective is actually one of the more obvious empirical occurrences on the social scene, though, again, one of the most neglected by social anthropologists, virtually all of whom have seen it happen countless times. Religious belief has usually been presented as an homogeneous characteristic of an individual, like his place of residence, his occupational role, his kinship position, and so on. But religious belief in the midst of ritual, where it engulfs the total person, transporting him, so far as he is concerned, into another mode of existence, and religious belief as the pale, remembered reflection of that experience in the midst of everyday life are not precisely the same thing, and the failure to realize this has led to some confusion, most especially in connection with the so-called 'primitive mentality' problem. Much of the difficulty between Lévy-Bruhl (1926) and Malinowski (1948) on the nature of 'native thought', for example, arises from a lack of full recognition of this distinction; for where the French philosopher was concerned with the view of reality savages adopted when taking a specifically religious perspective, the Polish-English ethnographer was concerned with that which they adopted when taking a strictly common-sense one. Both perhaps vaguely sensed that they were not talking about exactly the same thing, but where they went astray was in failing to give a specific accounting of the way in which these two forms of 'thought' – or, as I would rather say, these two modes of symbolic formulation – interacted, so that where Lévy-Bruhl's savages tended to live, despite his postludial disclaimers, in a world composed entirely of mystical encounters, Malinowski's tended to live, despite his stress on the functional importance of religion, in a world composed entirely of practical actions. They became reductionists (an idealist is as much of a reductionist as a materialist) in spite of themselves because they failed to see man as moving more or less easily, and very frequently, between radically contrasting ways of looking at the world, ways which are not continuous with one another but separated

36

by cultural gaps across which Kierkegaardian leaps must be made in both directions:

'There are as many innumerable kinds of different shock experiences as there are different finite provinces of meaning upon which I may bestow the accent of reality. Some instances are: the shock of falling asleep as the leap into the world of dreams; the inner transformation we endure if the curtain in the theatre rises as the transition to the world of the stageplay; the radical change in our attitude if, before a painting, we permit our visual field to be limited by what is within the frame as the passage into the pictorial world; our quandary relaxing into laughter, if, in listening to a joke, we are for a short time ready to accept the fictitious world of the jest as a reality in relation to which the world of our daily life takes on the character of foolishness; the child's turning toward his toy as the transition into the play-world; and so on. But also the religious experiences in all their varieties – for instance, Kierkegaard's experience of the "instant" as the leap into the religious sphere – are examples of such a shock, as well as the decision of the scientist to replace all passionate participation in the affairs of "this world" by a disinterested [analytical] attitude' (Schutz, 1962, p. 231).

The recognition and exploration of the qualitative difference – an empirical, not a transcendental difference – between religion pure and religion applied, between an encounter with the supposedly 'really real' and a viewing of ordinary experience in light of what that encounter seems to reveal, will, therefore, take us further toward an understanding of what a Bororo means when he says 'I am a parakeet', or a Christian when he says 'I am a sinner', than either a theory of primitive mysticism in which the commonplace world disappears into a cloud of curious ideas or of a primitive pragmatism in which religion disintegrates into a collection of useful fictions. The parakeet example, which I take from Percy (1961), is a good one. For, as he points out, it is unsatisfactory to say either that the Bororo thinks he is literally a parakeet (for he does not try to mate with other parakeets), that his statement is false or nonsense (for, clearly, he is not offering – or at least not only offering – the sort of class-membership argument which can be confirmed or refuted as, say, 'I am a Bororo' can be confirmed or refuted), or yet again that it is false scientifically but true mythically (because that leads immediately to the pragmatic fiction notion which, as it denies the accolade of truth to 'myth' in the very act of bestowing it, is internally self-contradictory). More coherently it would seem to be necessary to see the sentence as having a different sense in the context of the 'finite province of meaning' which makes up the religious perspective and of that which makes up the common-sensical. In the religious, our Bororo is 'really' a 'parakeet', and given the proper ritual context might well 'mate' with other 'parakeets' – with metaphysical ones like himself not commonplace ones such as those which fly bodily about in ordinary trees. In the common-sensical perspective he is a parakeet in the sense – I assume – that he belongs to a clan whose members regard the parakeet as their totem, a membership from which, given the fundamental nature of reality as the religious perspective reveals it, certain moral and practical consequences flow. A man who says he is a parakeet is, if he says it in normal conversation, saying that, as myth and ritual demonstrate, he is shot through with parakeetness and that this religious fact has some crucial social implications – we parakeets must stick together, not marry one another, not eat mundane parakeets, and so on, for to do otherwise is to act against the grain of the whole universe. It is this placing of proximate acts in ultimate contexts that makes religion, frequently at least, socially so powerful. It alters, often radically, the whole landscape presented to common sense, alters it in such a way that the moods and motivations induced by religious practice seem themselves supremely practical, the only sensible ones to adopt given the way things 'really' are.

Having ritually 'lept' (the image is perhaps a bit too athletic for the actual facts – 'slipped' might be more accurate) into the framework of meaning which religious conceptions define and, the ritual ended, returned again to the common-sense world, a man is – unless, as sometimes happens, the experience fails to register – changed. And as he is changed so also is the common-sense world, for it is now seen as but the partial form of a wider reality which corrects and completes it. But this correction and completion is not, as some students of 'comparative religion' (e.g. Campbell, 1949, pp. 236-237) would have it, everywhere the same in content. The nature of the bias religion gives to ordinary life varies with the religion involved, with the particular dispositions induced in the believer by the specific conceptions of cosmic order he has come to accept. On the level of the 'great' religions, organic distinctiveness is usually recognized, at times insisted upon to the point of zealotry. But even at its simplest folk and tribal levels – where the individuality of religious traditions has so often been dissolved into such desiccated types as 'animism', 'animatism', 'totemism', 'shamanism', 'ancestor worship', and all the other insipid categories by means of which ethnographers of religion devitalize their data – the idiosyncratic character of how various groups of men behave because of what they believe they have experienced is clear. A tranquil Javanese would be no more at home in guilt-ridden Manus than an activist Crow would be in passionless Java. And for all the witches and ritual clowns in the world, Rangda and Barong are not generalized but thoroughly singular figurations of fear and gaiety. What men believe is as various as what they are – a proposition that holds with equal force when it is inverted.

It is this particularity of the impact of religious systems upon social systems (and upon personality systems) which renders general assessments of the value of religion in either moral or functional terms impossible. The sorts of moods and motivations which characterize a man who has just come from an Aztec human sacrifice are rather different from those of one who has just put off his Kachina mask. Even within the same society, what one 'learns' about the essential pattern of life from a sorcery rite and from a commensual meal will have rather diverse effects on social and psychological functioning. One of the main methodological problems in writing about religion scientifically is to put aside at once the tone of the village atheist and that of the village preacher, as well as their more sophisticated equivalents, so that the social and psychological implications of particular religious beliefs can emerge in a clear and neutral light. And when that is done, overall questions about whether religion is 'good' or 'bad', 'functional' or 'dysfunctional', 'ego strengthening' or 'anxiety producing' disappear like the chimeras they are, and one is left with particular evaluations, assessments, and diagnoses in particular cases. There remain, of course, the hardly unimportant questions of whether this or that religious assertion is true, this or that religious experience genuine, or whether true religious assertions and genuine religious experiences are possible at all. But such questions cannot even be asked, much less answered, within the self-imposed limitations of the scientific perspective.

III

For an anthropologist, the importance of religion lies in its capacity to serve, for an individual or for a group, as a source of general, yet distinctive conceptions of the world, the self, and the relations between them, on the one hand – its model *of* aspect – and of rooted, no less distinctive 'mental' dispositions – its model *for* aspect – on the other. From these cultural functions flow, in turn, its social and psychological ones.

Religious concepts spread beyond their specifically metaphysical contexts to provide a framework of general ideas in terms of which a wide range of experience – intellectual, emotional, moral – can be given meaningful form. The Christian sees the Nazi movement against the background of The Fall which, though it does not, in a causal sense, explain it, places it in a moral, a cognitive, even an affective sense. An Azande sees the collapse of a granary upon a friend or relative against the background of a concrete and rather special notion of witchcraft and thus avoids the philosophical dilemmas as well as the psychological stress of indeterminism. A Javanese finds in the borrowed and reworked concept of *rasa* ('sense-taste-feeling-meaning') a means by which to 'see' choreographic, gustatory, emotional, and political phenomena in a new light. A synopsis of cosmic order, a set of religious beliefs, is also a gloss upon the mundane world of social relationships and psychological events. It renders them graspable.

But more than gloss, such beliefs are also a template. They do not merely interpret social and psychological processes in cosmic terms – in which case they would be philosophical, not religious – but they shape them. In the doctrine of original sin is embedded also a recommended attitude toward life, a recurring mood, and a persisting set of motivations. The Zande learns from witchcraft conceptions not just to understand apparent 'accidents' as not accidents at all, but to react to these spurious accidents with hatred for the agent who caused them and to proceed against him with appropriate resolution. *Rasa*, in addition to being a concept of truth, beauty, and goodness, is also a preferred mode of experiencing, a kind of affectless detachment, a variety of bland aloofness, an unshakeable calm. The moods and motivations a religious orientation produces cast a derivative, lunar light over the solid features of a people's secular life.

The tracing of the social and psychological role of religion is thus not so much a matter of finding correlations between specific ritual acts and specific secular social ties – though these correlations do, of course, exist and are very worth continued investigation, especially if we can contrive something novel to say about them. More, it is a matter of understanding how it is that men's notions, however implicit, of the 'really real' and the dispositions these notions induce in them, color their sense of the reasonable, the practical, the humane, and the moral. How far they do so (for in many societies religion's effects seem quite circumscribed, in others completely pervasive); how deeply they do so (for some men, and groups of men, seem to wear their religion lightly so far as the secular world goes, while others seem to apply their faith to each occasion, no matter how trivial); and how effectively they do so (for the width of the gap between what religion recommends and what people actually do is most variable cross-culturally) – all these are crucial issues in the comparative sociology and psychology of religion. Even the degree to which religious systems themselves are developed seems to vary extremely widely, and not merely on a simple evolutionary basis. In one society, the level of elaboration of symbolic formulations of ultimate actuality may reach extraordinary degrees of complexity and systematic articulation; in another, no less developed socially, such formulations may remain primitive in the true sense, hardly more than congeries of fragmentary by-beliefs and isolated images, of sacred reflexes and spiritual pictographs. One need only think of the Australians and the Bushmen, the Toradja and the Alorese, the Hopi and the Apache, the Hindus and the Romans, or even the Italians and the Poles, to see that degree of religious articulateness is not a constant even as between societies of similar complexity.

The anthropological study of religion is therefore a two-stage operation: first, an analysis of the system of meanings embodied in the symbols which make up the religion proper, and, second, the relating of these systems to social-structural and psychological processes. My dissatisfaction with so much of contemporary social anthropological work in religion is not that it concerns itself with the second stage, but that it neglects the first, and in so doing takes for granted what most needs to be elucidated. To discuss the role of ancestor worship in regulating political succession, of sacrificial feasts in defining kinship obligations, of spirit worship in scheduling agricultural practices, of divination in reinforcing social control, or of initiation rites in propelling personality maturation are in no sense unimportant endeavors, and I am not recommending they be abandoned for the kind of jejune cabalism into which symbolic analysis of exotic faiths can so easily fall. But to attempt them with but the most general, commonsense view of what ancestor worship, animal sacrifice, spirit worship, divination, or initiation rites are as religious patterns seems to me not particularly promising. Only when we have a theoretical analysis of symbolic action comparable in sophistication to that we now have for social and psychological action, will we be able to cope effectively with those aspects of social and psychological life in which religion (or art, or science, or ideology) plays a determinant role.

NOTES

1. The reverse mistake, especially common among neo-Kantians such as Cassirer (1953-57), of taking symbols to be identical with, or 'constitutive of', their referents is equally pernicious. 'One can point to the moon with one's finger,' some, probably well-invented, Zen Master is supposed to have said, 'but to take one's finger for the moon is to be a fool.'

2. That the chronic and acute forms of this sort of cognitive concern are closely interrelated, and that responses to the more unusual occasions of it are

patterned on responses established in coping with the more usual is also clear from Bateson's description, however, as he goes on to say: 'On another occasion I invited one of my informants to witness the development of photographic plates. I first desensitised the plates and then developed them in an open dish in moderate light, so that my informant was able to see the gradual appearance of the images. He was much interested, and some days later made me promise never to show this process to members of other clans. Kontum-mali was one of his ancestors, and he saw in the process of photographic development the actual embodiment of ripples into images, and regarded this as a demonstration of the clan's secret' (Bateson, 1958).

3. This is *not*, however, to say that everyone in every society does this; for as the immortal Don Marquis once remarked, you don't have to have a soul unless you really want one. The oft-heard generalization (e.g. Kluckhohn, 1953) that religion is a human universal embodies a confusion between the probably true (though on present evidence unprovable) proposition that there is no human society in which cultural patterns that we can, under the present definition or one like it, call religious are totally lacking, and the surely untrue proposition that all men in all societies are, in any meaningful sense of the term, religious. But if the anthropological study of religious commitment is underdeveloped, the anthropological study of religious non-commitment is non-existent. The anthropology of religion will have come of age when some more subtle Malinowski writes a book called 'Belief and Unbelief (or even "Faith and Hypocrisy") in a Savage Society'.

4. The term 'attitude' as in 'aesthetic attitude' (Bell, 1914) or 'natural attitude' (Schutz, 1962; the phrase is originally Husserl's) is another, perhaps more common term for what I have here called 'perspective'. But I have avoided it because of its strong subjectivist connotations, its tendency to place the stress upon a supposed inner state of an actor rather than on a certain sort of relation – a symbolically mediated one – between an actor and a situation. This is not to say, of course, that a phenomenological analysis of religious experience, if cast in inter-subjective, non-transcendental, genuinely scientific terms (see Percy, 1958) is not essential to a full understanding of religious belief, but merely that that is not the focus of my concern here. 'Outlook', 'frame of reference', 'frame of mind', 'orientation', 'stance', 'mental set', etc. are other terms sometimes employed, depending upon whether the analyst wishes to stress the social, psychological, or cultural aspects of the matter.

5. The Rangda-Barong complex has been extensively described and analysed by a series of unusually gifted ethnographers (Belo, 1949, 1960; deZoete & Spies, 1938; Bateson & Mead, 1942; Covarrubias, 1937) and I will make no attempt to present it here in more than schematic form. Much of my interpretation of the complex rests on personal observations made in Bali during 1957-1958 (see Geertz, 1964b).

ACKNOWLEDGEMENTS

Thanks are due to the individuals and publishers concerned for permission to quote passages from the following works: The Clarendon Press in respect of *Divinity and Experience* by G. Lienhardt; Harvard University Press in respect of *Philosophy in a*

New Key by S. Langer; Hutchinson and Barnes & Noble in respect of *The Concept of Mind* by Gilbert Ryle; Macmillan in respect of *The Ila-Speaking Peoples of Northern Rhodesia* by G. W. Smith and A. M. Dale; The New York Academy of Science in respect of *Balinese Character* by Gregory Bateson and Margaret Mead; Martinus Nijhoff in respect of *The Problem of Social Reality* by A. Schutz; The S.C.M. Press in respect of *Metaphysical Beliefs* edited by A. MacIntyre; Stanford University Press in respect of *Naven*, by Gregory Bateson.

REFERENCES

BATESON, G., 1958. *Naven*. Stanford: Stanford University Press, 2nd ed.

BATESON, G. & MEAD, M. 1942. *Balinese Character*. New York: N.Y. Academy of Sciences.

BELL, C. 1914. *Art*. London: Chatto & Windus.

BELO, J. 1949. *Bali: Rangda and Barong*. New York: J. J. Augustin.

—— 1960. *Trance in Bali*. New York: Columbia University Press.

BURKE, K. 1941. *The Philosophy of Literary Form*. n.p.: Louisiana State University Press.

CAMPBELL, J. 1949. *The Here with a Thousand Faces*. New York: Pantheon.

CASSIRIR, E. 1953-57. *The Philosophy of Symbolic Forms* (trans. R. Mannheim). New Haven: Yale University Press. 3 vols.

COVARRUBIAS, M. 1937. *The Island of Bali*. New York: Knopf.

CRAIK, K. 1952. *The Nature of Explanation*. Cambridge: Cambridge University Press.

EVANS-PRITCHARD, E. E. 1937. *Witchcraft, Oracles and Magic Among the Azande*. Oxford: Clarendon Press.

FIRTH, R. 1951. *Elements of Social Organization*. London: Watts; New York: Philosophical Library.

FORTUNE, R. F. 1935. *Manus Religion*. Philadelphia: American Philosophical Society.

VON FRISCH, K. 1962. Dialects in the Language of the Bees. *Scientific American*, August.

GEERTZ, C. 1958. Ethos, World-View and the Analysis of Sacred Symbols. *Antioch Review*, Winter (1957-58): 421-437.

—— 1960. *The Religion of Java*. Glencoe, Ill.: The Free Press.

—— 1962. The Growth of Culture and the Evolution of Mind. In J. Scher (ed.), *Theories of the Mind*. New York: The Free Press, pp. 713-740.

—— 1964a. Ideology as a Cultural System. In D. Apter (ed.), *Ideology of Discontent*. New York: The Free Press.

—— 1964b 'Internal Conversion' in Contemporary Bali. In J. Bastin & R. Roolvink (eds.), *Malayan and Indonesian Studies*, Oxford: Oxford University Press, pp. 282-302.

GOODY, J. 1961. Religion and Ritual: The Definition Problem. *British Journal of Sociology* 12: 143-164.

HOROWITZ, N. H. 1956. The Gene. *Scientific American*, February.

JAMES, WILLIAM. 1904. *The Principles of Psychology*. New York: Henry Holt, 2 vols.

JANOWITZ, M. 1963. Anthropology and the Social Sciences. *Current Anthropology* 4: 139, 146-154.

KLUCKHOHN, C. 1949. The Philosophy of the Navaho Indians. In F. S. C. Northrop (ed.), *Ideological Differences and World Order*. New Haven: Yale University Press, pp. 356-384.

—— 1953. Universal Categories of Culture. In A. L. Kroeber (ed.), *Anthropology Today*. Chicago: University of Chicago Press, pp. 507-523.

KLUCKHOHN, C. & LEIGHTON, D. 1946. *The Navaho*. Cambridge, Mass.: Harvard University Press.

LANGER, S. 1953. *Feeling and Form*. New York: Scribner's.

—— 1960. *Philosophy in a New Key*. Fourth Edition. Cambridge, Mass.: Harvard University Press.

—— 1962. *Philosophical Sketches*. Baltimore: Johns Hopkins.

LEACH, E. R. 1954. *Political Systems of Highland Burma*. London: Bell; Cambridge, Mass.: Harvard University Press.

LÉVY-BRUHL, L. 1926. *How Natives Think*. New York: Knopf.

LIENHARDT, G. 1961. *Divinity and Experience*. Oxford: Clarendon Press.

LORENZ, K. 1952. *King Solomon's Ring*. London: Methuen.

LOWIE, R. H. 1924. *Primitive Religion*. New York: Boni and Liveright.

MACINTYRE, A. 1957. The Logical Status of Religious Belief. In A. MacIntyre (ed.), *Metaphysical Beliefs*. London: SCM Press, pp. 167-211.

MALINOWSKI, B. 1948. *Magic, Science and Religion*. Boston: Beacon Press.

NADEL, S. F. 1957. Malinowski on Magic and Religion. In R. Firth (ed.), *Man and Culture*. London: Routledge & Kegan Paul, pp. 189-208.

PARSONS, T. & SHILS, E. 1951. *Toward a General Theory of Action*. Cambridge, Mass.: Harvard University Press.

PERCY, W. 1958. Symbol, Consciousness and Intersubjectivity. *Journal of Philosophy* 15: 631-641.

—— 1961. The Symbolic Structure of Interpersonal Process. *Psychiatry* 24: 39-52.

RADCLIFFE-BROWN, A. R. 1952. *Structure and Function in Primitive Society*. Glencoe, Ill.: Free Press.

RADIN, P. 1957. *Primitive Man as a Philosopher*. New York: Dover.

REICHARD, G. 1950. *Navaho Religion*. New York: Pantheon, 2 vols.

RYLE, G. 1949. *The Concept of Mind*. London: Hutchinson; New York: Barnes & Noble.

SANTAYANA, G. 1905-1906. *Reason in Religion*. Vol. 2 of *The Life of Reason, or The Phases of Human Progress*. London: Constable; New York: Scribner's.

SCHUTZ, A. 1962. *The Problem of Social Reality* (vol. I. of *Collected Papers*). The Hague: Martinus Nijhoff.

SINGER, M. 1955. The Cultural Pattern of Indian Civilization. *Far Eastern Quarterly* 15: 23-36.

—— 1958. The Great Tradition in a Metropolitan Center: Madras. In M. Singer (ed.), *Traditional India*. Philadelphia: American Folklore Society, pp. 140-82.

SMITH, C. W. & DALE, A. M. 1920. *The Ila-Speaking Peoples of Northern Rhodesia*. London: Macmillan.

DE ZOETE, B. & SPIES, W. 1938. *Dance and Drama in Bali*. London: Faber & Faber.

Victor W. Turner

Colour Classification in Ndembu Ritual

A Problem in Primitive Classification

There has recently been a marked revival of interest in what Durkheim (1963) called 'primitive forms of classification', a revival in which the names of Lévi-Strauss, Leach, Needham, and Evans-Pritchard have been prominent. Much attention has been focused on dichotomous classification in kinship and religious systems or on other kinds of isometrical arrangement such as quaternary and octadic divisions. Needham's resuscitation of Robert Hertz's (1960) work and Needham (1960) and Beidelman's (1961) recent studies in the symbolism of laterality, of the opposition of right and left and its sociological implications, represent this interest. During my own investigations of Ndembu ritual symbolism I came across many instances of lateral symbolism and indeed of other forms of dual classification with which the opposition of right and left might or might not be correlated. Since one of my major lines of inquiry was into the problem of social conflict and its resolution, I was sensitive at the time to the symbolization and formalization of such conflict. Many disputes involved opposition between the principles of matriliny and virilocality, and it seemed, therefore, reasonable to suppose that the opposition between the sexes would secure ritual and symbolic representation. I found that this was indeed the case, but I was not long in discovering that not only the dualism of the sexes but indeed every form of dualism was contained in a wider, tripartite mode of classification.

COLOUR CLASSIFICATION IN AFRICAN RITUAL

This tripartite classification relates to the colours white, red, and black. These are the only colours for which Ndembu possess

47

primary terms. Terms for other colours are either derivatives from these – as in the case of *chitookoloka*, 'grey', which is derived from *tooka*, 'white' – or consist of descriptive and metaphorical phrases, as in the case of 'green', *meji amatamba*, which means 'water of sweet potato leaves'. Very frequently, colours which we would distinguish from white, red, and black are by Ndembu linguistically identified with them. Blue cloth, for example, is described as 'black' cloth, and yellow or orange objects are lumped together as 'red'. Sometimes a yellow object may be described as *'neyi nsela'*, 'like beeswax', but yellow is often regarded as ritually equivalent to red.

When I first observed Ndembu rites I was impressed by the frequent use of white and red clay as ritual decoration. I assumed that only these two colours were ritually significant and that I had to deal with a dual classification. There was, indeed, a certain amount of support for such a view in the anthropological literature on the West Central Bantu. For example, Baumann, writing of the Chokwe of eastern Angola, had asserted that for these people: 'White is the colour of life, of health, of moonlight and of women. Red, on the other hand, has connections with sickness, the sun and men' (1935, pp. 40-41). He then attempted to equate the opposition between the colours with that between right and left, associating red with the right and white with the left. But Baumann also admitted that white clay 'figures as a life-principle' and is consequently forced by the logic of his dual scheme to regard red as the colour of 'death'. Yet when he discusses the red decoration of novices in the circumcision ceremony he writes: 'It seems as though the red colour were in itself not only the colour of illness, but also the colour of averting illness.' Other authorities on the West Central Bantu are by no means in agreement with Baumann's interpretation. C. M. N. White, for example, holds that 'red is symbolic of life and blood in various Luvale contexts' (1961, p. 15), and the Chokwe and Luvale are culturally very similar. White also writes that various red fruits and trees are 'constantly associated with fertility and life'.

My own field observations among the Ndembu tended to confirm White's interpretation rather than Baumann's, although it is true that there are a number of ritual contexts in

which red is associated with masculinity, as in the red ritual
decorations of war chiefs (*tumbanji*), circumcisers, and hunters,
and white with femininity, as in the case of the *mudyi* tree
which secretes a white latex and is the supreme symbol of
femininity and motherhood. But on the other hand, I came upon
at least an equal number of ritual occasions where white
represented masculinity and red femininity. For example, in the
Nkula rite, performed to rid a woman of menstrual disorder, red
clay and other red symbols represent menstrual blood, 'the
blood of parturition', and matriliny – all feminine things. In the
Wubwang'u rite, performed for a mother of twins or for a
woman expected to bear twins, powdered white clay, kept in a
phallus-shaped container and blown over the patient as she
stands on a log near a stream-source, is explicitly likened to
'semen'. On the other hand, powdered red clay, kept in the shell
of a river mollusc and blown over the patient after the white
powder, is said to represent 'the blood of the mother'. The white
clay is applied by a male, and the red clay by a female doctor.
I discuss this rite more fully in an essay to be published, but the
point is made. There is no fixed correlation between the colours
and the sexes. Colour symbolism is not consistently sex-linked,
although red and white may be situationally specified to represent the opposition of the sexes.

It is clear that Baumann's attempt to polarize the symbolic
values of white and red is artificial and constrained. This would
suggest that we are dealing here with something wider than a
dual classification. White and red are certainly opposed in some
situations, but the fact that each can stand for the same
object – in other words, they participate in one another's
meaning – suggests that more than a pair of opposites has to be
taken into account. As a matter of fact, as I have already
indicated, there is a third factor, or term. This is the colour
black, in some ways the most interesting of the three.

COLOUR CLASSIFICATION IN NDEMBU LIFE-CRISIS RITUAL

Let us now examine some contexts in which the three colours
appear together before we look at them singly or in contrasted

pairs. Ndembu assure me that the relationship between the colours 'begins with the mystery (or riddle – *mpangu*) of the three rivers – the rivers of whiteness, redness, and blackness (or darkness)'. This cryptic utterance refers to part of the secret teaching of the lodge during the circumcision rites (*Mukanda*) and during the phase of seclusion at the rites of the funerary associations of *Chiwila* and *Mung'ong'i*. It is said that girls were also, until recently, taught this mystery (*mpang'u*) during their puberty rites (*Nkang'a*), but I found no evidence of this.

I have not personally observed the instruction of novices in this mystery of the three rivers, but I have recorded several accounts from reliable informants. The first of these is from a member of the *Chiwila* society, which performs elaborate initiation rites for young people at the death of its female cult members. *Chiwila* is no longer held in Northern Rhodesia, but my informant had been initiated as a young girl among the Ndembu of Angola. She described to me how the novices were taught the mystery of one of the 'rivers' (*tulong'a*), in this case 'the river of blood' (*kalong'a kamashi*) or 'the river of redness' (*kachinana*). The prefix *ka-* sometimes signifies that the term it qualifies is a liquid, usually water. Thus *ku-chinana* means 'to be red (or yellow)', *chinana* is the radical, and *ka-chinana* means 'red fluid' or 'red river', and *keyila*, the 'black river'.

My informant told me that the novices, boys as well as girls, were taken to a long, roofed but unwalled shelter called *izembi*. The senior celebrant, entitled *Samazembi* ('father of *mazembi*'), then took a hoe and dug a trench inside the hut. It was shaped 'like a cross' ('*neyi mwambu*'), but could also be made in the form of an Ndembu axe (*chizemba*) or a hoe (*itemwa*). Next he took sharp reeds, such as are used for making mats, and planted them along both sides of the trench. This was followed by the planting of many small antelope horns, containing pounded leaf-medicine (*nsompu*), in lines on either side of the trench. He then filled the trench with water; *Samazembi's* next task was to behead (the term *ku-ketula*, 'to cut' is always used for this) a fowl and pour its blood into the 'river' to tinge it with red. Not content with this, he added other red colouring matter such as powdered red clay (*mukundu* or *ng'ula*) and powdered gum from the *mukula* tree. *Samazembi* then washed his body with medicine

made from root scrapings soaked in water and contained in his
personal calabash. What was left after washing he threw into
the 'river of redness'. Next he took some powdered white clay
(*mpemba* or *mpeza*), addressed the spirits of 'those who had
passed through *Chiwila* long ago', anointed himself by the
orbits and on the temple with *mpemba*, anointed the novices,
and then harangued them as follows:

> 'Pay attention! This river is blood. It is very important
> (literally, "heavy"). It is very dangerous. You must not speak
> of it in the village when you return. Beware! This is no
> ordinary river. God (*Nzambi*) made it long, long ago. It is the
> river of God (*kalong'a kaNzambi*). You must not eat salt for
> many days, nor anything salty or sweet (*-towala* means both).
> Do not speak of these matters in public, in the village; that is
> bad.'

When he had finished, each novice bent down and took one
of the small horns by the teeth, without using hands. They all
went outside and tried to perform the difficult feat of bending
over backwards and tossing the horn up in such a way as to be
caught by adepts standing just behind them without spilling
the medicine.

Samazembi collected up all these horns and secreted them in
his medicine-hut (*katunda*). The medicine was called *nfunda*, a
name also applied to the lodge-medicine of the *Mukanda* or
Boys' Circumcision rites. In addition to other ingredients it
contained ashes from the burnt hut of the deceased. *Nfunda* is
never thrown away but the portion left over at the end of each
performance of *Chiwila* or *Mung'ong'i* is used at the next
performance, where it is mixed with fresh medicine. The *nfunda*
used at the circumcision rites, though not in the *chiwila* rites,
contains ashes and powdered charcoal from the seclusion lodge,
which is burnt at the end of the seclusion period, and ashes and
charcoal from various sacred fires extinguished at the conclusion
of the rites. These are held to be 'black' symbols. It is interesting
to learn from Baumann (p. 137) that among the Chokwe *ufunda*
stands for 'interment' and is derived from the verb *ku-funda*,
'to bury'. The term *funda*, which seems to be the cognate of
nfunda, according to Baumann, stands for 'a bundle' and

'appears to be connected with the idea of the bundled corpse laced on to the carrying-post'. *Nfunda*, as used at *Mukanda, Mung'ong'i*, and *Chiwila*, rites of the Ndemba is certainly a medicine-bundle; but the possible etymological connection with death is suggestive in view of its connection with funerary rites, the destruction of sacred edifices, and black symbols.

My informant on *Chiwila* customs was unable or unwilling to venture much in the way of their interpretation. But other informants on *Mukanda* and *Mung'ong'i* ritual supplied further exegesis. At these rites, they told me, there are 'three rivers'. 'The river of blood', usually made in the shape of an axe, represents 'a man with a woman' (*iyala namumbabda*), or 'copulation' (*kudisunda*). 'The man' is represented by the axe-head with its tang, and the woman by the wooden shaft.[1]

But the main 'river' or 'trough', the 'elder' one as Ndembu put it, is the 'river of whiteness' (*katooka*). This 'runs in a straight line to the *izembi* shelter'. 'The river of red water is junior, and this is followed by the river of black water. The red river is a woman and her husband.' The crossing of the mother's and father's blood means a child, a new life (*kabubu kawumi* – *kabubu* stands for a small organism, such as an insect; it also stands for the navel-cord; *wumi* signifies generic life rather than the personal life-principle – thus an infant before it is weaned is thought to have *wumi* but not a *mwevulu*, a 'shadow-soul' which after death becomes an ancestor spirit of *mukishi*). One informant told me that the *katooka* is whitened with powdered white clay (*mpemba*), 'stands for *wumi*', and is 'the trunk to which the red and black rivers are attached like branches'. The black river (*keyila*), darkened with charcoal (*makala*) represents 'death' (*kufwa*).

During *Mung'ong'i* the novices are asked a number of riddles (*jipang'u*). One of them is, 'What is the white water restless by night?' (*katooka kusaloka*). The correct answer is 'Semen' (*matekela*). Thus one of the senses of the 'white river' is masculine generative power. This river, too, is described as 'a river of God'.

In *Mung'ong'i*, and also formerly in *Mukanda*, the novices are taught to chant a song, or rather incantation, full of archaic and bizarre terms. I record the text but cannot translate several of the words:

Katooki meji kansalu kelung'i chimbungu chelung'a belang' ante-e

White river, water of the country, cannibal monster (or hyena) of the country . . .

Mukayande-e he-e kateti kasemena mwikindu mwini kumwalula hinyi?

In suffering (?) the little reed of begetting in the medicine basket (?), the owner who may find him?

'The little reed of begetting' is probably the penis; '*Mwini*', the Owner, may refer to the name of a territorial spirit or demigod propitiated in the *Musolu* rite for bringing on belated rains and is perhaps connected with the 'water' motif. Incidentally, Ndembu describe semen as 'blood whitened (or purified) by water'. The verb 'to urinate' has the same radical *-tekela* as the noun *matekela*, 'semen'. Moreover, the urine of an apprentice circumciser is one of the ingredients of the *nfunda* medicine. It is clearly implied that the river of whiteness is untainted while the river of blood contains impurities. This difference will emerge more sharply when I present informants' interpretations of the individual colours.

While I was discussing the 'white river' with one informant he treated me to a short disquisition on the Ndembu theory of procreation, referring it directly to the initiation mysteries. 'A child', he said, 'means good luck (*wutooka*, which also means 'whiteness'). For a child gives things in the first place to his father who first begat him. The mother is like a pot only, the body and soul of a child come from the father. But it is *Nzambi*, God, who gives life (*wumi*) to the child.' I asked him why it was, then, that Ndembu traced descent through the mother. He replied, 'A man begets children, but they are the mother's because it is she who suckles and nurses them. A mother feeds a child with her breast; without it the child would die.' Then he cited the proverb: 'The cock begets, but the chickens are the hen's (*kusema kwandemba nyana yachali*).' He went on to point out that breast-milk (*mayeli*) is 'white' too, a 'white stream', and that the *mudyi* tree, dominant symbol of the girls' puberty rites, is a white symbol because it exudes white latex. Indeed, the primary sense of *mudyi* is breast-milk. Thus the *katooka* or 'white river' is bisexual in significance, representing both semen and milk. White symbols may then stand for both masculine and feminine objects, according to the context or situation, and are not reserved, as in Baumann's account of the Chokwe, for feminine objects.

Finally, at *Mung'ong'i* there is a long song, chanted by novices, the refrain of which runs: '*Yaleyi Nyameya lupemba lufunda antu wafunda nimumi niwayili*', which means literally, 'You the man Nyameya, the big *mpemba* which draws lines on people, you draw lines on the living and those who went (i.e. the dead)'. *Yaleyi* is a somewhat familiar term of address which may be applied to a person of either sex, like the South African English word 'man'. *Nyameya* means literally 'the mother of whiteness' in the Luvale language, but the prefix *nya-*, 'mother of', may be used honorifically of important men, such as chiefs or great hunters, with the flavour of 'one who nourishes'. *Lupemba* is *mpemba* or *pemba* with the additional prefix *lu-* which often denotes size. Nouns in the *lu-* class are commonly inanimate, and include many long articles. But here I am inclined to think that the 'greatness' of '*mpemba*', and of the 'whiteness' it represents, is being stressed. *Ku-funda*, in the Lunda language, means to 'draw lines' with white clay, red clay, or charcoal. When the father or mother of children dies, a line is drawn in white clay from the middle of the chest down to the navel, as a sign that the deceased is desired as a giver of names to his or her descendants. To give someone one's name, for Ndembu, implies a kind of partial reincarnation of certain traits of character or body. When a sterile person dies, however, a line of black is drawn with a stick of charcoal from the navel of the dead person downwards, between the legs and round to the sacrum. This is a sign to the dead not to visit the world of the living again, 'to die forever', as Ndembu say.

The living, too, in many rites are marked with white clay. To take one example, when Ndembu address the spirits of their ancestors at special quick-set shrine trees planted in their honour in the villages, they take white clay, mark the tree with white, then draw one, three, or four lines on the ground from the base of the tree towards them, and finally anoint themselves with this *mpemba* beside the orbits, on the temple, and above the navel. The *mpemba* is said to represent a state of good will or good feeling between living and dead. There are held to be 'no secret grudges' (*yitela*) between them, to 'blacken' (*kwiyilisha*) their livers (*nyichima*), the seat of the feelings.

COLOUR CLASSIFICATION IN NGONDE LIFE-CRISIS RITUAL

Other accounts of initiation rites in Central Africa mention many of the elements just described. For example, Lyndon Harries (1944) records several texts among the Ngonde of Southern Tanganyika which discuss the meaning of the colour triad in both male and female initiation. He asked native informants to interpret for him some of the cryptic songs of the seclusion lodge. One explanation ran as follows: 'A woman conceives through the semen of a man. If the man has black semen there will be no bearing of a child. But if he has white semen he will have a child' (p. 19). The esoteric teaching given to the novices includes the displaying by an elder of 'three things symbolic of sexual purity, sexual disease through impurity, and menstruation'. These symbols are white flour, black charcoal, and red *inumbati* medicine respectively. 'The boys are taught by means of these symbols' (p. 23). Incidentally, red *inumbati* medicine is used for 'anointing a newly-born child', and the novices' song 'I want *inumbati* medicine' Harries takes to mean 'I want to bear a child'. *Inumbati* medicine is made from the powdered gum or bark of a Pterocarpus tree; the species *Pterocarpus angolensis* plays a major role in Ndembu ritual where it figures as a red symbol. Again, we hear that 'the boys smear themselves with black clay (*cikupi*) so that "they may not be seen by passers-by in the bush" ' (p. 16). Blackness, among the Ndembu, is also connected with concealment and darkness. It stands not only for actual but also for symbolic or ritual death among the Ndembu, and it may well have this significance in the Ngonde practice just mentioned.

At girls' puberty rites among the Ngonde, newly initiated girls 'are taken by an older initiated girl to the well. Whenever they come to a cross-path, this older girl stoops down and draws three lines on the path, one red one with ochre to represent menses, one black one with a piece of charcoal to represent sexual impurity and one white one with cassava flour for sexual purity' (p. 39). Here once more we have a relationship between water, the cross motif, and the colour triad.

Dr Audrey Richards, in *Chisungu*, describes how among the Bemba colour symbolism plays an important role in the girls' puberty rites. Thus the *mbusa* pottery emblems used to instruct the novices in ritual esoterica are 'usually painted with white, black and red' (p. 59). Larger models of unfired clay are decorated with beans, soot, chalk and red camwood dye (p. 60). The red camwood powder 'is the blood', Dr Richards was informed (p. 66). It is rubbed on those who have passed through danger, such as lion-killers or those who have successfully undergone the poison ordeal. Red camwood powder, in some situations, is clearly a male symbol, as when the bridegroom's sisters, stained red, simulate bridegrooms (p. 73). Again, the *mulombwa*, the hardwood tree which exudes a red juice, 'represents the male, the lion, and in some cases the chief' (p. 94). But red among the Bemba, as among the Ndembu, also has feminine connotations, for it represents menstrual blood in many ritual contexts. Among the Bemba white represents the washing away of the menstrual blood (p. 81). All three colours are brought together in the cleansing rite of *ukuya ku mpemba* ('going to whitewash') where the novice is washed and cleansed and her body is covered with whitewash. At the same time a lump of black mud is put cross-shaped on her head and this is decorated with pumpkin seeds and red dye. Meanwhile the following song is sung: 'We make the girls white (like egrets). We make them beautiful . . . they are white now from the stain of blood . . . it is finished now the thing that was red.' This rite marks a definite stage in the puberty ritual (pp. 88-90). In another episode white beads stand for fertility (as indeed they do among the Ndembu) (p. 72).

In his book *Les Rites Secrets des Primitifs de l'Oubangui* (1936), A. M. Vergiat discusses colour symbolism he recorded at the circumcision rites of the Manja (or Mandja) in the following terms (p. 92):

'Black (in the form of powdered charcoal) is devoted to death. Warriors smear themselves with soot when they leave for war. People in mourning stay dirty, they do not wash any more. Black is a symbol of impurity. The colour white is that of rebirth. It protects from illness. At the end of the rites the initiated boys paint themselves white. These are new men. At the ceremony of the mourning gathering, the relatives of the dead do the same. White purifies. Red is a symbol of life, joy and health. The natives rub themselves with red for dancing and those who are sick pass it frequently over their bodies.'

COLOUR CLASSIFICATION AND THE HIGH GOD IN CENTRAL AFRICA

It is needless to multiply such citations; they are there in the literature on African initiation rites for all to read. But it is perhaps worth mentioning that Baumann (1935, p. 12) came across a ritual shelter (*izembi*) – called by him '*zemba*' – of the *Mung'ong'i* cult in a Chokwe village north of the upper Kasai, and was told that two large fires burning in it 'are called "Kalunga" (that means God); they reach "up to the sky" '. Thus we find the three colours fairly widely associated with initiations and life-crisis rites, and among the Ndembu and Chokwe at any rate with the High God. Of the three, white seems to be dominant and unitary, red ambivalent, for it is both fecund and 'dangerous', while black is, as it were, the silent partner, the 'shadowy third', in a sense opposed to both white and red, since it represents 'death', 'sterility', and 'impurity'. Yet we shall see that in its full significance black shares certain senses with both white and red, and it is not felt to be wholly malignant. The colours are conceived as rivers of power flowing from a common source in God and permeating the whole world of sensory phenomena with their specific qualities. More than this they are thought to tinge the moral and social life of mankind with their peculiar efficacies, so that it is said, for example, 'this is a good man for he has a white liver', or 'he is evil; his liver is black', when in physical fact a liver is dark red. Although the Ndembu, like many other simple societies, may be said to have 'an otiose God', nevertheless that God may be considered active in so far as from him stream unceasingly the three principles of being that are symbolized and given visible form in the white-red-black triad. Evidences of these principles or powers are held by Ndembu to be scattered throughout nature in objects of those colours, such as trees with red or white gum, bark, or roots, others with white or black fruit, white kaolin clay or red oxidized earth, black alluvial mud, charcoal, the white sun and moon, the black night, the redness of blood, the whiteness of milk, the dark colour of faeces. Animals and birds acquire ritual significance because their feathers or hides are of these hues. Even human beings, Negroes though they are, are classified as 'white' or 'black' in terms of nuances of pigmentation. There is here an implied moral difference and most people object to being classified as 'black.'

THE NDEMBU INTERPRETATION OF THE COLOUR TRIAD

What, then, are the novices taught about the meaning of the triad? I have collected a considerable number of texts from my Ndembu informants on colour symbolism recording what they have learnt, at initiation and in the course of their participation in rites of many kinds, about the significance of the colours. Let me begin by citing the basic senses of each.

White
Informants agree that white clay (*mpemba* or *mpeza*) and other 'white things' (*yuma yitooka*) stand for 'whiteness' (*wutooka*) which is:

1. goodness (*ku-waha*);
2. making strong or healthy (*ku-koleka* or *ku-kolisha*);
3. purity (*Ku-tooka*) [this merely signifies 'to be white' but is contextually recognizable as 'purity'];
4. to lack (or be without) bad luck or misfortune (*ku-bula ku-halwa*);
5. to have power (*kwikala nang'ovu*) [literally 'to be with power'];

6. to be without death (*ku-bula ku-fwa*) [i.e. not to have death in one's kin-group];
7. to be without tears (*ku-bula madilu*) [as above];
8. chieftainship or authority (*wanta*);
9. (when people meet together with ancestor spirits (*adi-bomba niakishi*);
10. life (*wumi*);
11. health (*ku-handa*);
12. begetting or bringing forth young (*lusemu*);
13. huntsmanship (*Wubinda*);
14. giving (or generosity) (*kwinka*);
15. to remember (*kwanuka*), i.e. one's ancestors with gifts and offerings at their muyombu shrines;
16. to laugh (*ku-seha*) [the mark of friendly sociability];
17. to eat (*ku-dya*) [Ndembu remark that both mother's milk and cassava meal, the main food, are white in colour];
18. to multiply (*ku-seng'uka*) [in the sense of the fertility of humans, animals, and crops];
19. to make visible or reveal (*ku-solola*);
20. to become mature or an elder (*ku-kula*) [Ndembu comment here on the fact that elders have white hair – it is their 'whiteness' becoming 'visible'];
21. to sweep clean (*ku-komba*) [i.e. to rid of impurities];
22. to wash oneself (*ku-wela*) [as above];
23. to be free from ridicule – 'people do not laugh at you because you have done something wrong or foolish.'

Red

'Red things (*yuma yachinana*)', say informants, 'are of blood (*mashi*) or of red clay (*ng'ula*).' There are different categories (*nyichidi*) of blood. These are:

1. the blood of animals (*mashi atunyama* or *mashi anyama*) [this stands for huntsmanship (*Wubinda* or *Wuyang'a*)], also for meat (*mbiji*);
2. the blood of parturition, of mothers (*mashi alusemu amama*);
3. the blood of all women (*mashi awambanda ejima*), i.e. menstrual blood (*mbayi* or *kanyanda*);

4. the blood of murder or stabbing or killing (*mashi awubanji hela kutapana*), the blood shed at circumcision comes under this heading as does the red decoration in the rites to purify a homicide or the slayer of a lion, leopard or buffalo;

5. the blood of witchcraft/sorcery (*mashi awuloji*), for Ndembu witchcraft/sorcery is necrophagous and in anti-witchcraft rites red stands for the blood exposed in such feasts.

'Red things belong to two categories, they act both for good and ill (these), are combined (*Yuma yachinana yakundama kuyedi, yela nikuwaha nukutama, yadibomba*).'

This statement well expresses the ambivalence of the red symbolism.

6. 'Red things have power (*yikweti ng'ovu*); blood is power, for a man, an animal, an insect, or a bird must have blood, or it will die. Wooden figurines (*nkishi*) have no blood and hence cannot breathe, speak, sing, laugh, or chat together – they are only carvings in wood. But if the figurines used by sorcerers (*aloji*) are given blood, they can move about and kill people.'

7. 'Semen (*matekela*) is white (lucky, pure) good blood (*mashi atooka amawahi*). If it is red (or) black, there is no begetting (*neyi achinana eyila kusema nehi*). Red semen is ineffective or impotent (*azeka*), it cannot penetrate fully (*ku-dita*).'

Black

'Black things include: charcoal (*makala*), river mud (*malowa*), dye from the *mupuchi* and *musamba* trees (*wulombu*, the word now used for "ink"), and the black fruits of the *muneku* tree.

'Blackness (*wuyila*) is:

1. badness or evil (*ku-tama*), bad things (*yuma yatama*);

2. to lack luck, purity, or whiteness (*ku-bula ku-tooka*);

3. to have suffering (*yihung'u*) or misfortune (*malwa*);

4. to have diseases (*yikweti yikatu*);

5. witchcraft/sorcery (*wuloji*), for if your liver is black, you can kill a person, you are bad (*muchima neyi wuneyili wukutwesa kujaha muntu, wunatami dehi*); on the con-

trary, if your liver is white, you are good, you laugh with your friends, you are strong together, you prop one another up when you would have failed alone;
6. death (*ku-fwa*);
7. sexual desire (*wuvumbi*);
8. night (*wufuku*) or darkness (*mwidima*).'

Commentary on the black symbolism
The inventory of 'black' attributes I have recorded here would inevitably give a false impression of how Ndembu regard this colour were I to omit all reference to the concept of mystical or ritual death and to the related concept of the death of passion and hostility. The Ndembu concept *ku-fwa*, 'death', does not have the note of finality that, despite Christianity, 'death' seems to possess in Western civilization. For the Ndembu 'to die' often means to reach the end of a particular stage of development, to reach the terminus of a cycle of growth. When a person 'dies' he is still active, either as an ancestor spirit who keeps watch over the behaviour of his living kin and manifests himself to them in various modes of affliction, or as partially reincarnated in a kinsman in the sense of reproducing in the latter some of his mental and physical characteristics. Such a person has undergone not merely a change in social status but also a change in mode of existence; here there is no question of annihilation. The term *ku-fwa* also stands for 'fainting', and, indeed, on many occasions Ndembu have told me that they had 'died' and recovered after treatment by a doctor (*chimbuki*). An English idiom which perhaps hits off the Ndembu sense best is 'to have a black-out'. Death is a 'black-out' – a period of powerlessness and passivity between two living states. There is also a connection between the concepts 'death' and 'maturation' (*ku-kula*) among the Ndembu. One tends to grow up by definite stages, each of which is the 'death' of the previous stage, by a series of 'deaths and entrances'. Thus when a girl first menstruates Ndembu say '*wunakuli dehi*', 'she has matured', and the same remark is made at her First Pregnancy rites and when she bears her first child. The connection between *ku-fwa* and *ku-kula* is strikingly illustrated also at the circumcision rites where the site of the operation is termed *ifwilu*, 'the place of

dying', while the place where the boys sit bleeding while they recover from the operation is a long *mukula* log, a red gum tree whose name is derived from *ku-kula*, 'to mature'. 'Through death to maturity' might well be the motto of *Mukanda*, the circumcision rites. The site where a girl lies motionless, covered with a blanket, for a twelve-hour ordeal on the first day of her puberty rites (*Nkang'a*) is also *ifwilu* or *chihung'u*, the place of suffering (see Black Symbolism, item 3,) and the aim of these rites is to endow the novice with sexual maturity.

Black symbolism plays an important, though unobtrusive part, in the boys' circumcision rites. I have already mentioned how certain black symbolic articles constitute important ingredients of *nfunda* medicine. Again, when the novices are returned to their mothers after seclusion, they beat two sticks over their heads while they are carried by their ritual guardians (*yilombola*). These sticks are striped by alternate bands of white and black which, according to informants, stand for 'life and death'. Black symbolism sometimes appears also on the face masks of the *makishi* maskers, who are believed by the boys to emerge from under the ground at the *ifwilu* site. There one sees three horizontal rectangular bands, rather like a small flag. One is white, one red, and one black, white being uppermost and black underneath. These are described as 'very important'. In explanation I was referred to a song of the *Nkula* rites, performed *inter alia* to cure a woman of the frigidity which is preventing her, so Ndembu think, from conceiving a child, and which is associated with such menstrual disorders as menorrhagia and dysmenorrhoea. The song runs:

'You destroy lines (stripes) mongoose, that is your habit which makes you refuse men, you destroy lines.'
(*wakisa nyilenji nkala chaku chey'ochu chiwalekelang'a amayala, wakisa nyilenji.*)

It was then explained that the *nkala* species of mongoose has 'red, white and black stripes down its back'. The song means that 'the woman patient is a bad, useless woman, she has no power (*hawaheta ng'ovuku*) – you are destroying yourself woman; you ought to have babies, you are unworthy (*hawatelelaku*), guilty. You are a frigid woman (*wafwa mwitala*, literally "dead in the hut"). The mongoose has stripes, but this woman, although she has been given her privy parts, has kept them useless.' Incidentally, the stub of wood carried at all times during their seclusion by the novices at *Mukanda* and representing their *membrum virile* is also called *nkala*, 'mongoose', and this animal is one of the tabooed foods of the lodge. It would seem to be a bisexual symbol for generative power and to represent the simultaneous action of all three colour principles. What does black mean in their combination, if it does not there mean evil or unlucky things?

There is undoubtedly a connection between the colour black and sexual passion (*wuvumbi*). For example, during seclusion older women take the sooty black bark of certain trees, such as the mudyi tree, and blacken the novice's vulva. This is thought to enhance her sexual attractiveness. Women with very black skins are said by Ndembu men to be very desirable as mistresses, though not as wives. Sexual passion is associated with darkness and secrecy also. Hence black represents that which is hidden (*chakusweka*, *chakujinda*), and is not only hidden, but an object of longing. The Wagnerian notion of a 'love-death', as exemplified in Tristan und Isolde, springs to mind here.

But black is also connected with licit love, and in several contexts represents 'marriage'. For example, just after the girl's puberty rites are over, the novice spends the night with her bridegroom (known as *kalemba*). The couple have frequent intercourse and if the bride considers herself satisfied she makes a secret sign of affirmation to her ritual instructress (*nkong'a*), who visits her early in the morning. The latter tiptoes away to collect some *malowa*, black alluvial mud, that she has fetched from a stream the previous evening at sundown and 'kept hidden away from the eyes of men'. Then she scatters a little *malowa* on the threshold of every hut in the village. This was explained to me as follows by an Ndembu informant: 'The *malowa* is a symbol (*chijikijilu*) of love (*nkeng'i*). For a young girl and her husband now love one another. But everyone in the village must connect with that same love. *Malowa* is used also because it is cold from the river. Their marriage must then be peaceful. *Malowa*, though it is black, does not stand for bad luck here, but marital peace or happiness (*wuluwi*).' Here blackness plus 'coldness' appear to represent the cessation of hostility between two intermarrying groups, a hostility previously mimed in the rites. Black can, therefore, sometimes represent the 'death' of an inauspicious or undesirable condition.

A brief survey of the senses attributed by informants to 'white' and 'black' respectively indicates that these can mostly be arrayed in a series of antithetical pairs, as for example: goodness/badness; purity/lacking purity; lacking bad luck/lacking luck; lacking misfortune/misfortune; to be without death/death; life/death; health/disease; laughing with one's friends/witchcraft; to make visible/darkness, etc.

This mode of arrangement reveals clearly that when the colours are considered in abstraction from social and ritual contexts Ndembu think of white and black as the supreme antitheses in their scheme of reality. Yet, as we shall see, in rite after rite white and red appear in conjunction and black is seldom directly expressed. In abstraction from actual situations red seems to share the qualities of both white and black. But in action contexts red is regularly paired with white.

The characteristics of the colours white and red
(a) *Whiteness*. Although each of the ritual colours has a wide fan of referents, nevertheless each has its own distinctive quality, which can be briefly expressed by saying that whiteness is positive, redness ambivalent, and blackness negative. To be 'white' is to be in right relation to the living and the dead. To be in right relation to these is to be whole and hale in oneself. One neither incurs the wrath or envy of others, nor does one feel animosity towards them. Hence one does not fear witchcraft/sorcery, nor is one inwardly tainted by the temptation to practise it. Such a one is admirably equipped to exercise authority (*wanta*), for he will not abuse his power. He will be generous with gifts and hospitality, and magnanimous. He will sweep away 'evil things' from the village or chiefdom in his charge, just as he piously sweeps away dust and impurities from the base of the *muyombu* tree where he makes libation to the

spirits of his ancestors (with the white maize or bullrush millet beer) and invokes their aid on behalf of his people. He will provide food for his people and nourish them with wisdom. For white is, *inter alia*, the symbol of nurture. This quality is 'made visible' (as Ndembu say) in such material forms as breast-milk, semen, and cassava meal. It represents smooth continuity from generation to generation, and is associated with the pleasures of eating, begetting, and suckling. Begetting and feeding are, indeed, processes that are often identified by Ndembu. For example, after a woman is known to be pregnant her husband continues to have intercourse with her for some time 'in order to feed the child' with his semen. The same term *ivumu* is used both for 'stomach' and 'womb', and a woman undergoing a long and difficult labour is often given food 'to strengthen the child'.

Another aspect of the white symbolism is the nature of the relationship between persons that it represents. This is a relationship of feeder and fed. Dominance and subordination are certainly implied by it, mastery and submissiveness, but it is a benevolent dominance and a mild mastery. The senior partner in the relationship gives nourishment and knowledge to the junior. Whiteness expresses the generosity of the dominant partner, and, at the same time, the gratitude of the subordinate. The situation of ancestor veneration brings out these features. The living bring wood, drink, and symbolic food in the form of *mpemba*, the white symbol par excellence, to the ancestor spirits at their shrine-trees, which possess a white wood. Thus at this phase of the proceedings the dead are dependent upon the living. But on the other hand the living are dependent upon the dead for long-term health, happiness, fertility, and good luck in hunting, for the ancestors are believed to have power to with-hold these blessings and 'to tie up' (*ku-kasila*) the fertility and huntsmanship (*wubinda*) of their living kin, if the latter neglect to make offerings to them. Furthermore, to get a hearing from the ancestors the whole congregation, the core of which consists of the matrilineal kin of the ancestors, should by rights be at peace and in agreement with one another. This harmony between living and dead and among the living is represented by white marks on the *muyombu* tree, white lines between tree and invoker, white marks on the invoker and finally on the other members of the congregation. Once the circuit of whiteness is established, as it were, material nourishment and benefits and invisible virtues are believed to flow through the whole group including its deceased members.

Whiteness not only has the note of social cohesion and continuity, but also stands for that which can be seen by the eye, what is open, and unconcealed. Ndembu morality is essentially corporate; the private is the suspect, probably the dangerous, possibly the deadly. Persons who eat or work alone, such as certain chiefs and great hunters, are always suspected of possessing sorcery powers. In a society living at bare subsistence level, all must be seen to pull their weight, to share goods and services fairly. Persistent selfishness may actually imperil the survival of the group, and must therefore be condemned. It is recognized that a person may live most of his life in full public view and yet have secret reservations about assisting his fellows. He may cherish grudges and nurse ambitions. Such a person, I have shown in a Rhodes-Livingstone Paper on Ndembu divination (Turner, 1961, pp. 61-62), if exposed by divination, is regarded as a sorcerer. Whiteness is thus the light of public knowledge, of open recognition. In fact, it represents daylight, and both sun and moon are said to be its 'symbols' (*yijikijilu*), contrary to what Baumann records of the Chokwe who, he says, regard white as 'the colour of moonlight' and red as 'having connections with the sun' (1935, p. 40). Sun and moon are also regarded as symbols of God (*Nzambi*) and once more we come back to the notion that whiteness, more than any other colour, represents the divinity as essence and source, as well as sustentation. But whiteness as light streaming forth from the divinity has, in the sense we are considering here, a quality of trustworthiness and veracity, for Ndembu believe that what is clearly seen can be accepted as a valid ground of knowledge.

White is also the unsullied and unpolluted. This quality of freedom from defilement may have either a moral or a ritual character. Thus I have heard an African storekeeper expostulate, when he was accused by his employer of embezzlement, 'My liver is white', much as an Englishman would say, 'My conscience is clear'. On the other hand, there are certain ritually polluting states or statuses. Thus an uncircumcised boy is known as *wunabulakutooka*, 'one who lacks purity or whiteness', and he may not eat food cooked in the same pot as an adult man's meal. If he did so, it is believed that the various mystical powers acquired by a man as a result of having undergone many rites, such as the power to slaughter game, would lose their efficacy. It is believed that the 'dirt under the foreskin' (*wanza* – regularly used as a term of abuse) of an uncircumcised boy is defiling in the extreme, regardless of his moral qualities as an individual. Water is regarded as 'white' because it cleanses the body from dirt, but more especially because washing symbolizes the removal of impurities inherent in a biological condition or social status which one is now leaving behind. For example, novices at both boys' and girls' initiations are thoroughly washed just before they return to society after the period of seclusion. At the end of the funerary rites a widow or widower is washed, anointed with oil, shaved around the hair line, given a new white cloth, and adorned with white beads, a series of acts which illustrate the close connection between washing and white symbolism. What is being washed off in these life-crisis rites is the state of ritual death, the 'liminal' condition, between two periods of active social life. Whiteness or 'purity' is hence in some respects identical with the legitimate incumbency of a socially recognized status. To behave in a way that transgresses the norms of *that status*, however innocuous that behaviour might be for the incumbent of another status, constitutes impurity. It is particularly impure to behave regressively, i.e. in terms of the norms of a status occupied earlier in the individual life-cycle. This is because the successive stages of life are felt to represent an ascent from the impurity of the uncircumcised to the purity of the aged in the case of men, and from the impurity of a menstruating maiden, through the increasing purity of the mother of many children, to the postmenopausal status of *kashinakaii*, the venerable leader of the village women. Ancestor-hood is purer still and albinos are regarded as peculiarly propitious beings because they have 'the whiteness of ancestor spirits' (*wutooka wawakishi*).

Behind the symbolism of whiteness, then, lie the notions of

harmony, continuity, purity, the manifest, the public, the appropriate, and the legitimate.

(b) *Redness*. But what are we to make of the red symbolism which, in its archetypal form in the initiation rites, is represented by the intersection of two 'rivers of blood'? This duality, this ambivalence, this simultaneous possession of two contrary values or qualities, is quite characteristic of redness in the Ndembu view. As they say: 'Redness acts both for good and ill.' Thus while it is good to combine the blood of the mother with that of the father it is bad to practise necrophagous witchcraft. Both the blood of childbirth and the blood relished by witches are represented by red oxidized clay or earth (*mukundu, ng'ula*). Red is peculiarly the colour of blood or flesh, the carnal colour. Hence it is redolent of the aggressiveness and pangs of carnality. It stands for the killing and cutting up of animals and for the pains of labour. There is something impure, too, about redness. A homicide has to be purified from the stain of the blood he has shed, though he is entitled to wear the red feather of Livingstone's lourie (*nduwa*) after the purification rites on subsequent ritual occasions. Red stands also for the menstruation of women in such rites as, for example, *Nkula*, a term which is sometimes used as a synonym for menstruation. The common term for menstrual discharge is *mbayi*, which may be connected with *ku-baya*, 'to be guilty', though *kanyanda* is often employed. *Kasheta* represents a menstrual period, but the circumlocution *ku-kiluka kwitala dikwawu*, 'to jump to the other hut', is quite commonly heard. For until recently each village had at least one grass hut near the edge of the bush, in which women stayed during their periods. Here they prepared their own food. They were forbidden to cook for their husbands and children or eat food with them during this time. Another woman of the village would undertake these offices for them during their absence. The blood of menstruation and murder is, therefore, 'bad' blood, and is connected by Ndembu with blackness.[2] But the blood shed by a hunter and offered at the graves and shrines of hunter ancestors is reckoned to be 'good' blood, and is associated ritually with white symbolism. Most rites of the hunters' cult are characterized by conjunction of white and red symbols.

There appears to be some correlation of the male role with the taking of life and of the female role with the giving of life, though both activities remain under the rubric of redness. Man kills, woman gives birth, and both processes are associated with the symbolism of blood.

Semen, as we have noted above, is blood 'purified by water'. The father's contribution to the child is, therefore, free from the impurity that invests female blood. And since whiteness is particularly closely associated with the ancestor spirits and with *Nzambi*, the High God, it might be said that the 'father's blood' is more 'spiritual' and less 'carnal' than the mother's blood. This greater purity is probably linked with the universal Ndembu belief that father-and-child is the one relationship completely free from the taint of witchcraft/sorcery. Mother-and-child, on the contrary, is far from free from this taint, and witches are thought to kill their own infants to provide 'meat' for the coven. Again, while a person has a strong jural bond to his maternal kin, he is considered by Ndembu to owe to his father and his father's kin important elements of his personality. For it is his father who has recourse to divination to find a name for him shortly after his birth, and it is from his father's deceased kin that he usually obtains it. It is believed that certain traits of character and physique of the name-giving spirit are reincarnated in the child. Again, the father plays an important role at *Mukanda*, the boys' circumcision rites, in providing care, instruction, and protection (against the carelessness of circumcisers) for his son during seclusion, while the mother is excluded from the lodge altogether. I mention these practices and beliefs to stress the 'pure' nature of the father-child tie. It is well-known among Ndembu that relationships between matrilineal kin are often strained, since competition is likely to develop between them over matters of inheritance and succession. Competition in kinship relations in African tribal society tends in the long run to give rise to accusations of sorcery and witchcraft, and sorcerers and witches, in Ndembu theory, are people 'with black livers' who lust after 'red human flesh' and harbour 'grudges' (*yitela*) which are classed among 'black things'. Thus while harmony lies on the 'white' father's side, competition lies on the 'red' mother's side (cf. Beidelman, 1961, pp. 253-254) – at least on the level of values if not of facts.

White and red as a binary system

This discussion of the sex-linking of white and red in the Ndembu theory of procreation leads inevitably to a consideration of these colours as a pair, as a binary system. For black is very often the neglected member of the triad. There are a number of reasons for this. In the first place, Ndembu regard symbols as articles or actions which 'make visible' or bring into play the powers inhering in the objects they signify.[3] Thus to employ a black symbol would be to evoke death, sterility, and witchcraft. Those contexts in which black is displayed openly, for instance the black and white striped sticks in *Mukanda* and the black band on the *ikishi* mask, usually refer to ritual death and are closely connected with the opposite notion of regeneration. When black symbols are used, as in the case of *malowa*, the black alluvial earth, they tend to be swiftly buried or hidden from view. *Malowa*, for example, is in several kinds of rites (*Kayong'u, Chihamba, Wubwang'u*) to propitiate ancestor spirits either plastered round the base of ritual objects, such as tree shrines, or buried under symbols of illness, 'to make them cool', i.e. to bring about the death of the 'hot' and hence mystically dangerous aspects of the affliction. It is alleged that sorcerers make use of materials considered 'black' and 'impure' such as the faeces of their intended victims, cindered foreskins stolen from circumcisers and the like, as ingredients of death-dealing 'medicine' (*wang'a*). But this very allegation illustrates how closely black symbolism is connected with socially un-desirable behaviour or with the privation of life and goodness. It is the extinction, whether willed or otherwise, of everything that moves, breathes, and has self-determination.

White and red, on the contrary, are associated with activity. Both are considered 'to have power'. Blood, the main denotation of 'redness', is even identified with 'power' (p. 14). White, too, stands for life-fluids; it represents milk and semen. Black, on the contrary, stands for body leavings, body dirt, and the fluids of putrefaction and for the products of katabolism. There is, however, an important difference between white and red, for the former represents the preservation and continuance of life, whereas the latter may represent the taking of life, and even where, as in the case of certain red symbols, such as the *mukula* tree, it represents continuity through parturition, it still has a note of danger and discontinuity. Killing is an activity of the living, giving birth is also such an activity. Hence, red, like white, falls under the general rubric of 'life'. When it is associated with purity, we may think of red as blood shed for the communal good. Red may be tinctured with white in Ndembu thinking, as in the case of normal semen, 'blood whitened by water', or with black, as in the case of an impotent man's semen, 'dead semen' (see p. 15). Now where a twofold classification of things as 'white' or 'red' develops, with black either absent or hidden, it sometimes happens that red acquires many of the negative and undesirable attributes of blackness, without retaining its better ones. It is, of course, of the essence of polarity that contrary qualities are assigned to the poles. Therefore, when the threefold colour classification yields to a twofold classification, we find red becoming, not only the complement, but also in some contexts, the antithesis of white. It might be apposite here to cite A. B. Kempe, the symbolic logician, who wrote: 'It is characteristically human to think in terms of dyadic relations: we habitually break up a triadic relation into a pair of dyads. In fact so ingrained is this disposition that some will object that a triadic relation is a pair of dyads. It would be exactly as logical to maintain that all dyadic relations are triads with a null member.' Thus in cases where white and red are regarded as complementary, rather than as antithetical pairs, we may very probably be dealing with a triadic relation of which black is the 'null member'. Since it is difficult, owing to Ndembu ideas about the nature of representation, to represent black visibly without evoking its inauspicious power, its absence from view may not necessarily mean its absence from thought. Indeed, its very absence may be significant since it is the true emblem of the hidden, the secret, the dark, the unknown – and perhaps also of potentiality as opposed to actuality. White and red, paired under the various aspects of male and female, peace and war, milk and flesh, semen and blood, are jointly 'life' (*wumi*); both are opposed to black as death and negativity.

SOME COMPARATIVE DATA

Since I have had little opportunity to comb through the literature systematically, what follows must necessarily be somewhat haphazard. I begin this comparative survey with ethnographic data on contemporary primitives, grouping them in broad regions.

Africa

M. Griaule (1950, pp. 58-81) describes the relationship among the Dogon of West Africa between a cosmological myth, masks, statuettes, ritual, rupestral painting and the colour rubrics, white, red, and black. Here black is associated with pollution, red with the menstrual blood of the Earth Mother who committed incest with her first-born, the Jackal, and white with purity. A large wooden image of a serpent, representing death and rebirth, is consecrated by blood sacrifices and decorated with these colours. Young male initiands wear masks coloured with white, black, and red. Wall paintings used in the rites are renewed with pigments of these hues. Red is also associated with the sun and fire.

Arthur Leib (1946, pp. 128-133) summarizes what he calls 'the mythical significance' of colours among the peoples of Madagascar as follows: 'With *black*, words like the following are associated: inferior, unpleasant, evil, suspicious, disagreeable, undesirable. With *white*: light, hope, joy, purity. With *red*: power, might, wealth.'

I have mentioned the ambivalence of black symbolism among the Ndembu. Black alluvial clay (*malowa*) is a symbol of fertility and marital love. Now, in many African societies black has auspicious connotations. Among the Shona of S. Rhodesia black represents *inter alia* the rain-bearing clouds which usher in the wet season, and sacrifices to spirit-guardians who send rain are made in black cattle, goats, or fowls while the spirit-mediums or priests wear black cloth. Thus in contiguous Bantu societies black may represent sterility in one and fertility in the other. According to Huntingford (1953a, p. 52) a black bullock is slaughtered over the grave of a rainmaker among the Kuku of Bari stock, while at the rainmaking ceremonies of the Lokoya a

72

black goat is killed and the contents of its stomach smeared on the stones at the grave of the rainmaker's father. It is Hunting-ford, too, who informs us that among the Sandawe of Tangan-yika 'priests (or diviners) are also rainmakers and offer sacrifices of black oxen, goats and sheep to bring rain' (Huntingford, 1953b, p. 138).

The Sandawe have often been alleged to have affinities with the Bushmen. Thus it is interesting to find that among the latter, according to Bleek and Lloyd (1911), a lustrous black powder made of pounded specularite, and known as //hara by the Cape Bushmen was used as body decoration and hair-dressing and appears to have been attributed with magical qualities. Thus, to quote one of Bleek's texts:

'They anoint their heads with //hara very nicely, while they wish that their head's hair may descend (i.e. grow long)' And it becomes abundant because of //hara; because they have anointed their heads, wishing that the hair may grow down-wards, that their heads may become black with blackness . . . //hara sparkles; therefore our heads shimmer on account of it. . . . Therefore, the Bushmen are wont to say . . . "That man, he is a handsome young man, on account of his head, which is surpassingly beautiful with the //hara's blackness" ' (p. 375, p. 377).

It is worth noting, in anticipation, that specularite (specular iron) was apparently 'an often sought after medium for paint in the Later Stone Age in the Cape, judging by the pieces that are found in the occupation sites' (Clark, 1959, p. 244). My own hypothesis is that black tends to become an auspicious colour in regions where water is short, for the black clouds bring fertility and growth (apparently of hair, as well as plants!). In regions where water is plentiful and food more or less abundant black may well be inauspicious. Thus it is not only among the Forest Bantu and Malagasy peoples that we find black to be inauspicious. For example, in a recent article Joan Wescott (1962, p. 346) writes: 'Black is associated (by the Yoruba) with the night and the night is associated . . . with evil. It is at night that sorcery and witchcraft are abroad and men are most vulnerable. Some Yoruba say simply that Elegba (the Trickster deity) is painted black because of his wickedness.'

Malay Peninsula

The Bushmen employ all three colours ritually. So also do the Semang, Sakai, and Jakun of the Malay Peninsula. Like the Bushman these peoples are hunters and gatherers. Skeat and Blagden (1906, p. 31) write that the Sakai paint their bodies in 'black, white, red, and occasionally yellow, which last two appear to be of equivalent value from a magical point of view' – incidentally just as they are among the Ndembu. When children are born among the Sakai the midwife applies stripes of pigment from the eyebrows to the tip of the nose, black in the case of girls, red in that of boys (p. 48). The black nose line is said to be for the protection of women against 'the Blood Demon' (Hantu Darah) which stops a woman's courses, and so prevents her bringing healthy children into the world. White is generally an auspicious colour, among the Sakai and other Malay peoples.

Australia

Charles P. Mountford (1962, p. 215) mentions that all three colours are used in the cave art of the Australian aborigines – black in the form of manganese oxide or one of the ferruginous ores, white from pipe-clay or kaolin deposits, and red ochre which may be secured by mining and trade – indeed men will travel a hundred miles or more to collect these ochres from special localities (such as Wilgamia in W. Australia and Blinman in the North Flinders Ranges of South Australia) (p. 210).

Mountford describes how white and red pigments are used in the cave paintings of the Wandjinas – tall mouthless figures with a halo-like design around their faces – sometimes these may be eighteen feet high. The face is always in white and surrounded by one, sometimes two, horseshoe-shaped bows which, in some examples, have lines radiating from them. These are usually in red. 'The aborigines believe,' says Mountford, 'that the paintings are filled with the essence of both water and blood; the water, so necessary for all living things, is symbolized by the white face and the blood, which makes men and animals strong, by the red ochre bows.' Note once more the close affinity with Ndembu exegesis of white and red. Water is 'white' for Ndembu, and blood of course is 'red'.

North American Indian

My last example from ethnographic sources is drawn from the New World, from Mooney's *Sacred Formulas of the Cherokees* (quoted by Lewis Spence in his article on the Cherokees in *Hastings Encyclopaedia of Religion and Ethics*). Mooney shows how, among the Cherokees, white represents peace, happiness and the south, red is equated with success, triumph, and the north, black with death and the west, and blue with defeat, trouble and the north. These senses probably indicate that, as in parts of Africa, blue is felt to have affinities with black. Certain Cherokee divinities and spirits corresponded in colour to the characteristics imputed to them. White and red spirits were usually regarded, when combined, as those from whom emanated the blessings of peace and health. The black spirits were invoked to slay an enemy. It is interesting to recall here how white and red in Ndembu ritual are used to betoken powers which may be combined for the benefit of the subject of the rites (e.g. in hunting and gynaecological ritual), while black is the colour of sorcery or witchcraft.

The Ancient World

Perhaps the most sophisticated exegesis of the colour triad and the most elaborate working out of its implications is to be found in the Chhāndogya Upanishad of ancient Hinduism and in the commentary by Śri Śankārachārya, the great eighth-century philosopher. Swami Nikhilinanda has recently translated the Upanishads and supplied notes based on Śankārachārya's explanations. I shall quote a few passages from the Chhāndogya Upanishad, VI, iv, 1, and follow each text with Nikhilinanda's notes:

'The red colour of (gross) fire is the colour of (the original fire); the white colour of (gross) fire is the colour of (the original) water (remember here the Ndembu and Aboriginal usages); the black colour of (gross) fire is the colour of (the original earth). Thus vanishes from fire what is commonly called fire, the modification being only a name, arising from speech, while the three colours (forms) alone are true.'

Commentary
'The three colours, or forms, constitute the visible fire. When these three colours are explained as belonging to the original fire, water, and earth, fire as it is commonly known disappears, and also the word "fire". For fire has no existence apart from a word and the idea denoted by that word. Therefore what the ignorant denote by the word "fire" is false, *the only truth being the three colours'* (my italics).

'The whole world is tripartite. Therefore, as in the case of fire (or in the cases of sun, moon, lightning, etc.) the only truth about the world is the three colours. Earth being only an effect of water, the only truth is water; earth is a mere name. So, too, water, being an effect of fire, is a mere name, the only truth being fire. Fire, too, being an effect of *Sat* or Pure Being, is a mere name, the only truth being Pure Being.'

In this Upanishad the colours are sometimes known as 'deities'. Examples are given of the way in which they manifest themselves in phenomena. Thus 'food when eaten becomes threefold (VI, v. 1). What is coarsest in it (the black part) becomes faeces, what is medium (the red part) becomes flesh, and what is subtlest (the white part) becomes mind'.

Also, 'water when drunk becomes threefold. What is coarsest in it (or black) becomes urine, what is medium (or red), becomes blood and what is subtlest (or white) becomes *prana* (= the vital breath which sustains life in a physical body or the primal energy or force, of which other forces are manifestations).'

The three colours appear to be identical with the *gunas* or 'strands' of existence (a metaphor from weaving) found in the Samkya-Karika, a work attributed to the sage Kapila. These are described by R. C. Zaehner (1962, p. 91) as 'permeating every corner of Nature's being *(praktri)'.* 'These three' are called *sattva, rajas* and *tamas* which can be literally translated as 'the quality of being, energy and darkness'. *Sattva* is the quality of purity and tranquillity (and may be equated with white); *rajas* is the active principle which initiates *karma* (and may be equated with red), while *tamas* is 'constrictive, obstructive, and

76

conducive to lethargic apathy (and may be equated with black)'. Zaehner quotes from Book 4, Chapter 5 of the great epic of the *Mahabharata* some verses which throw further light on the relationship between the *gunas* and the colours:

'With the one unborn Female, white, red, and black ("symbolizing the three *gunas*", as Zaehner writes) who produces many creatures like herself.

Lies the one unborn Male, taking his delight: another unborn Male leaves her when she has had her pleasure of him'.

It would seem probable that the notion of the colours is an inheritance from a remote (perhaps pre-Indo-European) past and that the Upanishadic texts are the speculations of a later philosophy on this primordial deposit.

It is again worth recalling at this point that the three colours or forms, in ancient Hinduism, are ultimately reducible to a single nature or being, to *Sat* or *Praktri*, for the Ndembu notion that the 'three rivers' of colour flow from Deity is not dissimilar. We find again in both cultures the notion that white is connected with purity and peace, and is the 'subtlest' or most 'spiritual' of the colours.

Much the same range of senses seems to be possessed by white in Semitic religions, for Robertson Smith records of the Arabs (1912, pp. 590, 583) that when a man disgraces himself by a breach of traditional custom or etiquette *his face becomes black*, whereas when he restores the omission, or makes up a quarrel, it again *becomes white*. There are also similarities between the senses of red in Hindu and Semitic cultures. Thus the common Hebrew word for passion (*quin'ah*) is derived from a verbal root which means primarily 'to be crimson'. And *rajas*, the second, 'red' 'strand' is often translated as 'passion' by English and American scholars. Maurice Farbridge (*Hastings Encyclopaedia*) writes that for the Old Testament Hebrews, 'red, as the colour of blood, represented bloodshed, war & guilt'.

THE THREE COLOURS IN ARCHAEOLOGICAL LITERATURE

In Africa many finds from the Stone Age from widely separated parts of Africa attest to the use of white, red, and black in ritual contexts. To pick a few at random: Roger Summers (1958, p. 295) excavated a shelter at Chitura Rocks in Inyanga District on the eastern border of Southern Rhodesia and found in association with Stillbay artifacts of the Middle Stone Age at the back of the shelter numerous small lumps of red ochre mixed with similar sized pieces of charcoal. Leakey (1931, p. 109) discovered in Gamble's Cave II at Elmenteita in Kenya several skeletons buried in the ultra-contracted position, males lying on the right side, females on the left, and all were freely sprinkled with red ochre. These skeletons resembled the Oldoway skeleton discovered in 1913 in Northern Tanganyika. Men of this type have been found in association with Chellean and even pre-Chelles-Acheul cultures with pebble choppers and flake tools.

Van Riet Lowe (quoted by Desmond Clark, 1959, p. 249) describes Later Stone Age Bushman burials at Smithfield in the Orange Free State in the following terms: 'An inverted half of an ostrich eggshell lay beneath the arms of the flexed skeleton, coated internally with (black) specularite (which, you will recall, is still used by Bushmen as a hair decoration) and externally with red ochre.' At Wilton in the Southern Region, Clark mentions that there were almost invariably a number of grave-stones, some of which were grindstones, some covered in ochre or even painted. The body was 'liberally covered with red ochre as were some of the grave goods'.

White, too, is used in early African rupestral art. For example, C. K. Cooke, writing of the prehistoric artist's materials and techniques in Southern Matabeleland (in Clark, 1957, p. 284) describes how bird droppings (still called *mpemba*, 'white clay', by Ndembu), vegetable substances, and kaolin are used in the manufacture of white pigments for cave and rock paintings.

In this paper I have no time to discuss the rich literature on burial practices and cave art in the European Palaeolithic. But it again seems clear that the colour triad white-red-black is always prominent, though other colours, such as yellows and browns are also used. Archaeologists are still undecided as to the significance of the colours. Their views may perhaps be typified by Annette Laming's (1959, p. 112) comments on the Lascaux cave paintings:

'The colours vary from group to group: sometimes one colour seems to have been more in favour than another. These preferences may have been due to the need for an economical use of some raw material which was particularly prized and difficult to obtain; or they may have been inspired by religious faith – by the belief in the greater efficacy of a certain red, or a particularly intense black, for example; or they may have been merely the result of a change in aesthetic taste.'

The hypothesis I am putting forward here is that magico-religious ideas of a certain kind were responsible for the selection of the basic colour triad and for the assiduity with which its constituent colours were sought or prepared. It is not the rarity of the pigments that makes them prized but the fact that they are prized for magico-religious reasons that makes men overcome all kinds of difficulties to obtain or manufacture them. I could cite much evidence to demonstrate the quite extraordinary lengths to which some societies will go to get red or black or white pigments. Sometimes to prepare a pure colour many ingredients are used, some of them probably with ritual intent. Thus, to make white paint for Dogon masks, limestone powder is mixed with cooked rice and the excrement of lizards or large snakes – the masks are used in rites connected with a mythical serpent. Among the Luluba, a Northern Nilo-Hamitic people, there is a big trade in a red ochreous substance made from biotite gneiss, which is powdered, buried for two months, and then after several processes roasted, when it can be mixed with simsim oil. Even black pigment may involve some degree of complexity in manufacture, as among the Dogon where it is obtained from the burnt seeds of *Vitex pachyphylla*, whose ashes are mixed with a tannin decoction. There are frequent records, both in prehistoric and in contemporary pre-industrial societies, of long trading expeditions being made to obtain red ochres.

THE SIGNIFICANCE OF THE BASIC COLOUR TRIAD

In the ethnographic literature it is noteworthy that among societies that make ritual use of all three colours the critical situation in which these appear together is initiation. Each may appear separately as a sign of the general character of a rite; thus red may be a persistent motif in hunting rites among the Ndembu, and white in rites dealing with lactation or village ancestral shades. But at the initiation of juniors into the rights and duties and values of seniors all three colours receive equal emphasis. In my view this is because they epitomize the main kinds of universal-human organic experience. In many societies these colours have explicit reference to certain fluids, secretions or waste-products of the human body. Thus red is universally a symbol of blood, white is frequently a symbol of breast-milk and semen (and sometimes of pus), while, as we have seen, the Chhāndogya Upanishad relates the black colour with faeces and urine (though other cultures connect urine with semen and both with whiteness). Each of the colours in all societies is multivocal, having a wide fan of connotations, but nevertheless the human physiological component is seldom absent wherever reliable native exegesis is available. Initiation rites often draw their symbolism from the situation of parturition and first lactation, where, in nature, blood, water, faeces, and milk are present.

I am going to throw caution to the winds for the sake of stimulating controversy and state boldly that:

1. Among the earliest symbols produced by man are the three colours representing products of the human body whose emission, spilling, or production is associated with a heightening of emotion – in other words, culture, the super-organic, has an intimate connection with the organic in its early stages, with the awareness of powerful physical experiences.

2. These heightened bodily experiences are felt to be informed with a power in excess of that averagely possessed by the individual; its source may be located in the cosmos or in society; analogues of physical experience may then be found wherever the same colours occur in nature; or else experience of social relations in heightened emotional circumstances may be *classified* under a colour rubric.

3. The colours represent heightened physical experience transcending the experiencer's normal condition – they are therefore conceived as 'deities' (Hindu) or mystical powers, as the sacred over against the profane.

4. The physical experiences associated with the three colours

are also experiences of social relationships: thus white = semen is linked to mating between man and woman; white = milk is linked to the mother-child tie; red = maternal blood is linked to the mother-child tie and also the processes of group recruitment and social placement, red = bloodshed is connected with war, feud, conflict, social discontinuities, red = obtaining and preparation of animal food = status of hunter or herder, male productive role in the sexual division of labour, etc., red = transmission of blood from generation to generation = an index of membership in a corporate group; black = excreta or bodily dissolution = transition from one social status to another viewed as mystical death, black = rainclouds or fertile earth = unity of widest recognized group sharing same life-values.

5. While it is possible to find many references to bodily fluids in white and red symbolism, few societies specifically connect black with processes and products of katabolism and decay e.g. with decayed or clotted blood. It is possible that black which, as we have seen, often means 'death' or a 'fainting fit' or 'sleep' or 'darkness' primarily represents falling into unconsciousness, the experience of a 'black-out'. Among Ndembu, and in many other societies, both white and red may stand for life. When they are paired in ritual, white may stand for one alleged polarity of life, such as masculinity or vegetable food, while red may represent its opposite, such as femininity or meat. Or white may represent 'peace' and red 'war'; both are conscious activities as distinct from black which stands for inactivity and the cessation of consciousness.

6. Not only do the three colours stand for basic human experiences of the body (associated with the gratification of libido, hunger, aggressive, and excretory drives and with fear, anxiety, and submissiveness), they also provide a kind of primordial classification of reality. This view is in contrast to Durkheim's notion that the social relations of mankind are not based on the logical relations of things but have served as the prototypes of the latter. Nor has society, Durkheim argues, been merely the model on which the classifying thought has wrought: the framework of society has been the very framework of the system of things. Men were themselves first grouped. For that reason they could think under the form of groups. The centre

of the earliest system of nature is not the individual: it is the society. Against this I would postulate that the human organism and its crucial experiences are the *fons et orgio* of all classifications. Human biology demands certain intense experiences of relationship. If men and women are to beget and bear, suckle, and dispose of physical wastes they must enter into relationships – relationships which are suffused with the affective glow of the experiences. These are the very processes which the Ndembu call 'rivers' – they stream from man's inner nature. The colour triad white-red-black represents the archetypal man as a pleasure-pain process. The perception of these colours and of triadic and dyadic relations in the cosmos and in society, either directly or metaphorically, is a derivative of primordial psychobiological experience – experience which can be fully attained only in human mutuality. It needs two to copulate, two to suckle and wean, two to fight and kill (Cain and Abel), and three to form a family. The multitude of interlaced classifications which make up ideological systems controlling social relationships are derivatives, divested of affectual accompaniments, of these primordial twos and threes. The basic three are sacred because they have the power 'to carry the man away', to overthrow his normal powers of resistance. Though immanent in his body they appear to transcend his consciousness. By representing these 'forces' or 'strands of life' by colour symbols in a ritual context, men may have felt that they could domesticate or control these forces for social ends. But the forces and the symbols for them are biologically, psychologically, and logically prior to social classifications by moieties, clans, sex totems, and all the rest. Since the experiences which the three colours represent are common to all mankind we do not have to invoke diffusion to explain their wide distribution. We do have to invoke diffusion to explain why other colours, such as yellow, saffron, gold, blue, green, purple, etc., are ritually important in certain cultures. And we must also look to processes of culture contact to explain differences in the senses attributed to the basic colours in different regions. The point I am trying to make here is that the three colours white-red-black for the simpler societies are not merely differences in the visual perception of parts of the spectrum: they are abridgements or condensations of whole realms of psychobiological experience involving the reason and all the senses and concerned with primary group relationships. It is only by subsequent abstraction from these configurations that the other modes of social classification employed by mankind arose.

NOTES

1. It is interesting to note that the art of iron-working is an exclusively masculine occupation and the use of the axe in bush-clearing is restricted to males. On the other hand, by far the greatest number of woodcarvings are of the female body.
2. Witches' familiars, called *tuyebela*, *andumba*, or *tushipa*, are commonly supposed to be kept in the menstruation hut.
3. A point I have discussed at length elsewhere, e.g. in *Ndembu Divination* (1961, p. 4).

REFERENCES

BAUMANN, H. 1935. *Lunda: Bei Bauern und Jägern in Inner Angola*. Berlin: Wurfel Verlag.

BEIDELMAN, T. 1961. Right and Left Hand among the Kaguru. *Africa* **31** (3).

BLEEK, W. H. I. & LLOYD, L. C. 1911. *Specimens of Bushman Folklore*. London: George Allen.

CLARK, J. D. 1959. *The Prehistory of Southern Africa*. Harmondsworth: Penguin Books.

COOKE, C. K. 1957. In J. Desmond Clark (ed.), *Prehistory*. Third Pan-African Congress, 1955. London: Chatto & Windus.

DURKHEIM, E. & MAUSS, M. 1963. *Primitive Classification*. R. Needham (ed.). London: Cohen & West; Chicago: University of Chicago Press.

FARBRIDGE, MAURICE 1922. Article on Symbolism (Semitic). In *Hastings Encyclopaedia of Religion and Ethics*, Vol. XII, p. 150. Edinburgh: T. & T. Clark.

GRIAULE, M. 1950. *Arts of the African Native*. London: Thames & Hudson.

HARRIES, LYNDON. 1944. The Initiation Rites of the Makonde Tribe. *Communications from the Rhodes-Livingstone Institute*, No. 3.

HERTZ, ROBERT. 1960. *Death and the Right Hand*. London: Cohen & West.

Victor W. Turner

HUNTINGFORD, G. W. B. 1953a. *The Northern Nilo-Hamites*. Ethnographic Survey of Africa, East-Central Africa, Part 6. London: International African Institute.

—— 1953b. *The Southern Nilo-Hamites*. Ethnographic Survey of Africa, East-Central Africa, Part 8. London: International African Institute.

KEMPE, A. B. 1890. On the Relation between the Logical Theory of Classes and the Geometrical Theory of Points. *Proceedings of the London Mathematical Society* 21.

LAMING, ANNETTE. 1959. *Lascaux*. Harmondsworth: Penguin Books.

LEAKEY, L. S. B. 1931. *The Stone Age Cultures of Kenya Colony*. London: Oxford University Press.

LEIB, ARTHUR. 1946. *Folklore* 57: 128-133.

NIKHILINANANDA, SWAMI (trans.) 1963. *Upanishads*. New York: Harper, Row.

MOUNTFORD, CHARLES P. 1962. *Oceania and Australia*. Art of the World Series, VIII. London: Methuen.

NEEDHAM, RODNEY. 1960. The Left Hand of the Mugwe. *Africa* 30 (1).

RICHARDS, A. I. 1956. *Chisungu*. London: Faber & Faber.

SKEAT, W. W. & BLAGDEN, C. O. 1906. *Pagan Races of the Malay Peninsula*. London: Macmillan.

SMITH, ROBERTSON. W. 1912. A Journey in the Hedjaz. In J. S. Black & G. Crystal, (eds.), *Lectures and Essays*. London: A. & C. Black.

SPENCE, LEWIS. 1911. Article on the Cherokees. In *Hastings Encyclopaedia of Religion and Ethics*, Vol. III, pp. 506-507.

SUMMERS, ROGER. 1958. *Inyanga*. London: Cambridge University Press.

TURNER, VICTOR W. 1961. *Ndembu Divination; Its Symbolism and Techniques*. Rhodes-Livingstone Institute Paper 31.

VERGIAT, A. M. 1936. *Les Rites Secrets des Primitifs de l'Oubangui*. Paris: Payot.

WESCOTT, JOAN. 1961. The Sculpture and Myths of Eshu-Elegba, The Yoruba Trickster. *Africa* 32 (4).

WHITE, C. M. N. 1961. *Elements in Luvale Beliefs and Rituals*. Rhodes-Livingstone Institute Paper 33.

ZAEHNER, R. C. 1962. *Hinduism*. London: Oxford University Press.

Melford E. Spiro

Religion : Problems of Definition and Explanation

INTRODUCTION[1]

Before examining various approaches to the explanation of religion, we must first agree about what it is that we hope to be able to explain. In short, we must agree on what we mean by 'religion'. Anthropology, like other immature sciences – and especially those whose basic vocabulary is derived from natural languages – continues to be plagued by problems of definition. Key terms in our lexicon – 'culture', 'social system', 'needs', 'marriage', 'function', and the like – continue to evoke wide differences in meaning and to instigate heated controversy among scholars. Frequently the differences and controversies stem from differences in the *types* of definition employed.

Logicians distinguish between two broad types of definition: nominal and real definitions (Hempel, 1952, pp. 2-14). Nominal definitions are those in which a word, whose meaning is unknown or unclear, is defined in terms of some expression whose meaning is already known. We all engage in such an enterprise in the classroom when we attempt to define, i.e. to assign meaning to, the new terms to which we expose our untutored undergraduates. Our concern in this case is to communicate ideas efficiently and unambiguously; and, in general, we encounter few difficulties from our students, who have no ego-involvement in alternative definitions to our own. We do have difficulties with our colleagues, however, because they – unlike us! – are ego-involved in their immortal prose and, intransigently, prefer their nominal definitions to ours. Despite their intransigence, however, the problem of achieving consensus with respect to nominal definitions is, at least in principle, easily resolved. We could, for example, delegate to an international committee of anthropologists the authority to publish a standard dictionary of anthropological concepts, whose

85

definitions would be mandatory for publication in anthropological journals.

The problem is more serious, and its resolution correspondingly more difficult, in the case of real definitions. Unlike nominal definitions which arbitrarily assign meaning to linguistic symbols, real definitions are conceived to be true statements about entities or things. Here, three difficulties are typically encountered in anthropology (and in the other social sciences). The first difficulty arises when a hypothetical construct – such as culture or social structure – is reified and then assigned a real definition. Since that which is to be defined is not an empirically observable entity, controversies in definition admit of no empirical resolution.

A second difficulty is encountered when real definitions are of the kind that stipulate what the definer takes to be the 'essential nature' of some entity. Since the notion of 'essential nature' is always vague and almost always non-empirical, such definitions are scientifically useless. Kinship studies represent a good case in point, with their – at least so it seems to a non-specialist – interminable controversies concerning the essential nature of marriage, descent, corporality, and the like.

Sometimes, however, real definitions are concerned with analyzing a complex concept – which has an unambiguous empirical referent – by making explicit the constituent concepts which render its meaning. These are known as analytic definitions. Thus, the expression 'X is a husband' can be defined as 'X is a male human, and X is married to some female human'. But the possible objections which such a definition would evoke among some anthropologists, at least, exemplifies the third definitional difficulty in anthropology: what might be called our obsession with universality. Since there are instances in parts of Africa of a phenomenon similar to what is ordinarily termed 'marriage', but in which both partners are female, some scholars would rule out this definition on the grounds that it is culturally parochial. This insistence on universality in the interests of a comparative social science is, in my opinion, an obstacle to the comparative method for it leads to continuous changes in definition and, ultimately, to definitions which, because of their vagueness or abstractness, are all but useless.

(And of course they commit the fallacy of assuming that certain institutions must, in fact, be universal, rather than recognizing that universality is a creation of definition. I am also at a loss to understand why certain institutions – marriage, for example – must be universal, while others – such as the state – need not be.)

THE PROBLEM OF DEFINITION IN RELIGION

An examination of the endemic definitional controversies concerning religion leads to the conclusion that they are not so much controversies over the meaning either of the term 'religion' or of the concept which it expresses, as they are jurisdictional disputes over the phenomenon or range of phenomena which are considered to constitute legitimately the empirical referent of the term. In short, definitional controversies in religion have generally involved differences in what are technically termed ostensive definitions. To define a word ostensively is to point to the object which that word designates. In any language community, the fiery ball in the sky, for example, evokes a univocal verbal response from all perceivers; and a stranger arriving in an English-speaking community can easily learn the ostensive definition of the word 'sun' by asking any native to point to the object for which 'sun' is the name. Similarly the empirical referent of 'table' can be designated unequivocally, if not efficiently, by pointing to examples of each sub-set of the set of objects to which the word applies.

The community of anthropologists, however, is not a natural language community – more important, perhaps, it does not share a common culture – and although there is little disagreement among anthropologists concerning the class of objects to which such words as 'sister', 'chief', 'string figure' – and many others – properly *do* apply, there is considerable disagreement concerning the phenomena to which the word 'religion' *ought* to apply. Hence the interminable (and fruitless) controversies concerning the religious status of coercive ritual or an ethical code or supernatural beings, and so on. From the affect which characterizes many of these discussions one cannot help but suspect that much of this controversy stems, consciously or unconsciously, from extra-scientific considerations – such as the personal attitudes to religion which scholars bring to its study. Since I am concerned with the logic of inquiry, I must resist a tempting excursion into the social psychology of science.

The scientific grounds for disagreement are almost always based on comparative considerations. Thus Durkheim rejects the belief in supernatural beings as a legitimate referent of 'religion' on the grounds that this would deny religion to primitive peoples who, allegedly, do not distinguish between the natural and the supernatural. Similarly, he rejects the belief in gods as a distinguishing characteristic of 'religion' because Buddhism, as he interprets it, contains no such belief (1954, pp. 24-36). Such objections raise two questions; one factual, the other methodological. I shall return to the factual question in a later section, and confine my present remarks to the methodological question. Even if it were the case that Theravada Buddhism contained no belief in gods or supernatural beings, from what methodological principle does it follow that religion – or, for that matter, anything else – must be universal if it is to be studied comparatively? The fact that hunting economies, unilateral descent groups, or string figures do not have a universal distribution has not prevented us from studying *them* comparatively. Does the study of religion become any the less significant or fascinating – indeed, it would be even more fascinating – if in terms of a consensual ostensive definition it were discovered that one or seven or sixteen societies did not possess religion? If it indeed be the case that Theravada Buddhism is atheistic and that, by a theistic definition of religion, it is not therefore a religion, why can we not face, rather than shrink, from this consequence? Having combatted the notion that 'we' have religion (which is 'good') and 'they' have superstition (which is 'bad'), why should we be dismayed if it be discovered that society *x* does not have 'religion', as we have defined that term? For the premise 'no religion' does not entail the conclusion 'therefore superstition' – nor, incidentally, does it entail the conclusion 'therefore no social integration', unless of course religion is defined as anything which makes for integration. It may rather entail the conclusion 'therefore science' or 'therefore philosophy'. Or it may entail no conclusion and, instead, stimulate some research. In short, once we free the word 'religion' from all value judgements, there is reason neither for dismay nor for elation concerning the empirical distribution of religion attendant upon our definition. With respect to Theravada Buddhism, then, what loss to science would have ensued if Durkheim had decided that, as he interpreted it, it was atheistic, and therefore not a religion? I can see only gain. First, it would have stimulated fieldwork in these apparently anomalous Buddhist societies and, second, we would have been spared the confusion created by the consequent real and functional definitions of religion which were substituted for the earlier substantive or structural definitions.

Real definitions, which stipulate the 'essential nature' of some phenomenon are, as I have already argued, necessarily vague and almost always non-empirical. What, for example, does Durkheim's 'sacred' – which he stipulates as the essential nature of religion – really mean? How useful is it, not in religious or poetic, but in scientific discourse? It is much too vague to be taken as a primitive term in a definitional chain, and it is useless to define it by equally vague terms such as 'holy' or 'set apart'. But if such real definitions are unsatisfactory when the phenomenal referent of the *definiendum* is universally acknowledged, they are virtually useless when, as in this case, it is the phenomenal referent which is precisely at issue. If there is no agreement about what it is that is being defined, how can we agree on its essential nature? Durkheim, to be sure, circumvented this problem by arguing that the sacred is whatever it is that a society deems to be sacred. But even if it were to be granted that one obscurity can achieve clarity by the substitution of another, real definitions of this type – like functional definitions to which I now wish to turn – escape the trap of overly narrow designata only to fall into the trap of overly broad ones.

Most functional definitions of religion are essentially a subclass of real definitions in which functional variables (the promotion of solidarity, and the like) are stipulated as the essential nature of religion. But whether the essential nature consists of a qualitative variable (such as 'the sacred') or a functional variable (such as social solidarity), it is virtually impossible to set any substantive boundary to religion and, thus, to distinguish it from other sociocultural phenomena. Social solidarity, anxiety reduction, confidence in unpredictable situations, and the like, are functions which may be served by any or all cultural phenomena – Communism and Catholicism, monotheism and monogamy, images and imperialism – and unless religion is defined substantively, it would be impossible to delineate its boundaries. Indeed, even when its substantive boundaries are limited, some functional definitions impute to religion some of the functions of a total sociocultural system.

It is obvious, then, that while a definition cannot take the place of inquiry, in the absence of definitions there can be no inquiry – for it is the definition, either ostensive or nominal, which designates the phenomenon to be investigated. Thus when Evans-Pritchard writes that 'objectivity' in studies of religion requires that 'we build up general conclusions from particular ones' (1954, p. 9), this caution is certainly desirable for discovering empirical generalizations or for testing hypotheses. But when he tells us that 'one must not ask "what is religion?" but what are the main features of, let us say, the religion of one Melanesian people . . .' which, when compared with findings among other Melanesian peoples, will lead to generalizations about Melanesian religion, he is prescribing a strategy which, beginning with the study of that one Melanesian people cannot get started. For unless he knows, ostensively, what religion is, how can our anthropologist in his Melanesian society know which, among a possible n, observations constitute observations of religious phenomena, rather than of some other phenomenal class, kinship, for example, or politics?

Indeed, when the term 'religion' is given no explicit ostensive definition, the observer, perforce, employs an implicit one. Thus, Durkheim warns that in defining religion we must be careful not to proceed from our 'prejudices, passions, or habits' (1954, p. 24). Rather, '. . . it is from the reality itself which we are going to define' (ibid.). Since any scientist – or, for that matter, any reasonable man – prefers 'reality' to 'prejudice', we happily follow his lead and, together with him, '. . . set ourselves before this reality' (ibid.). But since, Durkheim tells us, 'religion cannot be defined except by the characteristics which are found wherever religion itself is found', we must

'. . . consider the various religions in their concrete reality, and attempt to disengage that which they have in common' (ibid.). Now, the very statement of this strategy raises an obvious question. Unless we already know, by definition, what religion is, how can we know which 'concrete reality' we are to 'consider'? Only if religion has already been defined can we perform either this initial operation or the subsequent one of disengaging those elements which are shared by all religions.

In sum, any comparative study of religion requires, as an operation antecedent to inquiry, an ostensive or substantive definition that stipulates unambiguously those phenomenal variables which are designated by the term. This ostensive definition will, at the same time, be a nominal definition in that some of its designata will, to other scholars, appear to be arbitrary. This, then, does not remove 'religion' from the arena of definitional controversy; but it does remove it from the context of fruitless controversy over what religion 'really is' to the context of the formulation of empirically testable hypotheses which, in anthropology, means hypotheses susceptible to cross-cultural testing.

But this criterion of cross-cultural applicability does not entail, as I have argued above, universality. Since 'religion' is a term with historically rooted meanings, a definition must satisfy not only the criterion of cross-cultural applicability but also the criterion of intra-cultural intuitivity; at the least, it should not be counter-intuitive. For me, therefore, any definition of 'religion' which does not include, as a key variable, the belief in superhuman – I won't muddy the metaphysical waters with 'supernatural' – beings who have power to help or harm man is counter-intuitive. Indeed, if anthropological consensus were to exclude such beliefs from the set of variables which is necessarily designated by 'religion', an explanation for these beliefs would surely continue to elicit our research energies.

Even if it were the case that Theravada Buddhism postulates no such beings, I find it strange indeed, given their all-but universal distribution at every level of cultural development, that Durkheim – on the basis of this one case – should have excluded such beliefs from a definition of religion, and stranger still that others should have followed his lead. But this anomaly aside, is it the case that Buddhism contains no belief in super-human beings? (Let us, for the sake of brevity, refer to these beings as 'gods'.) It is true, of course, that Buddhism contains no belief in a creator god; but creation is but one possible attribute of godhood, one which – I suspect – looms not too large in the minds of believers. If gods are important for their believers because – as I would insist is the case – they possess power greater than man's, including the power to assist man in, or prevent him from, attaining mundane and/or supermundane goals, even Theravada Buddhism – Mahayana is clearly not at issue here – most certainly contains such beliefs. With respect to supermundane goals, the Buddha is certainly a superhuman being. Unlike ordinary humans, he himself acquired the power to attain Enlightenment and, hence Buddhahood. Moreover, he showed others the means for its attainment. Without his teachings, natural man could not, unassisted, have discovered the way to Enlightenment and to final Release.

The soteriological attributes of the Buddha are, to be sure, different from those of the Judaeo-Christian-Islamic God. Whereas the latter is living, the former is dead; whereas the latter is engaged in a continuous and active process of salvation, the former had engaged in only one active ministry of salvation. But – with the exception of Calvinism – the soteriological consequences are the same. For the Buddhist and the Western religionist alike the Way to salvation was revealed by a super-human being, and salvation can be attained only if one follows this revealed Way. The fact that in one case compliance with the Way leads directly to the ultimate goal because of the very nature of the world; and, in the other case, compliance leads to the goal only after divine intercession, should not obscure the basic similarity: in both cases man is dependent for his salvation upon the revelation of a superhuman being. (Indeed, there is reason to believe – I am now analyzing field data collected in a Burmese village which suggest that this might be the case – that Buddhist worship is not merely an expression of reverence and homage to the One who has revealed the Way, but is also a petition for His saving intercession.)

But superhuman beings generally have the power to assist (or hinder) man's attempts to attain mundane as well as supermundane goals, and when it is asserted that Buddhism postulates no such beings, we must ask to which Buddhism this assertion has reference. Even the Buddhism of the Pali canon does not deny the existence of a wide range of superhuman beings who intervene, for good and for ill, in human affairs; it merely denies that they can influence one's salvation. More important, in contemporary Theravada countries, the Buddha himself – or, according to more sophisticated believers, his power – is believed to protect people from harm. Thus Burmese peasants recite Buddhist spells and perform rites before certain Buddha images which have the power to protect them from harm, to cure snake bites, and the like. And Buddhist monks chant passages from Scripture in the presence of the congregation which, it is believed, can bring a wide variety of worldly benefits.

There are, to be sure, atheistic Buddhist philosophies – as there are atheistic Hindu philosophies – but it is certainly a strange spectacle when anthropologists, of all people, confuse the teachings of a philosophical school with the beliefs and behavior of a religious community. And if – on some strange methodological grounds – the teachings of the philosophical schools, rather than the beliefs and behavior of the people, were to be designated as the normative religion of a society, then the numerous gods and demons to be found in the Pali canon – and in the world-view of most Theravadists, including the monastic virtuosos – find more parallels in other societies than the beliefs held by the numerically small philosophical schools.

Finally – and what is perhaps even more important from an anthropological point of view – the Pali canon is only one source for the world-view of Buddhist societies. Indeed, I know of no society in which Buddhism represents the exclusive belief system of a people. On the contrary, it is always to be found together with another system with which it maintains an important division of labor. Whereas Buddhism (restricting this term, now, to Canonical Buddhism) is concerned with supermundane goals – rebirth in a better human existence, in a celestial abode of gods, or final Release – the other system is concerned with worldly goals: the growing of crops, protection from illness, guarding of the village, etc., which are the domain of numerous superhuman beings. These are the *nats* of Burma, the *phi* of Laos and Thailand, the *neak ta* of Cambodia, etc. Although the Burmese, for example, distinguish sharply between Buddhism and *nat* worship, and although it is undoubtedly true – as most scholars argue – that these non-Buddhist belief systems represent the pre-Buddhist religions of these Theravada societies, the important consideration for our present discussion is that these beliefs, despite the long history of Buddhism in these countries, persist with undiminished strength, continuing to inform the world-view of these Buddhist societies and to stimulate important and extensive ritual activity. Hence, even if Theravada Buddhi*sm* were absolutely atheistic, it cannot be denied that Theravada Buddhi*sts* adhere to another belief system which is theistic to its core; and if it were to be argued that atheistic Buddhism – by some other criteria – is a religion and that, therefore, the belief in superhuman beings is not a necessary characteristic of 'religion', it would still be the case that the belief in superhuman beings and in their power to aid or harm man is a central feature in the belief systems of all traditional societies.

But Theravada Asia provides only one example of the tenacity of such beliefs. Confucianist China provides what is, perhaps, a better example. If Theravada Buddhism is somewhat ambiguous concerning the existence and behavior of superhuman beings, Confucianism is much less ambiguous. Although the latter does not explicitly deny the existence of such beings, it certainly ignores their role in human affairs. It is more than interesting to note, therefore, that when Mahayana Buddhism was introduced into China, it was precisely its gods (including the Boddhisatvas), demons, heavens, and hells that, according to many scholars, accounted for its dramatic conquest of China.

To summarize, I would argue that the belief in superhuman beings and in their power to assist or to harm man approaches universal distribution, and this belief – I would insist – is the core variable which ought to be designated by any definition of religion. Recently Horton (1960) and Goody (1962) have reached the same conclusion.

Although the belief in the existence of superhuman beings is the core religious variable, it does not follow – as some scholars

94

have argued – that religious, in contrast to magical, behavior is necessarily other-worldly in orientation, or that, if it is other-worldly, its orientation is 'spiritual'. The beliefs in superhuman beings, other-worldliness, and spiritual values vary independently. Thus, ancient Judaism, despite its obsession with God's will, was essentially this-worldly in orientation. Catholicism, with all its other-worldly orientation is, with certain kinds of Hinduism, the most 'materialistic' of the higher religions. Confucianism, intensely this-worldly, is yet concerned almost exclusively with such 'spiritual' values as filial piety, etc. In short, superhuman beings may be conceived as primarily means or as ends. Where values are worldly, these beings may be viewed as important agents for the attainment and/or frustration of worldly goals, either 'material' or 'spiritual'. Where values are materialistic, superhuman beings may be viewed as important agents for the attainment of material goals, either in this or in an after life. Where values are other-worldly, mystical union with superhuman beings may be viewed as an all-consuming goal; and so on.

Although the differentiating characteristic of religion is the belief in superhuman beings, it does not follow, moreover, that these beings are necessarily objects of ultimate concern. Again, it depends on whether they are viewed as means or as ends. For those individuals whom Weber has termed 'religiously musical' (Gerth & Mills, 1946, p. 287), or whom Radin (1957, p. 9) has termed 'the truly religious', superhuman beings are of ultimate concern. For the rest, however, superhuman beings are rarely of ultimate concern, although the ends for which their assistance is sought may be. Hence, though their benevolent ancestral spirits are not of great concern to the Ifaluk, restoration of health – for which these spirits are instrumental – most certainly is. Similarly, while the Buddha may not be of ultimate concern to a typical Burmese peasant, the escape from suffering – for which He is instrumental – can certainly be so designated.

Conversely, while religious beliefs are not always of ultimate concern, non-religious beliefs sometimes are. This raises a final unwarranted conclusion, viz. that religion uniquely refers to the 'sacred', while secular concerns are necessarily 'profane'. Thus, if 'sacred' refers to objects and beliefs of ultimate concern, and 'profane' to those of ordinary concern, religious and secular beliefs alike may have reference either to sacred or to profane phenomena. For the members of Kiryat Yedidim, an Israeli *kibbutz*, the triumph of the proletariat, following social revolution, and the ultimate classless society in which universal brotherhood, based on loving kindness, will replace parochial otherhood, based on competitive hostility, constitutes their sacred belief system. But, by definition, it is not a religious belief system, since it has no reference to – indeed, it denies the existence of – superhuman beings.

Similarly, if communism, or baseball, or the stockmarket are of ultimate concern to some society, or to one of its constituent social groups, they are, by definition, sacred. But beliefs concerning communism, baseball, or the stockmarket are not, by definition, religious beliefs, because they have no reference to superhuman beings. They may, of course, serve many of the functions served by religious beliefs; and they are, therefore, members of the same functional class. Since however, they are, substantively dissimilar, it would be as misleading to designate them by the same term as it would be to designate music and sex by the same term because they both provide sensual pleasure. (Modern American society presents an excellent example of the competition of sports, patriotism, sex, and God for the title, perhaps not exclusively, of 'the sacred'. Indeed, if the dictum of Miss Jane Russell is taken seriously – God, she informs us, is a 'livin' doll' – I would guess that, whichever wins, God is bound to lose.)

A DEFINITION OF 'RELIGION'

On the assumption that religion is a cultural institution, and on the further assumption that all institutions – though not all of their features – are instrumental means for the satisfaction of needs, I shall define 'religion' as 'an institution consisting of culturally patterned interaction with culturally postulated superhuman beings'. I should like to examine these variables separately.

Institution. This term implies, of course, that whatever

phenomena we might wish to designate by 'religion', religion is an attribute of social groups, comprising a component part of their cultural heritage; and that its component features are acquired by means of the same enculturation processes as the other variables of a cultural heritage are acquired. This means that the variables constituting a religious system have the same ontological status as those of other cultural systems: its beliefs are normative, its rituals collective, its values prescriptive. This, I take it, is what Durkheim (1954, p. 44) had in mind in insisting that there can be no religion without a church. (It means, too, as I shall observe in a later section, that religion has the same methodological status as other cultural systems; i.e. religious variables are to be explained by the same explanatory schemata – historical, structural, functional, and causal – as those by which other cultural variables are explained.)

Interaction. This term refers to two distinct, though related, types of activity. First, it refers to activities which are believed to carry out, embody, or to be consistent with the will or desire of superhuman beings or powers. These activities reflect the putative *value system* of these superhuman beings and, presumably, they constitute part – but only part – of the actors' value system. These activities may be viewed as desirable in themselves and/or as means for obtaining the assistance of superhuman beings or for protection against their wrath. Second it refers to activities which are believed to influence superhuman beings to satisfy the needs of the actors. These two types of activity may overlap, but their range is never coterminous. Where they do overlap, the action in the overlapping sphere is, in large measure, symbolic; that is, it consists in behavior whose meaning, cross-culturally viewed, is obscure and/or arbitrary; and whose efficacy, scientifically viewed, is not susceptible of ordinary scientific 'proof'. These symbolic, but definitely instrumental, activities constitute, of course, a *ritual*, or symbolic *action, system.* Unlike private rituals, such as those found in an obsessive-compulsive neurosis, religious rituals are culturally patterned; i.e. both the activities and their meaning are shared by the members of a social group by virtue of their acquisition from a shared cultural heritage.

Superhuman beings. These refer to any beings believed to possess power greater than man, who can work good and/or evil on man, and whose relationships with man can, to some degree, be influenced by the two types of activity described in the previous section. The belief of any religious actor in the existence of these beings and his knowledge concerning their attributes are derived from and sanctioned by the cultural heritage of his social group. To that extent – and regardless of the objective existence of these beings, or of personal experiences which are interpreted as encounters with them – their existence is culturally postulated. Beliefs concerning the existence and attributes of these beings, and of the efficacy of certain types of behavior (ritual, for example) in influencing their relations with man, constitute a *belief system.*

This brief explication of our definition of 'religion' indicates that, viewed systemically, religion can be differentiated from other culturally constituted institutions by virtue only of its reference to superhuman beings. All institutions consist of *belief systems,* i.e. an enduring organization of cognitions about one or more aspects of the universe; *action systems,* an enduring organization of behavior patterns designed to attain ends for the satisfaction of needs; and *value systems,* an enduring organization of principles by which behavior can be judged on some scale of merit. Religion differs from other institutions in that its three component systems have reference to superhuman beings.

Having defined 'religion', our next task is to examine the types of explanation that have been offered to account for its existence. First, however, we must answer some elementary questions concerning the nature of anthropological explanation.

EXPLANATION IN SOCIAL ANTHROPOLOGY

What do anthropologists attempt to explain? Of what do explanations consist? How do these explanations differ from each other? Once we penetrate beneath our jargon, it appears that always the phenomenon to be explained is (*a*) the *existence* of some social or cultural variable, and (*b*) the *variability* which it exhibits in a cross-cultural distribution. These statements of course are really one, because the variable 'exists' in the range of values which it can assume. If a theory purports to explain the existence of religion, but its concepts are so general or so vague that it cannot explain the variability exhibited by its empirical instances, it is disqualified as a *scientific*, i.e. a testable, theory.

'Existence' is an ambiguous term. In asking for an explanation for the existence of religion, we might be asking how it came to exist in the first place – this is the question of religious origins – or how it is that it exists (i.e. has persisted) in some ethnographic present. Since a testable, i.e. scientific, theory of religious origins will probably always elude our explanatory net, this paper will be concerned with the persistence, not the origin, of religion.

In all of our explanations, to answer the second question, we stipulate a condition or a set of conditions in whose absence the variable to be explained would not exist. Now, to say that any sociocultural variable – religion, for example – 'exists' is, in the last analysis, to say that in some society – or, in one of its constituent social groups – a proposition is affirmed, a norm complied with, a custom performed, a role practiced, a spirit feared, etc. In short, the 'existence' of a sociocultural variable means that in any sense of 'behavior' – cognitive, affective, or motor – there occurs some behavior in which, or by which, the variable in question is instanced. Hence, a theory of the 'existence' of religion must ultimately be capable of explaining religious 'behavior'.

In general, theories of the existence – in the sense of persistence – of sociocultural variables are cast in four explanatory modes: historical (in the documentary, not the speculative, sense), structural, causal, and functional. When analyzed, the first two can be reduced to either the third or the fourth. Thus historical explanations are either no explanation at all, or they are causal explanations. Surely, the mere listing of a series of events which are antecedent to the appearance of the variable in question does not constitute explanation – unless it can be shown that one or more of these events was a condition, either necessary or sufficient, for its appearance. If this can be demonstrated, the explanation is based on a causal theory, the fact of its having originated in the past being incidental to the theoretical aim of explaining a certain type of social or cultural innovation.

The key term here is 'innovation'. Although a causal explanation of the historical type may account for the existence of some sociocultural variable during the period in which it made its appearance, it is not a sufficient explanation for its persistence into a later period – no more than a genetic explanation for the birth of an organism is a sufficient explanation for its persistence. Thus while a historico-genetic explanation is necessary to account for Burma's adoption of Buddhism, it cannot account for its persistence nine hundred years later. Alternatively, historical data explain why it is that the Burmese, if they practice any religion at all, practice Buddhism rather than, for example, Christianity; but they do not explain why they practice any religion at all – and, therefore, they do not explain why they practice Buddhism.

Structural explanations, too, can be reduced either to causal or to functional modes. Those structural accounts which delineate the configuration in, or relationships among, a set of sociocultural variables are essentially descriptive rather than explanatory – unless of course some theory, causal or functional, is offered to explain the configuration. Structural explanations which purport to explain some variable by means of a structural 'principle' – such as the principle of the unity of the sibling group – are either verbal labels which at best order a set of data according to a heuristic scheme; or they are phenomenological 'principles' of the actors (cognitive maps), in which case they comprise a cognitive sub-set in a set of causal variables. Similarly, structural explanations which stipulate some variable as a 'structural requirement' of a system, on the one hand, or as a 'structural implication', on the other, can be shown to be either causal or functional respectively.

This brings us, then, to causal and functional explanations. Causal explanations attempt to account for some sociocultural variable by reference to some antecedent conditions – its 'cause'. Functional explanations account for the variable by reference to some consequent condition – its 'function'. (For a detailed analysis of the logic of causal and functional explanation, cf. Spiro, 1963.)

How, then, is the existence of religion to be explained, causally or functionally? The answer depends, I believe, on which aspect of a religion is to be explained.

Typically, explanations for the existence of religion have been addressed to one or both of two questions. (*a*) On what grounds are religious propositions believed to be true? That is, what are the grounds for the belief that superhuman beings with such-and-such characteristics exist, and that ritual is efficacious in influencing their behavior? (*b*) What is the explanation for the practice of religion? That is, what is the basis for belief in superhuman beings, and for the performance of religious rituals? These questions, though clearly related – religious practice presupposes religious cognitions – are yet distinct; and they probably require different types of explanation.

THE 'TRUTH' OF RELIGIOUS BELIEFS

Every religious system consists, in the first instance, of a cognitive system; i.e. it consists of a set of explicit and implicit propositions concerning the superhuman world and of man's relationship to it, which it claims to be true. These include beliefs in superhuman beings of various kinds, of rituals of a wide variety, of existences – both prior and subsequent to the present existence – and the like. To the extent that documentary evidence is available, it is possible to discover a testable explanation for their origin and their variability. Since, for most of man's religions, however, such evidence is lacking, explanations are necessarily speculative. I shall be concerned, therefore, with explanations for their persistence.

This cognitive system, or parts of it, is of course acquired by the members of a group, and, on the individual level, it becomes a 'culturally constituted belief system'. It is a 'belief' system because the propositions are believed to be true; and it is 'culturally constituted' because the propositions are acquired from this culturally provided religious system. But the latter fact, surely, is not a sufficient basis for the belief that these propositions are true. Children are taught about many things which, when they grow up – often, before they grow up – they discard as so much nonsense. The fact that my personal belief system is acquired from my society explains why it is that the existence of the Lord Krishna rather than that of the Virgin Mary is one of the propositions I believe to be true; it does not explain the grounds on which I believe in the existence of superhuman beings of any kind, whether Krishna or the Virgin.

The notion of 'need' fares no better as an explanation. A need, in the sense of desire, may provide the motivational basis for the acquisition of a taught belief, but it cannot establish its truth. Similarly, a need, in the sense of a functional requirement of society, may explain the necessity for some kind of religious proposition(s), but – even if this need is recognized and its satisfaction is intended – it does not explain why the proposition is believed to be true.

Most theorists seem to agree that religious statements are believed to be true because religious actors have had social experiences which, corresponding to these beliefs, provide them with face validity. Thus Durkheim and Freud, agreeing that the cognitive roots of religious belief are to be found in social experience, disagree only about the structural context of the experience. Durkheim (1954) argues that the two essential attributes of the gods – they are beings more powerful than man, upon whom man can depend – are the essential attributes of society; it is in society that man experiences these attributes. These attributes are personified in superhuman beings, or imputed to extra-social powers, because of highly affective collective experiences in which the physical symbols of the group are taken to be symbolic of the one or the other. Freud (1928), emphasizing man's helplessness in a terrifying world, stresses the importance of personifying these terrifying forces so that, on a human analogy, they can be controlled. These personifications – the gods – reflect the child's experience with an all-powerful human being, his father.

In both Freud and Durkheim, then, society is the cause for the fixation of religious belief. It is ironical to observe, however, that it is Freud rather than Durkheim who anchors this experience within a specified structural unit, the family. In general, I believe that Freud has the better case. To be sure, his ethnocentric conception of patriarchal fathers, and of gods reflecting this conception of 'father', is entirely inadequate for comparative analysis: but the general theory which can be generated from this ethnocentric model is both adequate and, I believe, essentially correct. The theory, briefly, is that it is in the context of the family that the child experiences powerful beings, both benevolent and malevolent, who – by various means which are learned in the socialization process – can sometimes be induced to accede to his desires. These experiences provide the basic ingredients for his personal projective system (Kardiner, 1945) which, if it corresponds (structurally, not substantively) to his taught beliefs, constitutes the cognitive and perceptual set for the acceptance of these beliefs. Having had personal experience with 'superhuman beings' and with the efficacy of 'ritual', the taught beliefs re-enforce, and are re-enforced by, his own projective system (Spiro, 1953).

This theory is superior to Durkheim's, first, in its ability to explain these latter two nuclear religious variables. It is difficult to see how they can be deduced from Durkheim's theory. More important, even if they were deducible, it is difficult to see how Durkheim's theory can explain their cross-cultural variability. Since the antecedent condition – a power greater than man upon which man can rely – is a constant, how can it explain the consequent condition – religious belief – which is a variable? Hence, although the general theory may be true, there is a serious question concerning what empirical operations, if any, would permit us to decide whether it is true or false. The Freudian-derived theory, on the other hand, *is* capable of explaining cross-cultural differences and, therefore, it can be tested empirically. If personal projective systems, which form the basis for religious belief, are developed in early childhood experiences, it can be deduced that differences in religious beliefs will vary systematically with differences in family (including socialization) systems which structure these experiences. A number of anthropological field studies have been able to test – and have confirmed – this conclusion. And one need not go so far astray as personality-and-culture studies to find the evidence. In his illuminating analysis of Tallensi religion, Fortes (1959, p. 78) concludes that, 'All the concepts and beliefs we have examined are religious extrapolations of the experiences generated in the relationships between parents and children'.

As important as they are, case studies do not constitute rigorous proof of theories. The cross-cultural method, in which large samples can be used for statistical testing of hypotheses is more rigorous. A fairly large number of hypotheses, predicting religious variables – the character of supernatural beings, the means (performance of rituals or compliance with norms) which are believed to influence them, the conception of ritual (coercive or propitiatory) and the like – from child-training variables have been tested by this method, and many of them have been confirmed. (These studies are summarized in Whiting, 1961.)

Despite the differences between Freud and Durkheim, both propose causal explanations of the credibility of religious cognitions, in which society, as cause, produces a religious (cognitive) effect by means of psychological processes – in one case, in the *feeling* of dependency; in the other, in the feeling of dependency combined with the personal *projection* of nuclear experiences. For both theorists the independent, sociological, variable may be said to 'cause' the dependent, religious, variable by means of a set of intervening, psychological, variables.

Before passing to the next section it is necessary to counter one assumption which is often linked to this type of explanation, but which is not entailed by it. From the hypothesis that the antecedent condition for belief in superhuman beings is to be found in specified sociological variables, it does not follow that for the believer these beings are identical with, have reference to, or are symbolic of these variables. To put it bluntly, the fact that conceptions of God have their roots in society does not mean that *for the believer* society is God, or that God is merely a symbol of society, or that society is the true object of religious worship. Freud never said this, nor – despite some claims to the contrary – did Durkheim. Hence, it is no refutation of Durkheim's sociological hypothesis – as Horton (1960, p. 204) believes it to be – that for the Kalabari – and, I would add, for every other people – the statement ' "I believe in God" ' does not imply, ' "I subscribe to the system of structural symbolism of which this belief statement is part." ' [2]

Similarly it is not only among the Kalabari that a person who uses belief or ritual 'merely to make a statement about social relations or about his own structural alignment' is viewed as one who ' "does not really believe" ' (ibid., p. 203). Indeed the contrary notion is so absurd that it is difficult to believe that it could be proposed by anyone who has personally observed a Micronesian exorcising a malevolent ghost, a Catholic penitent crawling on hands and knees to worship at the shrine of Our Lady of Guadalupe, an Orthodox Jew beating his breast on Yom Kippur to atone for his sins, a Burmese spirit-medium dancing in a trance before a *nat* image. And yet, Leach, writing of Kachin spirits, insists (1954, p. 182) that 'the various nats of Kachin religious ideology are, in the last analysis *nothing more* than ways of describing the formal relationships that exist between real persons and real groups in ordinary Kachin society' (italics mine). For Leach, then, not only are religious beliefs derived from social structure, but the only referent of these beliefs, even for the believer, is social structure. Since Leach has, I am sure, observed as many manifestations of religious belief as I have, what are we to make of this extraordinary statement? I should like to suggest that this assertion reflects a confusion between the *practice* of religion and its *manipulation*; and although the former may be of as much interest to the student of religion as the latter, not to recognize this distinction is to sow confusion.

Leach, it will be recalled, interprets Kachin religion as almost exclusively an instrument in the political struggle for power and prestige. That theology, myth, or ritual may be manipulated for prestige and power, and that the latter drives may provide motivational bases for their persistence are documented facts of history and ethnology. But the manipulation of religion for political ends tells us more about politics than about religion. In the former, religion is used *as a means*, in the latter *religious means* are used, for the attainment of certain ends. (Indeed, they may both be instrumental for the same end.) This is an essential distinction. The differential characteristic of religious, compared with other types of instrumental, behavior consists in an attempt to enlist the assistance, or to execute the will, of superhuman beings. Indeed, by what other criterion *could* religious, be distinguished from non-religious, behavior? Surely not in terms of ends: with the exception of mysticism (confined to religious virtuosos) the range of mundane ends for which religion, cross-culturally viewed, is conceived to be instrumental is as broad as the range of all human ends. My argument, then, is not that political power is disqualified as a *religious end*, but that any attempt to achieve this end by means which do not entail a belief in the existence of superhuman beings is disqualified as *religious means*. A Kachin headman may attempt to manipulate myths and *nats* in order to validate his, or his clan's claim to power and authority; but this political behavior is to be distinguished from his religious behavior, which consists in his belief in the existence of the *nats*, and in his propitiation of them, both at local shrines and during *manaus*. Indeed, only because Kachins do believe that the verbal symbol '*nat*' has reference to an existential being – and is not merely a social structural symbol – is it possible to manipulate this belief for political ends.

THE PRACTICE OF RELIGIOUS BELIEF

The religious actor not only believes in the truth of propositions about superhuman beings, but he also believes in these beings – they are objects of 'concern': he trusts in God, he fears and hates Satan. Similarly, he not only believes in the efficacy of ritual, but he performs rituals. Explanations for religion, then, are addressed not only to the truth of religious propositions but also – and more frequently – to certain practices. In order to explain the practice of religion, we must be able to explain the practice of any sociocultural variable.[3]

All human behavior, except for reflexive behavior, is purposive; i.e. it is instigated by the intention of satisfying some need. If a given response is in fact instrumental for the satisfaction of the need, this 'reinforcement' of the response ensures its persistence – it becomes an instance of a behavior pattern. The motivational basis for the practice of a behavior pattern, then, is not merely the intention of satisfying a need, but the expectation that its performance will in fact achieve this end. Institutional behavior, including religious behavior, consists in the practice of repeated instances of culturally constituted behavior patterns – or customs. Like other behavior patterns they persist as long as they are practiced; and they are practiced because they satisfy, or are believed to satisfy, their instigating needs. If this is so, an explanation for the practice of religion must be sought in the set of needs whose expected satisfaction motivates religious belief and the performance of religious ritual.[4]

Needs

As a concept in the social sciences, 'need' has been borrowed from two sources: biology and psychology. Its ambiguity as a social science concept stems from a confusion in its two possible meanings. In biology 'need' refers to what might be termed a 'want', i.e. to some requirement which must be satisfied if an organism is to survive. In psychology, on the other hand, it refers to what might be termed a 'desire', i.e. a wish to satisfy some felt drive by the attainment of some goal. These two meanings may, of course, overlap. Thus water satisfies an organic want and it may also be the object of desire. Just as frequently, however, they do not overlap. The circulation of the blood is a want, but – for most animals, at any rate – it is not the object of desire. In sociological and, especially, in functionalist discourse, much confusion has resulted from not distinguishing these two meanings of 'need' when it is applied to society. In this paper I shall, when clarity does not suffer, use the generic 'need' to refer both to sociological wants and to psychological desires. Otherwise, I shall use 'sociological want' to refer to any functional requirement of society; and I shall use 'desire' in its motivational sense. I hasten to add that desires are not necessarily 'selfish', oriented to the welfare of the self. The goal, by whose attainment a drive is satisfied, may be – and, obviously, it often is – the welfare of an entire group, or of one or more of its constituent members.

We may now return to our question. If the practice of religion is instigated by the expectation of satisfying needs, by which set of needs – desires or wants – is its practice to be explained? It should be perfectly obvious that although behavior can *satisfy* both wants and desires, it is motivated by desires, not by wants. Wants in themselves have no causal properties. The absorption of moisture, for example, is a functional requirement

107

of plants; but this requirement cannot cause the rains to fall. Human behavior, to be sure, is different from the growth of plants. A social group may recognize the existence of some, at least, of its functional requirements, and these recognized wants may constitute a set of stimulus conditions which evoke responses for their satisfaction. Notice, however, that it is not the functional requirement – even when it is recognized – which evokes the response, but rather the wish to satisfy it. A functional requirement of society becomes a stimulus for a response, i.e. it acquires motivational value if, and only if (*a*) it is recognized, and (*b*) its satisfaction becomes an object of desire. If the functional requirement of social solidarity, for example, is not recognized, or, if recognized, it is not an object of desire, or, although both recognized and desired, it is not the desire whose intended satisfaction motivates the practice of the variable to be explained, it cannot be used to explain behavior, even though need-satisfaction may be one of its consequences. If social solidarity is a consequence – an unintended consequence – of the practice of religion, social solidarity is properly explained by reference to the religious behavior by which it is achieved; but religion, surely, is improperly explained by reference to social solidarity. An unintended consequence of behavior – however important it may be – can hardly be its cause. If religious behavior is to be explained by reference to those functions which it serves – and, indeed, it must be – the functions must be those that are intended, not those that are unintended (and probably unrecognized). We must, therefore, remind ourselves of some elementary distinctions among functions.

Functions

I should like, first, to distinguish between 'psychological' and 'sociological' functions. The psychological functions of behavior consist in the satisfaction of desires;[5] its sociological functions consist in the satisfaction of functional requirements.

Second, I should like to distinguish between 'manifest' and 'latent' functions. In his now-classic analysis of functional explanation, Merton (1957) distinguished between intended and recognized functions – which he termed 'manifest' – and unintended and unrecognized functions – which he termed 'latent'. Merton's dichotomous classification can be shown to yield a four-class functional typology. In addition to intended-recognized and unintended-unrecognized functions, we can also distinguish intended-unrecognized and unintended-recognized functions (Spiro, 1961a). The latter is a simple concept to grasp; social solidarity may be a recognized function of religious ritual, for example, although the intention of satisfying this functional requirement may not motivate its performance. An intended-unrecognized function, however, seems paradoxical. Assuming that intentions may be conscious as well as unconscious, this paradox is more apparent than real: if a behavior pattern is unconsciously motivated – or, more realistically, if its motivational set includes both conscious and unconscious intentions – one of its functions, although intended, is unrecognized.

The final distinction I should like to make is between real and apparent functions. 'Real functions' are those which, in principle at least, can be discovered by the anthropologist, whether or not they are recognized by the actors. 'Apparent functions' are those which the actors attribute to the sociocultural variable in question, but which cannot be confirmed by scientific investigation.

With these distinctions in mind, we may now attempt to answer the question with which we began this section. If institutional behavior in general is motivated by the expectation of satisfying desires, to what extent can religious behavior, specifically, be explained within this framework? That is, what desires are satisfied by religion? Since this question remains one of the unfinished tasks of empirical research, I can only make some tentative suggestions. As I interpret the record, I would suggest that there are at least three sets of desires which are satisfied by religion and which – for lack of better terms – I shall call cognitive, substantive, and expressive. The corresponding functions of religion can be called adjustive, adaptive, and integrative.

Cognitive

I believe that it can be shown that everywhere man has a desire to know, to understand, to find meaning;[6] and I would suggest –

although this is a terribly old-fashioned nineteenth-century idea – that religious beliefs are held, and are of 'concern', to religious actors because, *in the absence of competitive explanations*, they satisfy this desire. Religious belief systems provide the members of society with meaning and explanation for otherwise meaningless and inexplicable phenomena.

'Meaning', of course, is often used in two senses. It may be used in an exclusively cognitive sense, as when one asks for the meaning of a natural phenomenon, of a historical event, of a sociological fact. In this sense, it has the connotation of 'explanation', as that word is typically used. But 'meaning' is also used in a semantic-affective sense, as when one asks for the meaning of unequal life-fates, frustration, or death. The phenomena for which religion provides meaning, in this second sense of 'meaning', have been classified by Weber under the general rubric of 'suffering' (Gerth & Mills, 1946, Ch. 11). The main function of the higher religions, he argues, is to provide meaning for suffering (and some means to escape from or to transcend it).

Although the range of phenomena for which religious beliefs provide meaning in the first, explanatory, sense of 'meaning', occupies a broad spectrum, some structuralists hold to the peculiar notion that man's curiosity is so limited that religious explanations, regardless of their ostensible meaning, are concerned almost exclusively with phenomena of social structure. Again I should like to use an example from Leach – although the example concerns magical rather than religious belief – because, with his usual verve, he adopts what I would think to be an extreme position.

In his highly critical evaluation of Frazer, Leach (1961) tells us that Frazer (and Roth, too) is naïve in interpreting Australian explanations for conception as in fact referring to conception – and, therefore, as reflecting ignorance of physiological paternity. According to the 'modern interpretation', their notions of conception are to be seen, not as biological, but as sociological, statements. Let us examine the ethnographic facts, as Leach (p. 376) quotes them from Roth. Among the Tully River Blacks,

'A woman begets children because (*a*) she has been sitting

110

over the fire on which she has roasted a particular species of black bream, which must have been given to her by the prospective father, (*b*) she has purposely gone a-hunting and caught a certain kind of bull-frog, (*c*) some man may have told her to be in an interesting condition, or (*d*) she may dream of having the child put inside her.'

Both Frazer and Roth agree – and, I may add, I agree with them – that these statements are addressed to the problem to which they appear to be addressed – the problem of conception; and they agree that from these statements it may validly be deduced that the aborigines are ignorant of physiological paternity, believing rather that conception is the result of four kinds of 'magical' causation. Leach will have none of this. For him (ibid.) it is not

'a legitimate inference to assert that these Australian aborigines were ignorant of the connection between copulation and pregnancy. The modern interpretation of the rituals described would be that in this society the relationship between the woman's child and the clansmen of the woman's husband stems from public recognition of the bonds of marriage, rather than from the fact of cohabitation, which is a very normal state of affairs.'

The logic of this 'modern interpretation' is certainly not evident to me. Ignoring the fact that only two of the four explanatory beliefs have reference to a male – so that they, at least, are hardly susceptible of this modern interpretation – by what evidence or from what inference can it be concluded that the other two statements mean what Leach claims that they mean? Is this the interpretation which the aborigines place on these beliefs? There is certainly no evidence for this assumption. Perhaps, then, this is the meaning which they intended to convey, even though they did not do so explicitly? But even if we were to grant that, for some strange reason, aborigines prefer to express structural relationships by means of biological symbolism, how do we *know* that this was their intention? Perhaps, then, the symbolism is unconscious, and the structural meaning which Leach claims for these beliefs, although intentional, is latent? This interpretation is certainly congenial to

111

other 'modern interpretations'. Again, however, we are hung up on the problem of evidence. From what ethnographic data, or from what psychological theory of the unconscious, can this meaning be inferred? If, then, there is no way of *demonstrating* that either the manifest or the latent content of these symbols has reference to the structural relationship between a woman's children and the clansmen of her husband, I am compelled to discard this interpretation as not only implausible but false. I shall insist, instead, that the aborigines are indeed ignorant of physiological paternity, and that the four statements quoted in Roth are in fact proffered explanations for conception.

Substantive

The most obvious basis for religious behavior is the one which any religious actor tells us about when we ask him – and, unlike some anthropologists, I believe him. He believes in superhuman beings and he performs religious ritual in order that he may satisfy, what I am calling, substantive desires: desires for rain, nirvana, crops, heaven, victory in war, recovery from illness, and countless others. Everywhere man's mammalian desires (those which can be satisfied by naturalistic goals) must be satisfied, and *in the absence of competing technologies which confer reasonable confidence*, religious techniques are believed to satisfy these desires. Almost everywhere, moreover, the human awareness of the cessation of existence and/or of the unsatisfactory character of existence, produces anxiety concerning the persistence of existence (in some cases, it is desired; in others, it is not desired), and *in the absence of competing goals for the reduction of anxiety*, belief that one is successfully pursuing these religious goals (heaven-like or nirvana-like states) serves to reduce this anxiety.

Most, if not all, of these substantive desires, then, can be classified as attempts to overcome or transcend suffering. The religious actor wishes to overcome specific suffering – economic, political, physical, and the like; and he wishes to transcend more general suffering induced by some conception of life and the world as being evil, frustrating, sinful, and so on. Religion, as Weber (op. cit.) points out, not only provides an explanation for, but it also promises redemption from, suffering. Religious techniques – performance of ritual, compliance with morality, faith, meditation, etc. – are the means by which this promise is felt to be fulfilled.

For the religious actor, if we can believe him, the expectation of realizing this promise is the most important motivational basis for religious behavior; the realization of this promise is its function. For him, it is an intended and recognized function. Believing in its reality, he clings tenaciously to his religious beliefs and practices – however irrational they may seem, and however dysfunctional with respect to other ends their consequences may be. From the anthropologist's point of view – and this is what presents such a knotty problem to many classical functionalists – these functions are apparent; they are not real. Ritual cannot effect rainfall, prayer cannot cure organic diseases, nirvana is a figment of the imagination, etc. It is this seeming irrationality of religion and, therefore, the apparent – rather than real – nature of its intended functions, that has given rise, I believe, to misplaced emphases on the importance of its sociological functions. Thus, despite Merton's incisive analysis of functional theory, it is highly questionable if the persistence of Hopi rain ceremonies is to be explained by the social integration to which *he* (Merton) thinks their performance is conducive (their real, but latent, functions), rather than by the meteorological events to which *Hopi* think they are conducive (their manifest, but apparent, functions).

The Hopi belief in the efficacy of their rainmaking ritual is not irrational – although it is certainly false – because the conclusion, rain ceremonies cause the rains to fall, follows validly from a world-view whose major premise states that gods exist, and whose minor premise states that the behavior of the gods can be influenced by rituals. That the premises are false does not render them irrational – until or unless they are disconfirmed by evidence. But all available 'evidence' confirms their validity: whenever the ceremonies are performed it does, indeed, rain. Hence, given their 'behavioral environment' (Hallowell, 1955, pp. 75-110), Hopi beliefs are not irrational; and given their ecological environment, the apparent function of these ceremonies is surely a sufficient explanation for their persistence. (For further argument, see Spiro, 1964.)

If it is not sufficient, however, no appeal to unintended sociological functions will provide us with a better explanation – indeed, as we have already seen, it can provide us with no explanation at all. For how can the function of social solidarity explain the practice of these – or of any other – rituals? Notice that the objection to such an explanation is not that social solidarity may not be an object of desire – there is no reason why it cannot; and it is not that social solidarity is not achieved by the practice of these rituals – it often is. The objection, rather, is that the achievement of this end is *not* the desire which the practice of *these* rituals is intended to satisfy. Surely, not even the proponents of this type of explanation would suggest that Hopi rain ceremonies, sacrifices to Kali, exorcism of demons, celebration of the Mass, and the like are practiced with the conscious intention of achieving social solidarity. Is it suggested, then, that this is their unconscious intention? I would doubt that anyone would make this suggestion, for this suggests that if the efficacy of these rituals for the attainment of their designated ends were to be disbelieved, they would nevertheless be performed so that their solidarious functions might be served. This argument surely cannot be sustained. I can only conclude, then, that the persistence of these rituals is explicable by reference to what, for anthropologists, are their apparent, rather than their real, functions.[7]

Even if it were to be conceded that institutions must have real, rather than apparent, functions, anthropologists must surely be aware of those real functions of ritual which *are* recognized by religious actors and which may, therefore, re-enforce their practice. For although religious ritual may not, in fact, be efficacious for the elimination of poverty, the restoration of health, the bringing of rain, and the like, the belief that it does achieve these ends serves the important psychological (real) function of reducing hopelessness – and its attendant anxiety – concerning their otherwise impossible attainment.

Expressive

A third set of desires which, I would suggest, constitutes a motivational source of religious behavior consists of painful drives which seek reduction and painful motives which seek

114

satisfaction. By 'painful drives' I refer to those fears and anxieties concerning which psychoanalysis has taught us so much: fears of destruction and of one's own destructiveness, castration anxiety, cataclysmic fantasies, and a host of other infantile and primitive fears which threaten to overpower the weak and defenseless ego of the young child and which, if they become too overwhelming, result in schizophrenic and paranoid breakdown. By 'painful motives' I refer to those motives which, because culturally forbidden – prohibited forms of aggression, dependency, (Oedipal) sexuality, and the like – arouse feelings of shame, inadequacy, and moral anxiety. These drives and motives are much too painful to remain in consciousness and they are generally rendered unconscious. Although unconscious, they are not extinguished; they continue to seek reduction and satisfaction.

In the absence of other, or of more efficient means, religion is the vehicle – in some societies, perhaps, the most important vehicle – by which, symbolically, they can be handled and expressed. Since religious belief and ritual provide the content for culturally constituted projective, displacement, and sublimative mechanisms by which unconscious fears and anxieties may be reduced and repressed motives may be satisfied, these drives and motives, in turn, constitute an important unconscious source of religious behavior. Because the range of painful drives and motives which find expression in religion remains to be discovered by empirical research, I shall merely comment on two motives which I believe to be universally – but not exclusively – satisfied by religion; and since I have already attempted to deal with this problem elsewhere (Spiro, 1961b), I shall be brief.

Forbidden dependency needs inevitably seek satisfaction in religious behavior, in that the religious actor depends on superhuman beings for the gratification of his desires. Repressing his desire to remain in a state of childlike dependency on powerful adult figures, he can still satisfy this desire, symbolically, by his trust in and reliance upon superhuman beings.

Similarly, since all religions of which I am aware postulate the existence of malevolent, as well as of benevolent, superhuman beings, repressed hostility motives can be displaced and/or projected in beliefs in, and rituals designed for protection against, these malevolent beings. Prevented from expressing his hostility against his fellows, the religious actor can satisfy this desire symbolically through religion (Spiro, 1952).

These, then, are three sets of desires whose satisfaction by, partially explains the persistence of, religion. But though the persistence of religion is to be found in motivation – a psychological variable – the sources of motivation are to be sought, in part, in society. For just as the sociological causes (social structural variables) of the truth of religious beliefs achieve their effects through mediating psychological processes – feelings, projections, perceptions, and the like – so too the psychological causes (desires) of religious behavior may be explained by reference to those sociocultural (and biological) variables by which they are produced. With few exceptions, human drives are acquired rather than learned; and all human goals, it is probably safe to assume, are acquired. Since the crucial context for the learning of human drives and goals is social, and since most religious drives – but not most goals – are acquired in the child's early experiences, it is the family that once again is the nuclear structural variable.

Indeed, because these motivational variables are acquired within specified structural contexts, and because these contexts exhibit a wide range of variability, differences in the kinds and/or intensity of desires which constitute the motivational basis for religious behavior should vary systematically with differences in family systems (including socialization systems), *as well as with the alternative, non-religious means for their satisfaction.* The latter qualification is important. I have stressed, with respect to the three sets of desires which have been discussed, that in the absence of alternative institutional means, it is religion which is the means *par excellence* for their satisfaction. If cognitive desires, for example, are satisfied by science; if substantive desires are satisfied by technology; or if expressive desires are satisfied by politics or art or magic, religion should, by that extent, be less important for their satisfaction. In short, the importance of religion would be expected to vary inversely with the importance of other, projective and realistic, institutions.[8]

Holding other institutions constant, then, the kinds and intensity of drives which are satisfied by religion, the means by which they are believed to be satisfied, and the conceptions of the superhuman beings that are the agents of satisfaction should vary with variations in childhood experiences in which drives (and their intensity) are acquired, the means by which children influenced parents (and surrogates) to satisfy their drives, and the degree to which parents (and surrogates) do, in fact, satisfy them (Spiro & D'Andrade, 1958).

In short, a motivational explanation of religious behavior can, in principle, explain variability in behavior and, hence, can be tested empirically. A great deal of culture-and-personality research, too extensive to cite here, has been devoted to this very problem. Indeed, much of the research concerned with the structural bases for religious cognitions has, simultaneously, been devoted to the motivational bases for religious behavior. Unfortunately, however, cognitive desires have received less attention than expressive and substantive desires, possibly because we know comparatively little about how they are acquired.

CAUSAL AND FUNCTIONAL EXPLANATIONS

We may now return to the question with which we began this paper: is the existence of religion to be explained causally or functionally? I have suggested that the acquisition of religious beliefs is to be explained causally, and that the practice of these beliefs is to be explained in terms of motivation – which means that it is explained both causally and functionally. Religion persists because it has functions – it does, or is believed to, satisfy desires; but religion persists because it has causes – it is caused by the expectation of satisfying these desires. Both are necessary, neither is sufficient, together they are necessary and sufficient. The causes of religious behavior are to be found in the desires by which it is motivated, and its functions consist in the satisfaction of those desires which constitute its motivation.

Classical functionalist theory has, of course, tended to dismiss motivation and other psychological variables as being outside the domain of anthropology. Firth, for example (1956, p. 224), writes that in the study of ritual the anthropologist is not concerned with '. . . the inner state as such of the participants', but rather with 'the kinds of social relations that are produced or maintained'.[9] If 'inner states' were irrelevant for an explanation of religion, one might wish to defend the thesis that anthropology, whose central concern is the explanation of social and cultural institutions, should ignore them. But if by ignoring 'inner states', and other psychological variables, we cannot adequately explain religion, or, for that matter, the 'kinds of social relations' which it produces, we ignore them at our peril. Let me, beginning with the first proposition, take up each in turn.

An explanation of religion, or of any other sociocultural variable, consists in the specification of those conditions without which it could not exist. If religion is what is to be explained, if religion, that is, is the dependent variable, it can be explained only in terms of some independent variable, some condition by which it is maintained or sustained. I have argued that motivation is the independent variable. That religion, like other sociocultural variables, has sociological functions – it produces or maintains certain kinds of 'social relations' – is undeniable; and it is one of our tasks to study these sociological functions. Indeed, these sociological functions may be crucial for the maintenance of society. If, for example, social solidarity is a functional requirement of society, and if religion – as it is frequently argued – is one of the institutions that satisfies this requirement, religion is necessary (a cause) for the maintenance of society. Notice, however, that if religion does produce solidarious social relations, solidarity provides us with an explanation of society, not of religion. In this case, in short, social solidarity does not explain religion; religion explains social solidarity. For social solidarity is the dependent, and it is religion that is the independent, variable. In sum, if we are interested in the 'kinds of social relations' that are produced by religion, we are interested in explaining society; and religion – it is assumed – can supply us with an entire, or a partial, explanation.

But the functionalist argument sometimes assumes a different form. Religion, it is argued, not only satisfies certain functional requirements of society, but it is a necessary condition for their satisfaction. Since society cannot exist unless these requirements are satisfied, and since religion is a necessary condition for their satisfaction, these requirements 'cause' the existence of religion. It is not that the desire to satisfy some requirement motivates religious behavior – the latter may be accounted for by numerous other desires of the kind suggested, perhaps, in this paper. Rather, since religion is a necessary condition for the satisfaction of this requirement, the need for its satisfaction can explain the existence of religion. This argument, I think, is implicit in most functionalist interpretations of the Radcliffe-Brown variety. Thus Radcliffe-Brown himself (1948, p. 324) writes that religious ceremonies 'are the means by which the society acts upon its individual members and keeps alive in their minds a certain system of sentiments. Without the ceremonial these sentiments would not exist, and without them the social organization in its actual form could not exist.'

Notice, before we examine this type of explanation, that it is not a functionalist explanation at all; it is a causal explanation in which the cause happens to be a functional requirement. Notice, too, that despite the present tense of the predicates, this is really an explanation of the origin, not the persistence, of religion: the practice of religion – which is the only means by which religion persists – is not motivated by a desire to keep these sentiments alive, although the persistence of these sentiments is its consequence. But these questions aside, as an explanation of religion, this theory suffers from three defects: technical, methodological, and theoretical. Technically, no mechanism is specified by which the need for solidarity – and, therefore, the need for religion – gives rise to, or 'causes', religion. Methodologically, it cannot explain the variability of religion – how is it that the need to sustain social sentiments produces such a bewildering range of religious beliefs and rituals? – and, therefore, there is no way by which it can be tested. Theoretically, it is based on an unwarranted functionalist assumption, which Merton (1957) has aptly termed the assumption of 'indispensability'. What does this mean?

For some functional requirements any number of variables may be adequate for their satisfaction. Since none is necessary, although each may be sufficient, they are called 'functionally equivalent alternatives'. These are to be distinguished from a variable which is necessary or indispensable for the satisfaction of a requirement – without it the requirement could not be satisfied. The cross-cultural evidence strongly suggests that there are few, if any, indispensable variables; that, rather, for almost any sociocultural variable there are functional equivalents. Hence, even if it is the case that religion is the means by which Andamanese 'sentiments' are kept alive, it does not follow that religion is the only means by which this end could be accomplished, or that in other societies other institutions do not or cannot serve the identical function.[10]

In sum, from the fact that religion is a sufficient condition for the satisfaction of a requirement, it is invalidly deduced that it is a necessary condition. And, if it is not a necessary condition, its existence cannot be explained by arguing that without it society could not survive.

Although it is society, rather than religion, which is explained by the sociological consequences of religion, social anthropology – as the comparative study of social and cultural systems – is most certainly concerned with these functions; and psychological variables are not only necessary for the explanation of religion, but without them certain of its sociological functions would go unrecognized. (The classic example, of course, is Weber's (1930) analysis of the rise of capitalism, but it deals with the change in, rather than the persistence of, a social system.) Thus, the adjustive (real) function of religion, by satisfying the need for explanation, provides a society with a common 'behavioral environment' which, as Hallowell (op. cit) observes, satisfies a set of minimal requirements for the existence of any society: the requirement for a common object orientation, spatiotemporal orientation, motivational orientation, and normative orientation. It would be difficult to conceive of the possibility of social integration without a minimum level of such shared orientations.

The adaptive (apparent) function of religion, in satisfying the desire for the attainment of goals, provides – as Marxism has stressed – a most important basis for social stability. Disbelief in the efficacy of superhuman means for the achievement of this-worldly goals could certainly become a potential basis for

120

social discontent and socioeconomic change. At the same time, the (real) function of religion in reducing anxiety concerning the attainment of goals – especially those for whose attainment available technological skills are ineffective – and, thus, in providing a minimum level of psychological security, serves to release energy for coping with the reality problems of society.

Finally, the integrative (real) function of religion, in allowing the disguised expression of repressed motives, serves a number of sociological functions. By providing a culturally approved means for the resolution of inner conflict (between personal desires and cultural norms), religion (*a*) reduces the probability of psychotic distortion of desires, thereby providing a society with psychologically healthy members,[11] (*b*) protects society from the socially disruptive consequences of direct gratification of these forbidden desires, (*c*) promotes social integration by providing a common goal (superhuman beings) and a common means (ritual) by which the desires may be gratified.

CONCLUSION

It would appear from the foregoing discussion that an adequate explanation for the persistence of religion requires both psychological and sociological variables. If the cognitive bases for religious belief have their roots in childhood experience, their explanation must be found in social structural and, more specifically, family structure variables. Here religion is the dependent variable, and family structure is the independent sociological variable which effects religious belief by means of such intervening psychological variables as fantasies, projections, perceptions, and the like.

If religion persists because of its gratification of desires, explanations for the bases of religious behavior must be found in psychological and, specifically, motivational variables. Here, again, religion is the dependent, and motivation is the independent, variable. Since, however, motivation consists in the intention of gratifying desires, and since desires are rooted either in organic or in acquired drives, the motivational roots of religious behavior can, ultimately, be found in those biological and social structural variables, respectively, by which they are produced and/or canalized. Again, it is the family which emerges as the crucial sociological variable. Religion, then, is to be explained in terms of society and personality.

Many studies of religion, however, are concerned not with the explanation of religion, but with the role of religion in the explanation of society. Here, the explanatory task is to discover the contributions which religion, taken as the independent variable, makes to societal integration, by its satisfaction of sociological wants. This is an important task, central to the main concern of anthropology, as the science of social systems. We seriously err, however, in mistaking an explanation of society for an explanation of religion which, in effect, means confusing the sociological functions of religion with the bases for its performance.

In this paper, I have been concerned almost exclusively with the latter aspect of religion. I have not, except incidentally, dealt with its sociological functions or, what is perhaps more important, with how these are to be measured. I have not dealt, moreover, with the problem of religious origins because – despite the fact that numerous speculations have been proposed (and I have my own, as well) – these are not testable. Nor have I dealt with the problem of the cross-cultural variability in religion, except to suggest some motivational bases for the persistence of different types of belief and ritual. But the crucial problems – to which Max Weber has most importantly contributed – I have not even touched upon. If, for example, religion is centrally concerned with the problem of 'suffering' why is it that explanations for suffering run such a wide gamut: violation of ethical norms, sin of ancestors, misconduct in a previous incarnation, etc.? Or, if religion promises redemption from suffering, how are the different types of redemption to be explained? And, moreover, what is the explanation for the different means by which the redemptive promise is to be achieved? These are but a few of the central problems in the study of religion with which this paper, with its limited focus, has not been concerned.

NOTES

1. Work on this paper is part of a cross-cultural study of religion supported by research grant M-2255 from the National Institutes of Health, U.S. Public Health Service.

2. In any case, Durkheim's sociology of religion is unconcerned with structural symbolism. It is concerned with society as a collectivity, not as a configuration of structural units; with collective representations, not with social structure.

3. The notion that religion necessarily eludes the net of naturalistic explanation, though implicit in certain recent anthropological writing, is beginning to find explicit expression. Thus, Turner (1962, p. 92) claims that 'one has to consider religious phenomena in terms of religious ideas and doctrines, and not only, or principally, in terms of disciplines which have arisen in connection with the study of secular institutions and processes. . . . Religion is not *determined* by anything other than itself, though the religious find *expression* in sensory phenomena. . . . We must be prepared to accept the fruits of simple wisdom with gratitude and not try to reduce them to their chemical constituents, thereby destroying their essential quality as fruits, and their virtue as food.'

To say that religion is determined by religion is surely as meaningless as to say that tables are determined by tables, or that social structure is determined by social structure. But even if this statement is an ellipsis for a meaningful one, I would have thought that the determinants of religion are to be established empirically rather than by verbal assertion. I would have thought, too, that to 'reduce' religion to its 'chemical constituents' – which, I take it, refers to the discovery of its social and psychological bases – is precisely the task of the student of culture. I would not have thought that for the religionist – and the anthropologist, *qua* anthropologist, is of course neither a religionist nor an anti-religionist – the 'reduction' of religion to its social and psychological 'constituents' destroys its 'essential quality', any more than the 'reduction' of a Brandenburg concerto to its physical 'constituents' destroys its 'essential quality' for the lover of Bach.

4. There is, of course, no convincing evidence for the existence of a distinctively 'religious need'. That the belief in superhuman beings corresponds to and satisfies a 'need' for a belief in them is an unfounded instinctivist assumption. Nor is there any evidence for the assumption that the motivational basis for religious action, or the affect which it arouses, are unique. The meager evidence from religious psychology suggests that any drive or affect connected with religious behavior is also found in such activities as science, warfare, sex, art, politics, and others. The 'religious thrill' which Lowie (1924) and others have pointed to as a differentiating characteristic of religion is still to be documented. A clinical psychologist, commenting on still another set of data remarks: 'Some of our tests seem able to tap fairly deep levels of personality functioning, and yet we rarely encounter a clearly religious response to our Rorschach and Thematic Apperception tests. . . . For the psychology of religion this means that the clinical psychologist will not readily be able to furnish new data' (Pruyser, 1960, p. 122).

5. That a function is 'psychological' does not mean that the object of desire is psychological. The object of desire may be political, meteorological, economic, nutritional, sexual – and all other goals known to man. These goals are cathected because they satisfy some drive, acquired or innate. The attainment of the goal reduces the drive or, alternatively, satisfies the desire. The satisfac-

tion of the desire or, more realistically, the set of desires – whose intended (conscious or unconscious) satisfaction instigates behavior is its 'psychological' function.

6. The most striking evidence, on the simplest perceptual level, of this 'need' for meaning is provided by the cross-cultural use of the Rorschach test. As Hallowell has observed (1956, pp. 476-488), the most dramatic finding of cross-cultural Rorschach investigations is that at every level of technological and cultural development in which this test has been administered, subjects have attempted to offer 'meaningful' responses to what are, objectively, 'meaningless' ink-blots. The insistence, even on the part of 'primitive' peoples, on finding meaning in what is for them an exotic task – something concerning which many anthropologists had been skeptical – is certainly consistent with the assumption concerning a universal need for meaning.

7. One might, of course, wish to defend the weaker thesis, viz. that if these practices were sociologically dysfunctional, they would eventually disappear. Even this thesis is somewhat doubtful, however, when applied to multi-religious societies in which the practice of religion, however solidarious it may be for each religious group, has important dysfunctional consequences for the total social system. Still these religions persist, and with undiminished vigor, despite – one is tempted to say, because of – these consequences.

8. This does not imply, as some nineteenth-century thinkers believed, that as other institutions assume more of the traditional functions of religion, the latter will disappear. So far, at least, there has been no viable alternative to religion in providing a solution to the problem of 'suffering'; and the malaise of modern man, on the one hand, and the persistence of religion among many modern intellectuals, on the other, seem to suggest that a viable functional alternative is yet to be discovered.

9. I should hasten to add that, in a later publication (1959, p. 133), Firth changed his view and stressed the importance of the individual for a complete explanation of religion.

10. To cite but two counter-instances. First, there are the more than 150 atheistic *kibbutzim* in Israel, in which religious ceremonial does not exist (Spiro, 1956). Second, there are societies in which the important social sentiments are supported by secular rather than religious institutions. It would be difficult, for example, to discover even one sentiment important for the maintenance of capitalist democracy which is conveyed by the paramount Christian ceremony, the Eucharist. National celebrations, however, especially as interpreted by Warner (1959), serve this function *par excellence*.

11. Nadel, recognizing the 'defensive' function of religion, writes that in providing rituals by which forbidden impulses may be expressed, religion '. . . anticipates as well as canalizes the working of psychological mechanisms, which might otherwise operate in random fashion or beyond the control of society, in the 'private worlds' of neurosis and psychopathic fantasies' (1954, p. 275).

ACKNOWLEDGEMENT

Thanks are due to the author, the editor, and the American Academy of Arts and Sciences for permission to quote the passages from 'Golden Bough or Gilded Twig?' by E. R. Leach, in *Daedalus*, 1961.

124

REFERENCES

DURKHEIM, E. 1954. *The Elementary Forms of the Religious Life*. Glencoe, Ill.: Free Press.

EVANS-PRITCHARD, E. E. 1954. *The Institutions of Primitive Society*. Oxford: Blackwell.

FIRTH, R. 1956. *Elements of Social Organization*. London: Watts; New York: Philosophical Library.

—— 1959. Problem and Assumption in an Anthropological Study of Religion. *Journal of the Royal Anthropological Institute* **89**.

FORTES, M. 1959. *Oedipus and Job in West African Religion*. Cambridge: Cambridge University Press.

FREUD, S. 1928. *The Future of an Illusion*. London: Hogarth Press.

GERTH, H. H. & MILLS, C. W. (eds.). 1946. *From Max Weber: Essays in Sociology*. New York: Oxford University Press.

GOODY, J. 1961. Religion and Ritual: The Definitional Problem. *British Journal of Sociology* **12**.

HALLOWELL, A. I. 1955. *Culture and Experience*, Philadelphia: University of Pennsylvania Press.

—— 1956. The Rorschach Technique in Personality and Culture Studies. In B. Klopfer (ed.), *Developments in the Rorschach Technique*, Vol. 2. Yonkers-on-Hudson, N.Y.: World Books; London: Harrap.

HEMPEL, C. G. 1952. *Fundamentals of Concept Formation in Empirical Science*. Chicago: University of Chicago Press; London: Cambridge University Press.

HORTON, R. 1960. A Definition of Religion and its Uses. *Journal of Royal Anthropological Institute* **90**.

KARDINER, A. 1945. *The Psychological Frontiers of Society*. New York: Columbia University Press.

LEACH, E. R. 1954. *Political Systems of Highland Burma*. London: Bell.

—— 1961. Golden Bough or Gilded Twig? *Daedalus*.

LOWIE, R. 1924. *Primitive Religion*. New York: Boni & Liveright.

MERTON, R. K. 1957. *Social Theory and Social Structure* (revised edition), Glencoe, Ill.: Free Press.

NADEL, S. F. 1954. *Nupe Religion*. Glencoe, Ill.: Free Press.

PRUYSER, P. 1960. Some Trends in the Psychology of Religion, *Journal of Religion* **40**.

RADCLIFFE-BROWN, A. R. 1948. *The Andaman Islanders*. Glencoe, Ill.: Free Press.

RADIN. P. 1957. *Primitive Religion.* New York: Mayflower & Vision Press.

SPIRO, M. E. 1952. Ghosts, Ifaluk, and Teleological Functionalism. *American Anthropologist* **45**.

—– 1953. Ghosts: An Anthropological Inquiry into Learning and Perception. *Journal of Abnormal and Social Psychology* **48**.

—— 1956. *Kibbutz: Venture in Utopia.* Cambridge, Mass.: Harvard University Press.

—— 1961a. Social Systems, Personality, and Functional Analysis. In B. Kaplan (ed.), *Studying Personality Cross-Culturally.* Evanston, Ill.: Row, Peterson.

—— 1961b. An Overview and a Suggested Reorientation. In F. L. K. Hsu (ed.), *Psychological Anthropology.* Homewood, Ill.: Dorsey Press.

—— 1963. Causes, Functions, and Cross-Cousin Marriage: An Essay in Anthropological Explanation. *Journal of Royal Anthropological Institute* **97**.

—— 1964. Religion and the Irrational. In *Symposium on New Approaches to the Study of Religion.* (Proceedings of the American Ethnological Society). Seattle.

SPIRO, M. E. & D'ANDRADE, R. G. 1958. A Cross-Cultural Study of Some Supernatural Beliefs. *American Anthropologist* **60**.

TURNER, V. W. 1962. *Chihamba: The White Spirit.* Manchester: Manchester University Press.

WARNER, W. L. 1959. *The Living and the Dead.* New Haven: Yale University Press.

WEBER, M. 1930. *The Protestant Ethic and the Spirit of Capitalism.* London: Allen & Unwin; New York: Scribner's.

WHITING, J. W. M. 1961. Socialization Process and Personality. In F. L. K. Hsu (ed.), op. cit.

R. E. Bradbury

Fathers, Elders, and Ghosts in *Ẹdo* Religion

In recent years, our understanding of the nature and significance of African ancestor worship has been greatly advanced by the work of a number of British and American anthropologists. Among them, Fortes, Middleton, and Goody have all emphasized the connection between the identity and behavioural characteristics of those dead that are chosen as objects of worship, and the distribution and character of authority in both the domestic and political domains of the society. Fortes has stressed the importance of early childhood experiences in generating attitudes of dependence and filial piety which can be generalized through a lineage system in which, as Goody (1962, p. 413) puts it, 'the distribution of authority . . . is linked with the computation of the genealogy and with officiation at sacrifices'. It is the authority aspect of the relationship between successive generations of close kin that is projected onto the mystical plane, in such a way that the basic norms governing the behaviour of members of kin groups appear to the actors to be handed down from above, and therefore unchallengeable. Incontrovertibly just, yet arbitrary and aggressive in their dealings with the living, Tallensi ancestors reflect, not only the sentiments of piety and dependence, but also the underlying resentment that sons feel towards their fathers. The threat and experience of ancestral retribution for failures in submissiveness serve both to uphold the authority of the lineage heads, who control access to the ancestors, and to constrain them to act justly in their dealings with subordinates.

Goody (1962), accepting Fortes's basic propositions, has demonstrated that variability in the incidence of, and in the characteristic attitudes involved in, ancestor worship, as between the LoDagaba and the LoWiili, can be related to variability in the recurrent experiences of members of these societies in specific aspects of the relations between close kin of adjacent

127

generations. Thus a difference in the personnel of the holder-heir relationship, with regard to the transmission of wealth through the generations, is associated with differences in the incidence of sacrifice; and it is also correlated with the degree of hostility projected onto agnatic and uterine ancestors, which varies with the extent to which it is necessary for individuals to suppress resentment against living fathers (who are both household heads and property-holders) and mothers' brothers (who are normally only property-holders) (Goody, 1962, p. 410).

Comparing the findings of the writers I have mentioned, and others such as Colson (1955) and Gough (1958), it becomes clear that the distinguishing features of ancestor worship in different societies are related directly to rules of succession and inheritance, and to the distribution of authority in all the relevant sectors and levels of the social organization. These are factors which the individual experiences not so much in infancy as in later stages of life.

Goody (1962, p. 18) has expressed the view that 'in the morphological rather than the "evolutionary" sense, ancestor worship has been partially re-established as the elementary form of the religious life'. I take him to mean that in ancestor worship there is a readily discernible congruence between the form and organization of the cult (including relations with the ancestral beings) and the form of a social group, namely a kin group, membership of which is based on something other than mere common religious interests. It is a primitive religion in the sense that relations with the objects of worship derive very directly from the typical experiences of individuals in their relations with certain categories of living persons. When 'gods' are made, by men, out of men who have died and been re-incorporated into society by virtue of the status positions they occupied before death (and not by virtue of any supposed unique personal qualities), severe limits are set, I suggest, upon the imaginative capacities of the religious thinker. Similarly, in interpreting manistic cults of this kind, the social anthropologist is constrained to explain religious behaviour in terms of observed patterns of social interaction between persons occupying particular status positions. He cannot treat religious action and belief as something apart from other kinds of social behaviour as he may, to a greater extent, be able to do in dealing with some kinds of theistic cult.

Manistic cults, in the sense in which I use this term, are not, however, invariably associated with a genealogical ordering of the 'gods' and their congregation. One of the objects of this paper is to examine how far it may be possible to apply the Fortes/Goody type of interpretation to cults of the dead which cannot, strictly speaking, be labelled 'ancestral'. Most recent research into ancestor cults has been concerned with societies in which kinship plays a dominant role over a wide field of social and political relations. I propose to examine some of the cults of the dead that are found in a society of a very different kind, that of the Ẹdo of the Benin kingdom of Southern Nigeria who, for several centuries, have formed the nuclear population of a large and powerful centralized state. I shall not, however, be concerned with the way relations with the dead relate to the centralizing institutions of the state, but with the role of the dead in the village community, which is the basic unit of the political system.

THE ẸDO VILLAGE

The Ẹdo of the Benin Kingdom (see Bradbury, 1957, pp. 18-60, for an ethnographic outline) number about a quarter of a million. A quarter of them live in the capital, Ẹdo (Benin City), the remainder being spread over some 4,000 square miles in more than 600 villages ranging from about 20 to over 6,000 inhabitants. Only one-sixth of these have populations of more than 1,000 and a typical size is probably about 400.

The compact, discrete village community is generally divided into wards, each of which contains one or more patrilineal extended families, together with other compound and simple families whose heads may or may not be agnatically related. The widest effective patrilineage is, in general, rather shallow, the defining ancestor being usually not more than two or three generations back from living adults, though a wider range of patrikin may assemble for particular occasions, such as mortuary rites. Lineages as such play a rather minor role in village politics, where the interests of the community tend to overshadow those of its component kin groups. Community ties interact constantly with the private affairs of domestic groups. A family head, for example, will often call in one or more non-related village elders to help him settle disputes which involve only himself and his subordinate kin. The predominance of community interests is maintained through a strong, three-tier men's age-grade organization (Bradbury, 1957, p. 32) in which status and precedence are very largely determined by age itself. The oldest man, subject to 'citizenship' and sometimes other qualifications, is the village headman or *odionwere*. In consultation with other members of the elders' age-grade (*edion*) he makes policy, keeps order, settles disputes, and controls the warrior and executive grade of adult men (*ighele*) and the 'working' grade of youths (*iroghae*).

In many villages the *odionwere* is the sole village head but in others he shares political authority with a chief (*onogie*) who owes his office to descent, by primogeniture, in a ruling patriline (Bradbury, 1957, pp. 33-34). His chiefdom may consist of one village, or a number of villages, and he may or may not have subordinate hereditary or appointive title-holders. While the *odionwere's* authority springs from the gerontocratic character of village organization, the *onogie's* stems, to a greater degree, from the centralized political organization of the kingdom.

All villages are subject through their *odionwere* or *onogie*, and through one of the state counsellors in Benin City, to the *Oba* or sacred King of Benin.

CATEGORIES OF THE DEAD

Edo religious life is very complex (Bradbury, 1957, p. 52f.). It involves not only the dead but a supreme deity, other deities associated with the natural environment or with human skills, 'hero' figures that provide the focus of village and village-group cults, reifications of the components of human personality, and so on. Communication with the dead, however, accounts for a high proportion of all ritual activities and every kind of social group forms a congregation for the worship of its dead in some form or other. There are, in fact, many kinds of dead, each kind, as we shall see, corresponding to a status category among the living.

A primary division must first be made between what I may call the 'unincorporated' dead ('ghosts' of several varieties) and those dead who have been assigned a 'constitutional' position *vis-à-vis* the living, by a deliberate act of reincorporation. Both kinds interact with the living but they are distinguished from each other by the attitudes and behaviour of the living towards them. In general it may be asserted that, while relations between the living and the incorporated dead have a strong, positive, moral component, ghosts are dealt with almost entirely in terms of expediency. The incorporated dead are accepted as acting justly in their demands upon the living, who are morally obliged to submit to their authority and to sustain them; they are also believed capable of conferring positive benefits, in the form of vitality and prosperity, on their worshippers. Ghosts, on the other hand, while they may have just grievances against the living – for the very reason, perhaps, that their heirs have neglected to perform the rites that would convert them into ancestors and elders in the land of the dead – act out of anger and resentment, untempered with any capacity for exercising benevolence. The incorporated dead are the recipients not only of expiatory offerings but also of acts of thanksgiving and commemoration. Ghosts can only be bought off.

Of the incorporated dead we need mention here only three varieties, each associated with a separate field of authority. These fields of authority are distinguished from each other not only by their operational contexts (family and lineage; territorial communities and associations; the state) but also by different configurations of the principles – such as age, descent, citizenship, etc. – on which the right to command obedience and services is based. For all three types the act of incorporation is part of a complex series of mortuary and succession rites. From the actor's standpoint these rites do three main things:

1. They ensure the deceased his rightful place in *ẹrinbhin* (the world of the dead) in respect of the various authoritative statuses he occupied at the point of death.

2. They reformulate and regulate his relationships with those among the living for whom he has relevance by virtue of the same statuses.

3. They effect, or prefigure, or symbolize, the transmission of these statuses to one or more successors.

I shall refer to the three types of dead in the following manner (using capitals where the status is that of deceased persons):

A. FATHERS (*erha*, father) are named, individual, patrilineal ancestors, arranged genealogically in relation to each other and to their living descendants.

B. ELDERS (*ediọn*, elders; sing. *ọdiọn*) are the undifferentiated deceased elders of kinship, territorial, and associational groups.

C. CHIEFS (*enigie* and *ọba*) are the named predecessors of the living incumbents of hereditary political offices. Though the predecessors of a chief may be identical with his FATHERS, they are conceptually distinguished from them and may be worshipped at a separate shrine.

Only type A, FATHERS, can properly be called 'ancestors' if we restrict this term, as I think we should, to situations where relations between worshippers and worshipped are genealogically determined. The ELDERS of a kin group are, it is true, the collective ancestors of its living members but they are not identified as individuals and precise genealogical reckoning is, in this context, irrelevant. Kinship does not enter into the cults of ELDERS of territorial groups or associations; and, while CHIEFS are linked agnatically to their successors, in the cults of CHIEFS the congregation is neither confined to, nor necessarily structured round, a genealogically defined group. In this paper, then, the word 'ancestors' is used synonymously with FATHERS. It would also apply to MOTHERS (*IYE*) but this category of dead does not concern us here.

Space precludes a detailed consideration of the role of dead CHIEFS in Benin religion, for this would involve us in the complexities of sacred kingship. I shall concentrate, therefore, on FATHERS and ELDERS, and examine how they relate to each other and to the distribution of authority in the lineage and the village community. In those villages which have an hereditary *onogie* the cult of *ENIGIE* may be important, but its effect is to add a new dimension to the ritual life of the village without seriously altering the relationship between the cults of the ancestors and the ELDERS.

Fathers, Elders, and Ghosts in Ẹdo Religion

When a man who has no children dies, he is usually accorded only a perfunctory burial and no attempt is made to incorporate him as a FATHER. When a man leaves only daughters, the senior daughter's son, or her husband, acting on her behalf, may undertake to 'bury' him. But, in the normal course of events, it is the senior surviving son, and he alone, who should take responsibility for 'burying' (re) and 'planting' (ko) his father, that is for converting him into an ancestor and dedicating an altar at which to serve him. Those who are not 'buried' and 'planted' are implicitly assigned to the category of childless dead of the lineage who, whenever sacrifices are made to the lineage FATHERS and ELDERS, are thrown scraps of food, to appease them and discourage them from snatching what is intended for the incorporated dead.

Even those who do leave sons go through a period of discorporation between death (and interment which usually follows death very closely) and the completion of the funeral rites, or 'second burial', a period which may vary, according to the age and wealth of the senior son, from a few days to upwards of twenty years. Lonely, and resentful, and jealous of those who have been translated to a higher status, the father's ghost may, in the meantime, commit acts of aggression against his former dependants, making them sick, causing them to have accidents or to lose their money, attempting, even, to 'draw them after him'. He must, therefore, be pacified by offerings made, in the absence of an altar dedicated to him, over the right foot of his heir. On the strength of promises of an early funeral the son may, it is true, ask his father to show benevolence, but his willingness, and indeed his ability, to confer benefits are in constant doubt. For children, health and prosperity come not simply from one's own FATHER but, through him, from his father and father's fathers back along the patriline. For effective contact with his ancestors, then, he must go to another altar in the lineage, presided over by a close kinsman who has already 'planted' his FATHER. At this stage, then, the heir's authority over his father's other descendants and their **wives** lacks effective mystical backing. Nor, until he has accorded his father ancestorhood, has he validated his claim to be the heir to his father's property, in the form of a house, permanent crops, inheritable wives, and movable wealth. It is true that the lineage elders may permit him to make use of this property, or parts of it, but he cannot have full control over it nor, should he die before planting his father, can he transmit his rights over it to his own son. His next surviving brother might then step in, perform the funeral, and divert the seniority of descent to his own line.

Once he has made his father into an ancestor, the first son assumes rightful authority over his father's other children, and their access to the FATHER is through him. In the division of his father's property, supervised by the lineage elders, he receives much the biggest share and if his father held an hereditary office he succeeds to that.

One result of the rule of primogeniture is that much of the ambivalence, described for other patrilineal societies, in the relationship of fathers and sons, is concentrated, among the *Edo*, on the relationship between a man and his first son, for it brings about an exceptionally close identity and conflict of interests between these two. I have described in another paper (Bradbury, 1965) how the funeral rites serve to resolve this ambivalence, by drawing a dramatic parallel between the progress of the dead man's death journey towards ancestorhood, and the son's gradual assumption of his father's authoritative role in the domestic domain. The typical attitudes of a senior son during the funerary rites are discernibly different, in degree, if not in quality, from those of his brothers. Boastful, self-assertive, he is expected to show pride rather than sorrow. 'The child who eats the inheritance', say the *Edo*, 'does not weep for the dead.'

The rites themselves serve constantly to separate the first son off from his father's other children. On the final night of the funeral a wake is held in which the father himself, impersonated by one of his close kin, shares kola nuts and dances with his children for the last time. At the same time, it is believed, his kin in *erinbhin* (the spirit world) welcome him with similar festivities. Towards dawn the elders of the lineage perform a test to determine whether he has indeed been accepted as

FATHER and ELDER, and whether he is himself satisfied with the rites that have been performed for him. When this is affirmed the father's impersonator is led by his son to a nearby patch of bush where the unwanted, ghostly aspects of the father are finally dismissed. Then a piece of chalk, representing his ancestral spirit, is dragged, on a piece of string, back into the house, where it is placed on the altar built to receive it. The son is now free to dedicate the altar, in the rite of *ukọbhẹn* ('planting'), and to officiate there as his FATHER's priest.

But before this climax is reached other rites have to be performed which reformulate the position of the dead man and his son, in regard to the former's status of elder of the lineage. Throughout the funeral rites the children-of-the-deceased (*ibhi-ẹrinbhin*), led by the senior son, are set apart from, and opposed to, the elders of the lineage (*ediọn-ẹgbẹe*), led by its oldest man, the *ọkaẹgbẹe*. Only those who have 'planted' their fathers are recognized as true elders of the lineage but they rank among themselves according to age. Between the elders and the sons, especially the first son, there is constant tension and friction, as the former try to exert their authority and the son seeks to free himself, as far as possible, from it. He can never do so completely, however, for not only do they know how to perform details of the ritual that are hidden from him – and which they may contrive to keep hidden from him, even when the funeral is completed – but their cooperation is necessary for the translation of the dead man into an ELDER. One of the heir's first acts, when he begins the funeral, is to present a goat, through the *ọkaẹgbẹe*, to the *EDIỌN* of the lineage, requesting their help in achieving this aim.

Two other episodes in these rites require mention here. In the rite of *izaxwẹ-ẹgbẹe* the senior son presents to the elders a cow or goat (according to his father's rank and prestige) which is sacrificed to the *EDIỌN-ẸGBẸE*, the dead elders of the lineage, on the threshold of the deceased's house. This serves to assimilate the deceased to the *EDIỌN* and, at the same time, it affords recognition, by the elders, of the son's right to assume his father's domestic authority. Two days later, in the *isotọn* rite, the elders sit in a row on the verandah of the deceased's house to inspect and receive a collection of offerings (the *otọn*) from each of the bereaved children. The *otọn* which, together with decorated boxes, represent the wealth and prestige the dead man accumulated during his life, are first carried round the town or village in a procession led by the senior son. When he arrives back at the house he presents his *otọn* for the elders' inspection. But before this takes place a curious dialogue is usually carried on between the son and the elders, through a 'messenger'. The son inquires why the elders have sent for him. They tell him that his father is sick and that he should find a 'doctor' to attend him. After a brief silence the son replies that he has found a doctor but that, whether he tries to pass through this world or through *ẹrinbhin*, he can find no way to approach his father. He believes that it is they, the elders, who are preventing him from assisting his father. The elders then tell him that his father is already dead and that he should take steps to 'bury' him.

In this exchange it is clearly implied that hitherto the elders – those who have already 'buried' their fathers – have stood in the way of the son's direct access to their common ancestors. Now they are prepared to allow him access through his own FATHER, and to give recognition to his assumption of the latter's fatherly roles. But more than this, they are also prepared to accept him as an elder, as one of them. For after his *otọn* have been perfunctorily inspected and carried into the house (to be retained by the son himself) he takes his seat alongside them. So that, when his brothers and sisters come to present their *otọn*, their senior brother is no longer one of them, but one of the elders who receive their gifts. The *otọn* will, in fact, be shared by the senior son and the elders in two more or less equal parts. The other sons do not necessarily become elders immediately but will gradually and informally be accepted as such as they grow older. What I want to emphasize here, however, is that while the first son succeeds to his father's elderhood he does so only in a general sense, for his position *among* the elders will not be that which his father held. Thus, to take the extreme case, if his father had been the oldest man in the lineage, *ọkaẹgbẹe* and priest of the *EDIỌN-ẸGBẸE*, this office would pass not to the son, but to the next oldest man. The son, that is, does not succeed to his father's *specific* status

136

as elder, even in the necessarily qualified sense in which he succeeds to his fatherly roles.

From this brief and simplified account it will, I hope, begin to be clear that, among its other functions, *Ẹdo* mortuary ritual serves as an exegesis, for the actors, of the distinctiveness and the interconnectedness of the specific, individual authority of fathers and the more general, collective authority of elders in the family and lineage contexts. The death of a father and elder, who needs to be replaced in respect of both these statuses and who, in order to preserve the continuity of fatherly and elderly authority, must himself be made a FATHER and an ELDER, provides the obvious occasion for such an exegesis. In the day-to-day affairs of kin groups the interplay of these two types of authority is apparent. The relative autonomy of senior sons as intermediaries with their FATHERS, on behalf of the latters' children, is balanced against and limited by the overall authority of the elders as intermediaries with the *EDIQN*, on behalf of the lineage at large. It is not possible, within the space allowed for this paper, to examine, in detail, how these types of authority are exercised. It can be said, however, that the elders exercise a supervisory control over the dealings of household heads with their subordinates, restraining or supporting them according to their assessment of the justice of their actions and decisions. Men often succeed to their fathers' positions as family heads at an early age, and they need both encouraging and restraining if they are to perform this role successfully. Family heads rarely adjudicate between their subordinates without calling in other elders of the lineage, nor are they expected to be judges in their own disputes with their younger siblings. Moreover, while they are still young they have no effective voice in the councils of the village elders and it is through the lineage elders who, by virtue of their age, are also village elders, that the community exerts its pressures on the younger members of its component kin groups. These external pressures are, to my mind, a potent factor in holding together a lineage group when the rule of primogeniture, and the lack of a lineage estate, are working in the opposite direction. For the lineage, as a group, holds no property in common, not even land. Its elders do, however, control property collectively during the interval between the

death of a holder and the completion of his mortuary rites, and
it is they who, once the FATHER is 'planted', supervise its
division, in unequal proportions, between the first son and the
children of his father's other wives. It is no accident that the
solidarity of the lineage, and the authority of its elders, are
more apparent during the mortuary rites of one of its members
than at any other time.

Both the FATHERS' altar (*aru-erha*) and the lineage ELDERS'
altar (*aru-ediọn-ẹgbẹe*) are the scene of periodic commemorative
rites, of confirmatory rites, and of expiatory sacrifices and
offerings arising out of sickness and other disasters, which are
divined to be the result of quarrels and other sins of omission
and commission involving lineage members and their wives.
But by far the greater number of these expiations are directed
towards FATHERS rather than ELDERS. It would be possible to
produce evidence to suggest that this preponderance is in
accordance with a greater amount of suppressed resentment and
hostility in relations between fathers and sons, and sons of the
same father – relationships in which the control, transmission,
division, and use of property are a constant potential source of
conflicting interests – than in relations between the lineage
elders and their subordinates. The direct, demanding aggressiveness of FATHERS, and their equally positive capacity for exercising benevolence, stand out in contrast against the more
shadowy, vaguer mystical powers of the *EDIỌN*. The latter, it
is true, are fairly often divined to be the cause of troubles,
particularly those that fall upon the kin group as a whole or
indiscriminately on a series of its members, but also of individual disasters, generally as a result of a younger person ignoring
or flouting the elders' authority or following the breach of clan
taboos. Very frequently, however, they are seen as a secondary
cause, as lending their authority and their support to the
demands of the individual ancestors most directly concerned.

To bear out these assertions would take up the rest of this
paper and this is not my main intention. I have drawn attention
to the expression, in ritual, of two types of authority in the
lineage context, principally in order to pave the way for an
exploration of the part played in *Ẹdo* religion by another kind
of elderhood, namely elderhood in the village community. The

elders of the lineage and the forerunners they serve on the lineage's behalf share common descent and, though precise genealogical reckoning is not directly expressed in the ritual that joins them, it still may be thought permissible to speak of them as 'collective ancestors'. In the secular and religious notions of elderhood to which we now turn, the ideology of descent has only a peripheral part to play.

'ELDERS' OF THE VILLAGE

Whenever the *Ẹdo* speak of the *ediọn* of any group they have in mind those members of it who stand at the upper levels of a formal or informal hierarchy, graduated according to age or length of membership. The root *diọn* means 'to be older than'. Not only descent groups but groups formed on territorial or associational principles all set their senior members apart as *ediọn*, and the same men (and women in their own organizations) can be *ediọn* in a number of different groups at the same time. In each group the *ediọn* make policy, settle disputes, and serve as the repository and defenders of the group's traditions and regulations. They accept responsibliity for its well-being and good name, represent it in its relations with other groups and individuals, and expect the deference and obedience of its members who are not yet elders. If the group holds any property in common it is the *ediọn* who control its use. Among themselves the elders are generally arranged in recognized order of precedence, according to age or length of membership, and the oldest man, or the one who has been an elder longest, is usually designated *odiọnwere*.

Corresponding to every set of *ediọn* there are the *EDIỌN*, their forerunners, who demand that the living elders should uphold the customs and rules they have transmitted to them, and afford them mystical sanctions to assist them in dealing with infractions. The *EDIỌN* not only demand regular proof, in the form of offerings, of the group's continued respect for them but they also punish breaches of the rules they have laid down by bringing sickness and other disasters upon the group as a whole or its individual members. The *EDIỌN* are thought of in two slightly different senses, as: (*a*) the original founders of the group who laid down its customs and taboos; and (*b*) those members of the group who have, since its foundation, achieved elderhood, upheld its rules and conventions, modified them in accordance with changing circumstances, and passed them on to their successors. One by one, as the generations pass, elders die and are assimilated to the collectivity of their predecessors through the rites performed by their descendants and successors.

Descent groups, territorial communities at all levels up to that of the nation, occupational guilds, associations of retainers in the *Oba*'s palace, cult groups worshipping particular deities – all these have their 'altars of the *EDION*' (*aru-edion*) where the living elders communicate with and give sustenance to the collectivity of their forerunners.

Forde (1962) has described how, among the Yakö, each of the associations of which a dead man was a member intervenes in his mortuary rites, demanding from his heirs that they should feast its members and take steps to fill the gap he has left in its membership. In Benin each of the groups in which a dead man was *odion* makes similar demands. I have already referred to the rite of *izaxwe-egbee* which assimilates the deceased to the *EDION* of the lineage; but the sons must also perform *izaxwe* for each of the other groups in which their father had achieved elderhood, by presenting the living elders of the group with a cow or goat (according to rank and prestige), yams, cooked meats, kola nuts, palm wine, etc. These are sometimes explained by informants as repayments to the group for the benefits the dead man himself received as an elder, that is for his share of whatever accrued to the elders as a group. But they have a religious as well as a secular purpose, for they are directed not only to the living elders but also to the *EDION*, who receive them as offerings and sacrifices. The demand that the heir should fulfill these obligations comes from the dead man's survivors but also from his forerunners and, moreover, from the dead man himself. For, without the support of both the community he has left and the community he is seeking to join, he cannot accomplish the hazardous death-journey between the two. Thus the *izaxwe* offerings are both repayments for what he has received as an elder in this world and, as it were, entrance fees into the society of the various groups of *EDIQN* in the land of the dead.

We have seen that, in the mortuary ritual, the deceased's progress to ancestorhood is paralleled by the son's assumption of the 'father' roles he has vacated in this world. Also he replaces his father as an elder of the lineage, though in a much more general sense, for although he is accorded nominal elderhood his ability to exercise it will depend on his age relative to that of the other lineage elders. I now wish to examine the manner in which the mortuary ritual serves to effect, or rather symbolize, succession to village elderhood. I limit myself to the village variety, because to consider the *edion* of other groups would introduce too many complications, and also because I believe this to be the context in which many of the basic notions concerning the activities and interests of dead elders are generated. First it is necessary to give a little more detailed information about the age-grade organization (Bradbury, 1957, p. 32).

Youths around sixteen years of age become *iroghae*, usually in small batches and at irregular intervals, at the discretion of the *edion* and *odionwere*. Their passage into this grade is marked by a usually simple confirmatory rite, involving offerings of kola nuts and coconut at the shrine of the village *EDIQN* (*ogwedion*), which is normally the meeting-house of the village elders. Henceforth they are liable to be called out, along with the other *iroghae*, by their leaders, the *ikairoghae*, who, acting under the instructions of the *odionwere*, direct them in such menial 'public works' as road-clearing, trampling mud and carrying water for building operations, and, in the past, carrying tribute to the capital. After ten to fifteen years of this, by which time they are the oldest *iroghae*, they are promoted, in another simple ceremony, into the *ighele* grade where, under the *ikaighele*, they take part in those communal tasks demanding more skill and experience, perform 'police' duties as agents of the elders, and supervise the activities of the lower grade. In pre-colonial days it was from the *ighele* that detachments were generally chosen for service in the military campaigns of the state. We shall return to the *ighele* later for, as we shall see, they are the living counterparts of one of the varieties of unincorporatcd dead, namely the *ighele-erinbhin*. What I wish to emphasize here, however, is that, in the normal course of events, promotion from *ighele* to *edion*, as from *iroghae* to *ighele*, takes place right outside the context of mortuary rites.

When an elder dies, each of the elders junior to him moves up one step in the order of precedence, but as the body of elders becomes generally depleted the oldest *ighele* begin to pressure the *edion* to promote them. When an understanding is reached, each of the candidates visits either all the *edion*, or the most senior *edion*, in turn, and presents him with a small bundle of yams, seeking his approval. Then, after a number of mimetic rites symbolizing the completion of their obligations as *ighele*, they present offerings at the *aru-edion* and each of them is lowered seven times over the altar. They are pronounced *edion* of the village (and of other villages in the same chiefdom or village group) by the *odionwere*. Henceforth they have a rightful voice in the village council of elders, a right to share in such payments as are made to the elders, to share the elders' portion of feasts provided by individuals for the whole community, and so on. As they become older still, and reach the top ranks of elderhood, they will be recognized as eligible to deputize for the *odionwere* in making offerings to the *EDION*.

This is the normal process by which *edion* are 'made'. Yet in some villages in which I have lived elderhood is also conferred during mortuary rites. In the village of Ekho *izaxwe-egbee* (for the lineage elders) and *izaxwe-evbo* (for the village elders), used to be performed on the same day. The senior son of the deceased would produce two goats and the village elders would choose the bigger one, leaving the other for the lineage elders – an interesting token of the predominance of village interests. When the *izaxwe* offerings have been handed over to the village elders, the latter call upon the dead man's heir to nominate two persons, from among his patrikin, to be made *odion*. If he is not already a village *odion* himself, which he may well be, he will come forward himself with his immediately junior brother. If he is *odion* already, then he can nominate other brothers or patrilineal cousins for the honour. Presenting plates of coconut and kola nuts to the *edion*, assembled in the village street facing the deceased's house, the candidates kneel before the *odionwere* and are pronounced *ediọn* of the village. Generally speaking, the candidates put forward turn out to be young men, youths, even boys and it soon becomes clear that the elderhood conferred on them is of a largely 'honorary' or 'nominal' nature. It in no way cancels their obligations to continue to work with the *iroghae* or *ighele* until such time as, being among the oldest *ighele*, they are eventually promoted to substantive elderhood. It is true that when that time comes they will be absolved from making gifts of yams to the other elders but that is the only material effect of their 'promotion'.

Fortes (1962, p. 87), pointing out the office-like quality of all significant statuses, has recently described initiation ceremonies as 'the means of divesting a person of his status as a child in the domestic domain and of investing him with the status of actual or potential citizen in the politico-jural domain'. The relevance of this to the stage-by-stage process of making elders among the Ẹdo is readily apparent, but it is the word 'potential' that catches my eye here, for it implies that such rites are not always designed to effect immediate transitions from one effective status to another, or to fill immediate gaps in the network of social relations. The conferment of honorary elderhood in the Benin village does not materially affect the recipients, nor does it do anything to restore the balance in the representation of kin groups in village affairs. Two honorary *ediọn* do not compensate for one substantive *ọdiọn*. This becomes abundantly clear when it is found that after the kin group has nominated its own 'replacements' for the dead man, both the *ọdiọnwere* and, if the village has one, the hereditary *onogie* have the right to put forward new *'ediọn'* from their own kin groups. Moreover, any other elder in the village may, by making a token gift to the dead man's heir, have one of his own sons made *'ọdiọn'* too. What is going on here, then, or so it seems to me, is not an act of succession to the specific *ọdiọn* status of a dead man. It is rather a symbolic recognition that the village community as a whole, its component kin groups, and its main authorities, are jointly responsible for seeing that, as the elders, who embody the community's values, die away, their authority is transmitted to a new generation of elders. It is succession to elderhood in its collective aspect, not in its individual manifestations,

143

that is at stake. So the mortuary ritual not only affords an exegesis of the interplay of lineage and elderly authority in the lineage but links these two types of authority with a third, that of the village elders, in a more complex web of social relations. Village elderhood is essentially a community interest but, at the same time, it is symbolically recognized that, while the village can order its personnel, it remains dependent upon its component kin groups for their replacement.

It may seem pointless to view the collective authority of village elders, and its mystical coefficients, in the same theoretical terms that, in the hands of Fortes and Goody, have proved so fruitful for the analysis of the relationship between the character and variability of ancestor worship, and the jural and property aspects of nuclear kin relations. Yet I think it is worth making the attempt, for it is of the nature of authority and property rights that, whether held by individuals or collectivities, they must be transmitted through the generations. I shall try to show, therefore, that there is a sense in which the holder/heir concept can illuminate not only the nature of ELDER-worship but also the relations of the living with one of the categories of the unincorporated dead, the *ighele-erinbhin* (lit. *ighele*-dead), whose characteristics, as we shall see, are a negation of those of the *EDION*.

The *edion*, as a collectivity, hold jural authority over the rest of the community, men and women; authority which is passed on down the generations, individuals coming to share in it when they pass from the ranks of the *ighele* into the *edion* age-grade. They do not hold tangible movable property of the kind that Goody finds so crucial in his analysis of LoDagaa ancestral and mortuary rites. They do, however, hold rights over land which, in the Benin kingdom, belongs to village communities as a whole and is not divided up between their component kin groups. They also own ritual paraphernalia and shrines, though these have no economic value. As land is generally abundant and any member of the community can farm wherever he likes, provided the tract he chooses is not already under cultivation, or earmarked for it, by someone else, the rights of the elders in land at first sight appear to carry no great benefits. They do, however, collect and share out dues from strangers who wish to work the land or its tree-crop resources, such as palm oil. They also collect court fines and fees and take to themselves a major part of anything else that accrues to the village community as a whole. It is rights of this kind, and the right to command non-elders, that are transmitted down the generations. Here the holder and the heir are both collectivities, namely the elders as a group and those who will succeed them as elders. And the act of succession does not take place at particular points of time – as it does among some related *Ẹdo*-speaking peoples, where the senior age-grade retires, after a number of years, in favour of a succeeding age-group – but it is, rather, a process continuing throughout time; a process which, I have suggested, is symbolized in the making of 'honorary' *ediọn* during mortuary rites.

The alleged misuse of their rights and the arbitrary way in which they are seen, by their juniors, to use their authority to command, gives rise to constant resentment and accusations against the elders as a group. There is much in common between a father's authority over his sons and the authority of the elders over the other men in the village. The overt, expected behaviour of junior to senior villagers is much like that of sons towards their fathers, though necessarily lacking the same quality of affection and solicitude. Resentment of the elders' alleged selfishness can, on the other hand, be more easily admitted, and even openly expressed, for the collective nature of the elders' authority provides a general rather than a specific target. The younger men constantly meet in caucus to formulate their grievances and make plans for confronting the *ediọn* with their misdeeds or demanding their share of the proceeds of some alleged secret agreement with strangers, involving village land or trees. They are rarely very successful, for the public solidarity of the *ediọn*, combined with their mystical and magical superiority, and their individual authority in their respective domestic groups, give the old men considerable advantage. They are also usually adept at buying off some of their more vociferous juniors, either by quiet gifts or promises of promotion. The position of the official leaders of the *ighele*, who are expected to champion the cause of their fellows and at the same time to see that the will of the *ediọn* is carried out, is a particularly anomalous one and this is recognized in the special protection that is sought for them, from the *EDIQN*, on their installation.

Just as relations with the ancestors image father-son relations, so do relations between the village *EDIQN* and their congregation reflect the corresponding aspects of the relationship between the living *ediǫn* and their apparent heirs. We have seen that, in the domestic context, the relationship of a senior son with his father is of special importance. Of somewhat analogous significance for the cult of village ELDERS is the relationship between the living elders and those who, as a group, are their obvious and immediate successors, namely the *ighele*. It is the *ighele*, the chief agents of the elders' authority, that are most resentful of that authority. Their hostility and opposition to the elders is coloured by their stereotype as the most virile and physically powerful section of the community, men in their prime of life and, moreover, warriors.

Linked closely, in *Ędo* belief, with notions about the incorporated, collective *EDIQN* are others concerning the unincorporated, collective *ighele-ęrinbhin*. These are the men who have died in the prime of life, before passing out of the warrior phase into wise and experienced elderhood. Leaving no sons to 'plant' them, or sons who are as yet too young to do so, they have also been denied the opportunity of becoming *EDIQN* in *ęrinbhin*. Thus they are the collective, village expression of the ghostly fathers and childless dead of the lineage. They wander about in the bush, and it is they whom the foolhardy will see if they go to their farms on a rest-day. Removed from subordination to the living elders, the *ighele-ęrinbhin* are free to express their resentment in whatever way they can. The obvious target for their anger and jealousy is provided by those men who have died as elders, and whose translation into FATHERS and *EDIQN* has not yet been accomplished; those, that is, who are temporarily outside society but have the right and the promise of being taken back into it. Thus the *ighele-ęrinbhin* are thought to constitute the chief obstacle to the dead father and elder as he makes his dream-like death-journey, through the forest and across the waters, to seek acceptance among his kin and associates who have gone before him. One of the overt aims of mortuary ritual is to protect the deceased against their activities.

Protection is afforded in various ways. Prayers are addressed to the *EDIQN*, asking them to help the dead man on his way, and to accept him. Cowrie shells and other offerings are strewn along the route of funeral processions in a direct attempt to appease the *ighele-ẹrinbhin* themselves. But some of the mimetic acts of the participants in these rites are of particular interest, for they afford the living *ighele* a splendidly ambiguous role. While they are constrained by their position in the community to afford their assistance to a man who was recently their elder, and who will soon be assimilated to their *EDIQN*, they are, nevertheless, given the opportunity to express their resentment against elders in general. Thus they play the part of dutiful village *ighele*, supporting one of their number in his obligations towards his dead father and, at the same time, they play the part of their dead counterparts who cannot be controlled, but must be bought off. Let us examine their role more closely.

It is the senior son who marks out the line of his father's grave and strikes the ground with a hoe along it, to 'cut a road' by which his father will travel. But it is the *ighele* of the village who actually dig the grave and in doing so they find numerous, usually imaginary, roots, which cannot be cut through until they have received a 'bribe' from the heir. Thus they join their counterparts among the dead in hindering the progress of the dead elder. Then again, as the funerary procession makes its way from ward to ward of the town or village, symbolically escorting the dead man on his journey, the *ighele* of each ward hold it up and demand a ransom before they will allow it to pass. The *ighele* and the *iroghae* also take part in these processions. First they move on ahead, 'clearing a way' for it to pass. Then, turning about, they charge back towards it, in menacing fashion, stamping out the steps of a war dance as they confront the dead man's senior son. So, from moment to moment, their role changes as first they lead, then oppose, the dead man's progress.

In some villages of the Iyekorhiomwo district in the southeast of Benin Division, the *ighele* play an important part in a phase of the funerary ritual for dead elders, known as *igbizu*. This corresponds, in part, to the *ilẹga* rite which is carried out, night and morning, for several days, in the deceased's house, by

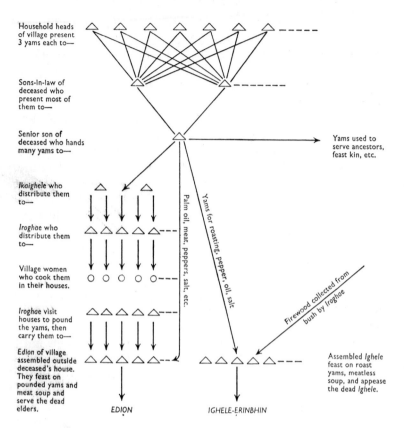

Household heads of village present 3 yams each to—

Sons-in-law of deceased who present most of them to—

Senior son of deceased who hands many yams to— → Yams used to serve ancestors, feast kin, etc.

Ikaighele who distribute them to—

Iroghae who distribute them to—

Village women who cook them in their houses.

Iroghae visit houses to pound the yams, then carry them to—

Edion of village assembled outside deceased's house. They feast on pounded yams and meat soup and serve the dead elders.

Palm oil, meat, peppers, salt, etc.

Yams for roasting, pepper, oil, salt

Firewood collected from bush by *Iroghae*

Assembled *Ighele* feast on roast yams, meatless soup, and appease the dead *Ighele*.

EDIQN

IGHELE-ERINBHIN

Movement of yams in the 'igbizu' rite at Ugboko

his children and lineage members. In *ilega* the participants first give food to the 'feet' of the dead man, represented by a piece of white 'chalk' placed in a small hole, to encourage them to carry him on his journey. Then they dance round the hole, singing seven songs, escorting him on his way. In the village of Ugboko a similar episode takes place, but with reference to the deceased's status as village elder. The chain of events involved with it is complicated, but it can be summarized thus:

First, the senior son, accompanied by his brothers, must carry kola nuts and coconuts to the *ogwediqn* where the *EDIQN* are enshrined. There, through the *odiqnwere*, he informs the

EDIQN that he is now ready to begin his father's funeral. The *EDIQN* are asked to allow the deceased to 'find a road by which to pass to *ẹrinbhin*'. But the accomplishment of this journey depends not only upon the *EDIQN*, but on the co-operation of all those members of the living community, kin and affines, men and women, elders, adults, and youths, with whom the deceased has associated and who have rights and obligations in respect of him. What happens is this (see *Figure*): All household heads present 3 yams each to each of the dead man's sons-in-law living in the village (those living elsewhere may get them from their own fellow-villagers if the latter follow this custom). Each son-in-law then ceremonially presents the bulk of the yams he receives (some say 200) to the dead man's heir, dancing along with them to his compound. At this stage the yams are a token of the esteem of the sons-in-law, of gratitude to the father for conferring his daughters upon them, of recognition that the child-bearing capacities of these women are still the concern of their own patrilineal ancestors. The heir sets some of the yams aside to feast his kin at various points in the rites, but a large number of them are handed over to the *ikaighele*, who give them to the *iroghae*, who, in turn, redistribute them to all households in the village, placing them on the thresholds. The women of these households cook them and the *iroghae* go round pounding them into 'fufu'. Then, in the evening, they carry the 'fufu' to the front of the deceased elder's house, where the assembled elders junior to the deceased feast on them, with soup and meat provided by the heir. This feasting, which some interpret as symbolizing a meal prepared by the dead man for his fellow *EDIQN*, may go on for from two to seven days. During the same period the *ighele* of the village also assemble, each night, outside the same house, where they remain, eating, singing, and sleeping till morning. Here, on a fire made by the *iroghae* from wood they have collected from the bush, the *ighele* roast yams and cook a simple soup of palm oil, pepper, and salt. The ingredients of this meal, roast yams and meatless soup, are, appropriately enough, the kind of offering that is made to those nameless, amoral spirits – such as the *ighele-ẹrinbhin* themselves – who, because they have failed to achieve full social destiny, are placed outside the confines of human society. Night and

149

morning the *ighele* dance *ilega*, singing 'Dance and meet the *EDIQN*', as they escort the deceased on his journey. By keeping watch over him, and encouraging him, they fulfil their pious obligations to one of their seniors, in the same way that children do so for their father. Yet, in the character of the meal they prepare and eat, there is a reminder of the less harmonious relations that underlie the proper attitudes of elders and juniors towards each other.

I have chosen to emphasize the role of the *ighele-erinbhin*, not because they are in themselves a particularly important feature of Benin religion, but because, in their interaction with the living and with dead fathers and elders, they serve to throw into sharper relief the meaning, for the *Edo*, of the *EDIQN*, of whom they are the negation. For the essential difference between the *EDIQN*, who demand service and expiation for infractions of village norms and the flouting of the elders' authority, and the *ighele-erinbhin*, who can only be appeased, is that while the former achieved and passed on the authority-status of elder, the latter died while they were still only heirs to it. Here, therefore, not only do we have the legitimate authority of elders projected onto the *EDIQN* whose actions are incontrovertibly just, but the resentment of their 'heirs', and the elders' fear of that resentment, are projected onto a separate category of dead, whose actions are neither just nor legitimate.

The *EDIQN* are of the village, the ordered, controlled, social world. They are those who have, in achieving elderhood, triumphed over disorder and evil. The *ighele-erinbhin* are those who have failed in this respect and, as a result, have found themselves outside the social order. They are of the bush, which is a constant threat to order and control – the source, it is true, of vitality and growth (food, 'medicines') but, at the same time, something that cannot be allowed to run wild, something that must be tamed, if possible; and, if it cannot be tamed, kept at bay. The shrine of the *EDIQN* is the centre of community life and it is often at the geographical centre of the village. The *ighele-erinbhin* have no shrine, nor can they be worshipped, but only appeased. The vigour and vitality that the word *ighele* connotes must be made to operate within the bounds of order.

Once it gets outside them, into the bush, as a result of men dying before they have socially fulfilled themselves, then it becomes an unmitigated menace. So the *ighele-ęrinbhin* must be fought back, or bought off, by individual and collective action because they represent failure, measured in terms of the society's evaluation of old age and fatherhood.

Outside the context of mortuary ritual, where it is simply assumed that the *ighele-ęrinbhin* will take every opportunity to hinder the dead elder's progress, interaction with these spirits occurs only in limited contexts. It is when an elder persistently fails to conduct himself with appropriate wisdom and self-control, or when a living *ighele* behaves recurrently in a manner which the elders see as a threat to them (i.e. when he steps outside the bounds of legitimate *ighele*-hood) that divination is likely to reveal the actions of the *ighele-ęrinbhin*. The remedy is to appease them by offerings and pleadings. But the offerings given to them are of the same nature, and made in the same spirit, as those given to witches and unknown living enemies. While offerings to FATHERS, ELDERS, and CHIEFS are partaken of by their worshippers, those given to the *ighele-ęrinbhin* are simply cast away, secretly, usually at night, outside the village, very often at the junction of two bush paths that symbolizes the junction of this world and *ęrinbhin* (*ad'agbọn ad'ęrinbhin*). The *EDIỌN*, by contrast, are worshipped in the daytime, publicly, in their shrine or in the middle of the village street. They make their demands on the living when people fail to fulfil their moral obligations towards them, when they break the village taboos laid down by the *EDIỌN* themselves, when they flout the community rules that the elders hold in trust. But they are also worshipped regularly and willingly, and they are called upon to witness and sanctify various kinds of *rites de passage*.

It is, to my mind, clear that the ritual episodes I have described constitute, for the *Ędo* themselves, explanatory models for their own society. These are simple models, at a low level of abstraction, constructed by drawing out from the totality of behaviour in certain fields the essential features of particular sets of social relations. These models can be, and are, extended to embrace other sets of social relations in other fields of authority – associations (with their ELDERS), state institutions (with their CHIEFS) – and to link them together in a meaningful synthesis. All this is done in terms of beliefs and actions concerned with the various categories of dead. Nor are they static models for it would be possible to produce evidence to show that they are deliberately altered, by what amounts to a legislative process, to meet circumstances which are recognized to have changed. To take a simple example, in discussing the *izaxwe* rites at Ekho village I have said that the deceased's heir produced two goats of which the village elders would choose the largest, leaving the inferior one for the lineage. During my stay there, however, the procedure was changed. It was recognized that under modern conditions the village community was no longer in a position to maintain its dominance over the interests of its component kin groups. The kin group was no longer willing to take second best and *izaxwe* often became the occasion for quarrelling. So it was decided that henceforth the two goats should be presented quite separately and that each group should be free to accept or reject what it was offered on its own merits.

In my last paragraphs, in discussing the contrasts between the character and behaviour of the *EDIǪN* and the *ighele-ęrinbhin* I have hinted at the implicit existence, in *Ędo* thought, of another kind of model, of a more abstract, ideal order. Its terms are no longer simple status-categories and social relationships but sets of opposed ideas such as 'day' and 'night', 'bush' and 'village', 'growth' and 'control', under which a wider range of human experience can be ordered. The opposition between day and night refers not only to the *EDIǪN/ighele-ęrinbhin* opposition but also to the dichotomy between the elders and the 'elders of the night' – i.e. the witches. Bush/village and growth/order are conceptual dichotomies which enable the *Ędo* to deal with some of the ideas we have already set out and some of the features of divine kingship and its ritual in terms of the same explanatory schema. But models and explanations of this type are not a substitute for the kind of conceptualization which, following Fortes and others, I have stressed in this paper. They are, rather, complementary to it. It is as necessary for the observer as it is for the actors to operate at both levels of abstraction.

REFERENCES

BRADBURY, R. E. 1957. *The Benin Kingdom*. Ethnographic Survey of Africa, Western Africa, Part 13. London: International African Institute.

—— 1965. Father and Senior Son in Edo Mortuary Ritual. In M. Fortes & G. Dieterlen (eds.), *African Systems of Thought*. London: Oxford University Press.

COLSON, E. 1954. Ancestral Spirits and Social Structure among the Plateau Tonga. *International Archives of Ethnography* **47**: 21-68.

FORDE, C. D. 1962. Death and Succession: An Analysis of Yako Mortuary Ritual. In M. Gluckman (ed.), *Essays on the Ritual of Social Relations*. Manchester: Manchester University Press.

FORTES, M. 1959. *Oedipus and Job in West African Religion*. London: Cambridge University Press.

—— 1961. Pietas in Ancestor Worship. *Journal of the Royal Anthropological Institute* **91**: 166-191.

—— 1962. Ritual and Office in Tribal Society. In M. Gluckman (ed.), *Essays on the Ritual of Social Relations*. Manchester: Manchester University Press.

GOODY, J. 1962. *Death, Property, and the Ancestors*. Stanford, Calif: Stanford University Press; London: Tavistock Publications.

GOUGH, E. K. 1958. Cults of the Dead among the Nayars. *Journal of American Folklore* **71**: 446-478.

MIDDLETON, J. 1960. *Lugbara Religion*. London: Oxford University Press.

Edward H. Winter

Territorial Groupings and Religion
among the Iraqw

INTRODUCTION

This essay is concerned with a particular type of social structure. The discussion will be conducted primarily in terms of the Iraqw of Tanganyika. Since I shall devote considerable attention to supernatural beliefs and practices, I shall take this opportunity to make a few general remarks about the study of religion by social anthropologists. Then I shall present some information concerning the Iraqw. While so doing, I shall make reference to another East African people, the Amba of Uganda in order to clarify, or throw into relief, points that I wish to make in terms of the Iraqw. Finally, I shall make some remarks about the recent history of the study of social structure.

In the last few years, during which we have witnessed a quickening of interest in the subject of religion, though there have been a number of publications dealing with religion in general, the bulk of the literature has been concerned with the religions of particular peoples. In studies of the latter type it is possible to delineate two approaches. Some scholars have interested themselves in religion, viewed as an isolable aspect of culture, for its own sake; *Nuer Religion* is a product of this approach. Other anthropologists have interested themselves not in religion *per se* but rather in the interrelationships between religion and social structure; Middleton's *Lugbara Religion* and Fortes's *Oedipus and Job* may be cited as examples of this approach. These varying lines of inquiry probably reflect fundamental differents of opinion as to what social anthropology is all about. Some people would hold that the study of various religions, viewed as cultural systems, is an integral part of the discipline, whereas others would maintain that social anthropology is primarily concerned with the study of social structure. Proponents of the latter view, with which I myself sympathize,

155

would claim that social anthropologists, because of their knowledge of social structure, are in a position to make an important specialist contribution to the study of religion. Though it is important to recognize these differences of opinion, because by so doing a number of misunderstandings can be avoided, there is little to be gained by arguing about what anthropologists should do; the important thing is for the individual to get on with the job as he defines it.

The study of the interrelationships between religion and social structure is still in its infancy. For one thing, it is only very recently that satisfactory analyses of particular social structures have been available in any number. Again, the study of the religious beliefs and practices of any group of people is inherently very difficult. As Paul Bohannan (1963) has written,

'. . . the anthropology of religion is the most difficult of all the branches of the subject. Not only does it require a most rigorous discipline to do well: in field research it is the religion of the people that the fieldworker learns last, and usually after greatest probing. Even when he has been shown the ritual early in his field research, it is only when he knows the culture the ritual reflects and can understand the theology as it is explained to him, that he can comprehend any except the superficialities of what is being shown and told him.'

To this admirable statement I can only add that some of us, particularly those who have worked in societies which practice extremely elaborate rites, rites which may be performed only at infrequent intervals, have left the field before reaching the level of understanding of which Bohannan speaks. I say some of us because many aspects of the religion of the first people with whom I worked remain mysterious to me to this day and I cannot believe that my situation is unique. In view of these considerations, I would maintain that, though it is perfectly legitimate to suggest new approaches to the problems encountered in this realm of inquiry and to devise new concepts for their study, there is relatively little which can be said at a highly generalized level about the interrelationships between the two systems, in the absence of a significant number of studies in depth of both the social structures and religious systems of particular peoples.

Since most contemporary social anthropologists believe that neither religion nor social structure can be considered an epiphenomenon of the other, the study of their interrelationships clearly has two facets; the impact of religion upon social structure and the influence of social structure upon religious beliefs and practices. Though it is probably impossible fully to separate these two aspects in the study of any particular body of data, nevertheless individual anthropologists have chosen to address themselves to one aspect of the matter rather than the other. This may be illustrated by reference to two studies which have been previously cited; Middleton is primarily concerned with the influence of Lugbara religion upon the social structure, whereas Fortes is primarily, although admittedly not entirely, concerned with the problem of understanding Tallensi religious ideas in terms of his knowledge of their social structure.

Insofar as the present essay will be concerned with religion, attention will be focused upon the influence of a religious system upon a particular social structure. I trust that it will become apparent that one cannot proceed very far in the attempt to understand the social structure of the Iraqw without acquiring some knowledge of their ideas in regard to the supernatural world. I am not, however, trying to say that an understanding of religious notions is vital to the understanding of every social structure; I am in fact trying to make precisely the opposite point, namely that in some societies religion plays a much more important role in group structure than it does in others. This point might seem to be so obvious as to be not worth mentioning were it not for the fact that since the days of Durkheim and Weber, one scholar after another has put forward a theory of *the* impact of religion upon social structure.

THE IRAQW

The Iraqw live in northern Tanganyika in the highlands above the western escarpment of the Rift Valley in country which, at least by the standards of Tanganyika, offers favourable conditions for the growth of crops and for livestock. Tanganyika's

Northern Province is a very complex region. Within its boundaries are Bantu, Nilo-Hamitic, Cushitic, and Click speaking groups. There are a few hunters and gatherers, two entirely pastoral peoples, and a number of societies which combine agriculture with stock-raising. The Iraqw, who speak a Cushitic language, belong to this last category. They depend for the bulk of the food upon grain crops, maize, millets, and sorghum. But they also keep herds of cattle, sheep, and goats and a few donkeys as well. Traditionally, wealth has been measured in terms of the size of an individual's livestock holdings. Under modern conditions most of the cash which comes into the area does so as the result of the sale of bulls and oxen and to a lesser extent small stock, because, with the exception of a few areas, cash crops are not of great importance.

A census taken by the government in 1957 showed that there were more than a hundred and thirty thousand Iraqw. Of greater importance is the fact that this figure represented an increase of some thirty thousand over that obtained in 1948 when the first census with any pretensions to accuracy was taken. Though reliable figures are available only for the post-war period, there is good evidence that an increasing population has been a characteristic of the Iraqw for a considerable period of time. This has had important repercussions upon the social structure because it has resulted in a steady movement of people out of previously occupied areas into new localities and the creation of a constantly moving frontier.

At one period the Iraqw were confined to a relatively small area now known as Kaynam, but in the latter part of the nineteenth century they began to spill out of it and, as new settlers sought living-space, the frontiers began to expand. The movement out of the more congested central areas is still in progress. Today, the Iraqw occupy an area which is many times the size of their original homeland. They were fortunate in two respects. In the first place, there were extensive adjacent areas which were either uninhabited or at most lightly occupied by pastoral peoples, areas which were suitable for settlement in terms of their techniques for exploiting the natural environment. Second, although they began to enter new areas before the arrival of the first Europeans, much of the expansion has taken place in a period when the settlers have been afforded protection by the German and British régimes against cattle-raiding by other people, particularly the Masai.

For the most part expansion has taken place on an individual rather than a group basis. Ideally, the process takes place as follows: as a man's sons reach adulthood and marry, they set up their own homesteads in more recently settled and less densely occupied areas. The youngest son remains at the parental home, and he and his wife care for his mother and father in their declining years. Whether this ideal pattern is followed or not, it commonly happens that men who are closely related, either as father and son or as brothers, live at considerable distances, fifty miles or more, from one another.

The Iraqw do not live in nucleated settlements; instead the houses are scattered over the landscape, although not in a completely random manner, since they are usually situated on sloping ground. Their house style, it might be mentioned in passing, is one of their most distinctive features, for, although in some areas they build thatched-roof houses of a conventional African type, most of them live in earth-roofed, semi-subterranean dwellings, the sites for which have been excavated from hillsides.

Although one or two other people such as the man's parents may be attached to it, the household group inhabiting such a dwelling consists typically of a man, his wife, and their children. The household is the basic unit of production and consumption, and each household attempts to be self-supporting. Viewed as a productive unit, the household is organized on the assumption that it contains at least one adult man and one adult woman whose tasks complement one another. Other members of the household, such as children and elderly people, are fitted into this basic framework, according to sex, as helpers. The members of the household working together on the agricultural land of the homestead try during the growing season to raise large enough crops to sustain the group throughout the year. From a subsistence point of view the most important product of the herd attached to the homestead is the milk given by the cows, for the Iraqw hold that a proper diet must include milk. The man of the house is responsible for herding the livestock, while the woman milks the cows and cleans the room in which the animals are kept, since the Iraqw do not build kraals but instead sleep under the same roof with their livestock. The question of the self-sufficiency of the household is a more complicated matter, in the case of cattle, though, than is the case with agricultural produce. Every household has cattle attached to it and thus has direct access to a supply of milk. This situation, it might be noted, contrasts with that among many other peoples of the interior of Tanganyika who may be classified as having pastoral-agricultural modes of subsistence. In many of these societies, although large numbers of cattle are present, significant proportions of the homesteads have no herds attached to them, and the people living in them are entirely dependent upon agricultural produce for their subsistence. The fact that each homestead among the Iraqw has a herd of cattle does not result from a rather even distribution of cattle in terms of ownership, for such is not the case – some men own great numbers of cattle whereas others own none at all. It results, rather, from the operation of a system of cattle loans. This is a complex subject, and in the present context only a few aspects of it will be mentioned. The operation of the system depends, of course, upon the willingness of the wealthier stock-owners to lend their animals to others who are less fortunate. They are willing to do so for a number of reasons of which a couple may be cited. For one thing, if a man has a very large number of cattle he cannot keep all of them in his house and he is forced to find other accommodations for them. Even when it is possible for a man to keep a medium-sized herd in his own house, he is usually reluctant to do so. In the past there was always the danger of a sudden cattle raid, and lingering fears of this persist. Then, too, there is the fear of a localized epidemic. If the herd is dispersed there is much less danger of it being wiped out in its entirety by some sudden and unforeseen catastrophe. As these remarks would suggest, cattle-lending arrangements are often made by men who live at considerable distances from one another, men who do not have close kinship ties. Thus such loans serve to forge important bonds between people living in different localities. The overall result is the creation of both a complex interlocking network among men throughout the entire area occupied by the Iraqw and a situation such that many men have important economic interests in distant peoples and places. These considerations are, I believe, positive forces which help to create an interest in the affairs and welfare of the Iraqw people as a whole and prevent a parochialism of thought and interest which is characteristic of many other African societies.

The Iraqw, who differ sharply from all of the other peoples, with one exception, with whom they are in contact in language and in most other aspects of culture, have a very lively awareness of their distinctiveness and of their identity as a single people. Furthermore, the individual has a feeling of loyalty towards the entire people. In the pre-European period this loyalty was never symbolized by allegiance to a common chief or king, for such figures did not exist. There are some individuals whom I shall call Great Diviners who occupy extraordinary positions within the system but, as the term which I have used would indicate, they were and are in no sense chiefs, although some of the early European administrators mistakenly thought them so and attempted to utilize their services in this capacity. As far as holders of traditional positions of authority are concerned, though there was no single position which acted as a focal point for the loyalties of the people, by the same token there were no petty independent chiefs whose presence might have caused a division of the Iraqw people into a number of hostile or potentially hostile units. One of the most important rights of an Iraqw, and, in terms of the present discussion, a crucial one, is that he may live wherever he wishes in Aya Iraqw – the land of the Iraqw.

The Iraqw are divided into unilineal kinships groups. Although they do have shallow unnamed matrilineages which are of little importance, the Iraqw are otherwise a classic African patrilineal people. Not only do they contract marriages by the payment of bridewealth in the form of livestock, but they also practice the true levirate and ghost marriage. Iraqw elders are able to trace their genealogies back nine or ten generations in the male line. The entire population is divided into some hundred named clans. Any individual can give the names of a large number of them, and a man is able to give the clan affiliation of

161

most of the people with whom he has any contact. The clans themselves are divided into lineages, the founders of which are placed four to six generations above present-day adults. While these units are also named, outsiders tend to be unaware of them. Furthermore, no individual can give a list of the lineages which constitute his own clan. Kinship terms are generalized within the lineage and clan so that a man refers to everyone in his father's generation by the same term which he uses for the father himself, every man of his own generation by the same term which he uses for his brother, and so on. An adult man can usually name all the descendants of his grandfather, but no one can list all of the members of his lineage, much less of his clan. The members of any given clan or lineage are dispersed throughout the Iraqw country. Though lineages and clans are exogamous, they are not corporate groups: they control no property, they conduct no ceremonies, they hold no meetings. It might be asked why people are so well versed about the clan affiliations of others if those affiliations are of such little importance. One answer is that a knowledge of them provides a means by which individuals can erect scaffolds upon which they can build acquaintanceships and friendships. In much the same way that middle-class Englishmen or Americans, upon meeting, inquire about such matters as place of birth, schools or universities attended, and occupation, so do the Iraqw in similar situations inquire about clan affiliations. It is virtually impossible for two Iraqw to fail to find a kinship link within a very short time; ultimately, given the extension of kinship terminology, all Iraqw are relatives. It is not, I should hasten to add, that the Iraqw, as has been reported for some peoples, need to fit someone into a kinship category so that they will know what attitudes or behaviour patterns they should adopt. For instance, if *A* recalls that a woman of his clan, a woman to whom he is unable to trace his relationship in precise genealogical terms, married someone in *B*'s clan, he and *B* do not treat each other in ways which are specially appropriate for men who are brothers-in-law; rather it is merely that once some link has been established they feel more comfortable about the situation.

In terms of territorial groupings there are two levels at which people are organized above that of the household. The first of these is the local community. Individual households are grouped together to form neighborhoods or villages, one of which may contain as many as three or four hundred people. People who live in the same villages have duties and obligations towards one another and they have a strong sense of interdependence. For example, building a house, or repairing one should part of it have collapsed as the result of a heavy rain, is a major undertaking and requires an amount of labor far beyond the resources of the household. On an occasion of this sort each household supplies at least one worker to the household in need. The village, however, is very loosely organized, having no institutionalized position of authority nor any formal conciliar arrangements. Again, while rites are carried out within villages, they are performed on a household basis. The village as a collective entity does not engage in ritual activity.

The second level of territorial organization is that of the county. The county, which often covers an area of thirty or forty square miles, contains a number of villages and has a population of several thousand. Each county has a council of elders which meets frequently and conducts its affairs in a formal manner. One individual occupies a position of *primus inter pares* and is held primarily responsible for maintaining good relations with the Great Diviners, but otherwise he has little authority. These councils do not consist of representatives of subgroups found within the county, either villages or kin groups; instead any elder, roughly speaking, anyone above the age of fifty, is welcome, indeed urged, to attend its meetings. The meetings are held in the open air away from any house. Although these meetings are readily visible – one group regularly holds its meetings within fifty yards of the main road running through the district – there is nevertheless an air of secrecy surrounding them. The elders do not discuss their affairs with younger men, and during the German and British periods there was a conspiracy of silence designed to keep the government from gaining too much knowledge of their activities and, in particular, their relations with the Great Diviners. The acts of the German administrators, and some of the earlier British ones as well, led the Iraqw to consider it possible that the Europeans might take away their Great Diviners, which, given their premises, would have left them in an impossible situation.

The county councils are concerned entirely with ritual matters. The elders see themselves as being collectively responsible for carrying out the proper rites, rites whose performance they consider to be essential for the welfare of the inhabitants of the county. The most important aim of these rites is to insure a proper amount of rain at the right season, rain for the crops, rain which will produce pasturage, and rain which will provide surface supplies of water. If the rites are not carried out, they believe they would face drought, famine, and death.

In order to understand these rites it is necessary to outline the religious beliefs of the Iraqw. They believe themselves to be in contact with three categories of supernatural beings, *Loa*, the spirits of the dead, and certain earth-dwelling spirits who are numerous but who are usually referred to by the singular form *Netlangw*.

Loa, a female deity, dwells in the sky and is associated with the sun. She is seen as being responsible for the steady state of the universe, for such things as the alternation of day and night, the orderly progression of the seasons of the year, and the like. But, despite Her importance, the vast bulk of the ritual practiced by the Iraqw at both the individual and communal level is concerned either with the spirits of the dead or with the earth-dwelling spirits.

In the present context little need be said about the spirits of the dead. The spirits of the dead, and I use this term rather than ancestors because a man may perform a rite directed towards his deceased wife, should be honored and can cause misfortunes. Sacrifices which are directed towards them are made at the homestead and on behalf of the members of the household; they are not, and this is a point which I wish to emphasize, made by or on behalf of large lineage segments.

The earth-dwelling spirits, although they are thought to live within mountains, under groves of trees, or under certain isolated, gigantic trees, are associated primarily with water. They live in the earth beneath streams or any body of water. Water, in fact, is dependent upon their presence. If a source of water dries up, it is said to have done so because the spirit has moved away. Furthermore, these spirits can interfere with the rainfall, of which more will be said later. Their importance in the daily lives of the Iraqw goes far beyond this, though, since most illnesses are attributed to them.

As a result of certain events, individuals contract states of ritual impurity: when a man dies, his wife becomes impure; when a woman gives birth to an illegitimate child, she becomes impure; when a man is clawed by a leopard, he becomes impure. For each of these states the Iraqw have a separate word. When an individual contracts one of these states of impurity, his well-being, indeed his life, is in jeopardy. It is the earth-dwelling spirits who are disturbed by these states of ritual impurity and they are the ones whom an individual fears. A purification ceremony, which usually involves the sacrifice of a sheep or a goat, must be held. After this has taken place the individual must remain in seclusion for a period which may vary from a few days to a year depending upon the type of ritual impurity involved. The reason for this is that once the purification rite has taken place, the person constitutes a danger to others, since the ritual impurity which is leaving him may be contracted by other people if they should come into contact with him.

When a man is ill or when someone in his household is ill, he consults a diviner. Very often he is told that the person who is ill has contracted a state of ritual impurity from someone else, and it is suggested to him, again after divination, that a ceremony be carried out to appease the earth-dwelling spirits. A person who has contracted ritual impurity at second hand is usually not required to sacrifice livestock, and furthermore the ritual impurity drains away very rapidly once the purification rite has been carried out.

There now remains the matter of the relevance of these ideas to the rites conducted by the councils of elders. As we have seen, individuals are endangered by ritual states of impurity and they are responsible for setting matters right by appropriate ritual action. However, it is assumed in an area as large as a county that one or more individuals, despite the risk which they run, have not performed the necessary rites of purification. As a result, the earth-dwelling spirits are angered and they may, in addition to punishing the guilty individuals, interfere with the rain. The Iraqw explain rainfall in the following way: they say it originates in the mists which rise from the earth. The mists form clouds from which rain falls in due course. The earth-dwelling spirits, stationed as they are at the point where the whole process begins, can prevent it from following its normal course. It thus becomes necessary for the elders to perform rites which will cleanse the county, although these rites do not cleanse the individuals whose impurities make them necessary. The rites themselves, which involve the sacrifice of a sheep or a goat, are very simple. They are usually conducted by a few elders accompanied by a small number of youths in a secluded place. Other people in the county need not concern themselves with these rites; they are content in their belief that the elders are conducting affairs to the best of their ability on behalf of all.

Although the rites themselves are, as I have said, extremely simple and every elder knows how to conduct them, yet in any particular instance the elders, by themselves, are at a loss as to how to proceed. They do not know for certain from what particular types of ritual impurity they must cleanse the county, nor do they know what type of animal must be sacrificed. In one case it may be necessary to sacrifice a brown sheep with one white ear; in another instance it may be necessary to offer a white sheep with one brown spot on its flank. Information of this type can be obtained only from the Great Diviners. Ordinary diviners who carry out divination for individuals are thought not to have the power to do so for counties. The power to divine on behalf of counties is restricted to a certain lineage, and within it only certain individuals are thought to possess the proper gifts. Diviners, including the Great Diviners, are considered to be diagnosticians, and it is significant that the Iraqw, who have had contact with European administrators, missionaries, and physicians, apply their own word for diviner (*qwaslarmo*) only to the last category. The Great Diviners are not tied into the territorial system in a rigid or direct manner. A Great Diviner may live in the county for which he prescribes ritual procedures or he may not, he may prescribe for one county or for many. Furthermore, a county council may, in order to be on the safe side, follow the prescriptions of more than one Great Diviner. The Great Diviners, then, are not only not chiefs, but they are not rainmakers in the sense of being individuals who control the elements by magical means. However, they are accorded a tremendous amount of respect and rewarded with presents for their efforts.

I have now described certain features of the social structure of the Iraqw and I have given an outline of their supernatural beliefs and practices. I have also tried to show the rationale behind the rites carried out at the county level. I now want to pursue further the matter of the interrelationships between the social structure and the religious system. I find this difficult to do, partly because of an inadequate vocabulary. I think that I can clarify the points which I am trying to make by comparing the Iraqw data with facts drawn from another people, the Amba, with whom I have also worked.

The Amba, of whom there are some thirty thousand, are an agricultural people who live in Uganda in the forest country at the foot of the Ruwenzori Mountains. They live in small villages containing a few hundred people at most. These small units were, until the advent of the European era, when the area in which they live came under the control of Toro, one of the Interlacustrine kingdoms, independent political bodies. A village consists of a set of men who can trace their descent patrilineally from a common ancestor plus their wives (who come from other villages since the lineages are exogamous) and their children. The village community is then the territorial expression of the lineage. Men live in one village and not in another because the one in which they live is the place which belongs to their lineage; a place in which they have both a right and an obligation to live.

Although the Iraqw, like the Amba, utilize patrilineal kinship principles, the vital point is that they do not utilize them in the construction of territorial groupings. Clans and lineages are not localized. Furthermore, no particular lineage occupies a special status in any locality; there are no dominant lineages. An Iraqw by virtue of his status as a member of a given lineage does not have a stronger right than anyone else to take up residence in a given locality. By the same token, he is not excluded from residence in a locality by virtue of his lineage affiliations or

o   167

kinship status. In extreme cases one can find a village in which every householder belongs not only to a different lineage but to a different clan. People are fellow-villagers, fellow-members of the same county, purely and simply because they live in the same area. I am not trying to say that there are not kinship links between villagers or between people who live in the same county. I have previously indicated that, given the extended usage of kinship terminology, all Iraqw are ultimately related to one another. The point is that kinship links are recognized between people who are neighbors because they are neighbors; they are not neighbors because of them. Rights and duties of people who live in the same village are defined in terms of neighborliness, not in terms of kinship. Thus one man helps another to repair his house because the latter is his neighbor, not because they have some remote kinship link. By contrast, among the Amba, one helps one's neighbor in similar situations because he is an agnatic kinsman, and he is your neighbor because he is a kinsman.

The structural principle utilized within Iraqw territorial groups is *spatial contiguity* itself. Although anthropologists working in Africa have not isolated this as a principle in the way in which they have isolated the lineage principle, there seems to be no intrinsic reason why it should not be utilized. However, when it is used, certain peculiar problems are raised for the analyst which are not raised when a lineage principle is employed. Granted the people within a territorial group are held together by ties of neighborliness, there is still the problem of why such a group exists in the form that it does; why it is the size that it is. Again, why should a people such as the Iraqw be organized territorially at three levels, the household, the village, and the county; why not four levels or why not two? To answer these questions recourse must be had to an additional organizational principle.

Again, I may be able to clarify the point which I am trying to make by reference to the Amba. If one inquires why, in a given part of their country, there are eighteen villages and not ten or thirty, the answer is very simple: there are eighteen villages, no more and no less, because eighteen lineages are localized in the area. If one asks why some villages have larger populations than others, the answer is that some lineages are larger than others. As a final example, if one asks why four adjacent villages are not united into a larger social entity, the answer is that the four villages are occupied by unrelated lineages, and in terms of the system there is no mechanism which could unite them. Similar questions are not so readily answered among the Iraqw because the principle of contiguity by itself does not answer them.

The smallest territorial unit, the household, is not problematical here because it is a kinship group, and its analysis presents no peculiar problems. The levels of organization which are problematical are those of the village and the county. At these levels, the principle involved is one which, for want of a better word, I have called *utilitarian*. The groups take the form they do because of the services they perform for the individual households, for the benefits which they confer upon them. The individual household, though it strives for self-sufficiency, could be seriously harmed or even destroyed were it not for the existence of a wider community from which help can be obtained in emergencies. Such a community must be of a certain minimum size, perhaps a dozen or so households. At the other end of the scale it seems that if the population increases, a point is reached at which people begin to lose contact with one another in terms of the system of reciprocity, and the village splits into two.

Thus I would hold that there are good practical reasons why a unit such as the village should exist, and why a particular village should not grow too large. Nevertheless, such practical reasons do not account for the existence of the counties from the point of view of the anthropological observer. However, from the point of view of the Iraqw, the reasons for the existence of a county level of organization are equally practical, equally, perhaps even more, important. As they see it, if the proper rites were not performed, rain would not fall.

Granting the necessity of these rites for the Iraqw, we may raise the question of why they should be carried out at the level of the county. Two alternatives immediately spring to mind; they could be carried out at the village level, each village performing its own rites, or they could be carried out at one place for the Iraqw people as a whole. Here again I think the answers can be sought in practical terms. For one thing, in any territorial unit larger than a county many of the elders, some of whom are very old men, would find it too difficult to walk to the meeting-place. Furthermore, and I think this is a more important reason, the organization of communal ritual on a county basis makes sense in terms of the patterns of rainfall. Rainfall varies considerably throughout the country occupied by the Iraqw. Some areas receive much more rain than others, the basic pattern being that areas near the edge of the escarpment receive a good deal of rain, while areas further away from it receive less. However, even areas which receive about the same amount of rainfall, when it is averaged over a number of years, may, in any given year, have quite different experiences in this regard. Often one can stand in the sunlight in one county and see the rain falling heavily a few miles away in another county. Villages, however, are so small that it is very rare for one of them to receive rainfall when others in the same vicinity remain dry. Thus it makes sense that the group of people who see themselves as facing the same rainfall conditions should cooperate ritually to solve the problems, as they visualize them, which are involved, and that, since a group of this sort is invariably larger than a village and yet smaller than the entire Iraqw people, this cooperation should take place on some intermediate level. The effect of this concern with rain, coupled with their view of the role of the supernatural in its control, is the creation of corporate groups above the village level.

Reverting to a point made earlier about the relative importance of religious ideas and practices in regard to the social structure (not, I must emphasize, in terms of their importance to the total way of life of a given people, which is quite a different question), I would argue that among the Iraqw they occupy a *pivotal* role while in many other African societies their role is *peripheral*.

Among the Amba, for instance, while a rite carried out by the largest territorial unit, the village, can be seen as aiding its integration in a simple Radcliffe-Brown sense of inculcating and strengthening the proper sentiments of loyalty and identification with the collectivity, or while it can be seen as stating and

170

resolving conflicts within the group, yet the village itself is defined and organized in other terms. Thus the religious system occupies a peripheral role since it is at most a prop to the social structure or a means by which certain organizational problems can be solved. By contrast, among the Iraqw the widest territorial group which acts in a unitary fashion, the county, is defined and organized in purely ritual terms. Putting this another way, if men's minds in the two societies could be selectively brain-washed so that all knowledge of supernatural matters were lost, the social structure of the Amba would remain the same but the social structure of the Iraqw would not; the counties would disappear. To put the matter still a third way, a society in which religion plays a pivotal part in the social structure is one in which one cannot describe the social structure without paying considerable attention to religious matters. By contrast, a society in which religion plays a peripheral role is one in which religion need not be mentioned. The social structure of the Iraqw cannot be described without taking religion into account; that of the Amba can. A well-known example of a lineage-based society in which religion plays a peripheral role is provided by the Nuer. Evans-Pritchard was able to write two volumes about their social structure without finding it necessary to involve himself in a discussion of their supernatural beliefs.

CONCLUSION

Fortes (1953) once wrote, 'It has taken twenty years for the Trobrianders to be placed in a proper comparative perspective. . . .' It might equally well be said that a major preoccupation of social anthropologists in recent years has been that of placing the Nuer and the Tallensi in perspective.

Evans-Pritchard and Fortes have had a profound effect upon the thought of the social anthropologist who have been trained in the post-war period, especially those who have worked in Africa. Though it is characteristic of the social sciences that a few key figures exert a great influence over the work of their colleagues, anthropologists are also influenced to an enormous extent by the nature of their field experience, by the characteristics of the societies which they themselves have studied at first hand; it is this which sets them apart from other social scientists and often from each other. The tensions created between the received intellectual tradition and the field experience give rise to new problems, new insights, and new controversies. Some of the controversies which have arisen in social anthropology within recent years can be attributed, in large measure, to the fact that the disputants have worked in societies of quite different types.

However, if we confine the discussion to Africa, it can be said, to put the matter in the simplest possible terms, that, in the last decade and a half, fieldworkers have found themselves confronted by two types of society, those which are like the Nuer or the Tallensi and those which are not. When societies similar to the Nuer and the Tallensi have been encountered it has been possible for the anthropologists concerned to build upon the work of their predecessors in a precise manner. I speak from experience because the Amba, the first people with whom I worked, were very much like the Tallensi in particular. It is only a slight exaggeration to say that I was able to observe the people by day and read about them at night in the pages of Fortes. This meant that I could formulate hypotheses about the organization and operation of a particular type of system and then gather the data to test them. For instance, I was convinced that the organizational form of a society of this sort could not be maintained unless genealogies were not only telescoped but manipulated in a number of other ways on a rather extensive scale. I was able to collect data which indicated that this was in fact happening among the Amba (Winter, 1955).

The type of the theoretical stimulation provided by contact with new types of social structure is best illustrated by the work of the Manchester group under the leadership of Gluckman. For example, we find the members of this group developing and sharpening the basic notions of conflict and opposition contained in the works of Evans-Pritchard and Fortes. Again, we find them gaining new insights, not only into the societies with which they have worked, but into society in general, by trying to explain, as has been done explicitly and brilliantly by Turner (1957) in *Schism and Continuity* precisely how the systems which

172

they studied differed from the classic descriptions of patrilineally based societies.

However, although radically different societies have provided inspiration for some, they provide pitfalls for the unwary. For one thing, there is the temptation to fit the facts into the framework developed by Evans-Pritchard and Fortes, a procedure not unlike that of attempting to fit the facts of other languages into Indo-European grammatical categories, something which has long been abandoned by linguists. Somewhat more subtle is the temptation to assume, as a basic principle, that kinship linkages are all-important and that once one has demonstrated that the members of a particular group are related to one another, one has laid bare the group's structure.

In the substantive part of this essay, I have attempted to show that while territorial groupings among the Iraqw could be described in terms of kinship linkages, such a procedure would be most misleading. I have argued that spatial contiguity itself is a structural principle. I have argued, further, that utilitarianism works as a secondary principle and that, given their definition of the problems which must be solved, religious beliefs and practices play a crucial role in the delineation and integration of territorial groups of a certain type. I do not believe that the social structure of the Iraqw is unique. Instead, I believe that there are many similar systems in Africa and that their analysis constitutes a considerable challenge.

The foregoing statement leads to a final point. Sir Henry Maine drew a distinction between societies based upon kinship and those based upon territoriality. In its day this was a useful dichotomy but that day has passed, even though some anthropologists appear to be unaware of the fact. If *The Nuer* did nothing else, it showed, in detail, that in many societies one is faced not with determining whether or not the system is based upon a kinship *or* a territorial basis but rather with the problem of showing how kinship principles are utilized to structure territorial groups. Once this point of view was understood by a number of social anthropologists, it became possible for them to analyze a number of systems in a highly illuminating manner. This point of view can be pushed too far, though, if it is assumed that in all tribal societies territorial groups are based upon

173

kinship principles. What must be adopted is what might be termed a neo-Mainian position. While recognizing the fact that all societies have both territorial and kinship modes of organization, and that in some kinship principles may be used to structure territorial groups, we must be prepared to face the fact that even in many of the so-called simpler societies, all localized groups above the level of the household may be organized in terms of principles other than those of kinship, and that among these principles may be that of spatial, or to use Maine's own term, local contiguity (Maine, 1861).

REFERENCES

BOHANNAN, P. 1963. *Social Anthropology.* New York: Holt Rinehart & Winston.

EVANS-PRITCHARD, E. E. 1956. *Nuer Religion.* Oxford: Clarendon Press.

FORTES, M. 1953. The Structure of Unilineal Descent Groups. *American Anthropologist* **55**: 17-41.

—— 1959. *Oedipus and Job in West African Religion.* Cambridge: Cambridge University Press.

MAINE, H. 1861. *Ancient Law.* London: J. Murray.

MIDDLETON, J. 1960. *Lugbara Religion.* London: Oxford University Press.

TURNER, V. W. 1957. *Schism and Continuity in an African Society.* Manchester: Manchester University Press.

WINTER, E. 1955. *Bwamba.* Cambridge: Heffer.

NOTES ON CONTRIBUTORS

BRADBURY, ROBERT ELWYN. Born 1929, England; studied at London University, B.A., Ph.D.

Research Fellow, International African Institute, 1952; Research Assistant, University College, London, 1954; Research Fellow, University College, Ibadan, 1956; Lecturer, University College, London, 1961; Lecturer in West African Anthropology, University of Birmingham, 1964.

Author of *The Benin Kingdom and the Edo-speaking Peoples*, 1957.

EGGAN, FRED. Born 1906, Seattle, Washington; studied at The University of Chicago, B.A., M.A., Ph.D.

Harold H. Swift Distinguished Service Professor of Anthropology and Director, Philippine Studies Program, University of Chicago.

Author of *Social Organization of the Western Pueblos*, 1950; 'Social Anthropology and the Method of Controlled Comparison' (*American Anthropologist*, Vol. 56, 1954); 'Social Anthropology: Methods and Results' (in *Social Anthropology of North American Tribes*, 1955).

Editor of *Social Anthropology of North American Tribes*, 1937, Enlarged Edition, 1955.

GEERTZ, CLIFFORD. Born 1926, U.S.A.; educated at Antioch College, B.A.; Harvard University, Ph.D.

Instructor in Anthropology, Harvard University, 1956-7; Fellow, Center for Advanced Study in the Behavioral Sciences, Palo Alto, 1958-9; Assistant Professor of Anthropology, University of California, Berkeley, 1958-60; Assistant Professor of Anthropology, 1960-2, Associate Professor 1962-4, Professor, 1964, University of Chicago.

Author of *The Religion of Java*, 1960; *Agricultural Involution* 1964; *Peddlers and Princes*, 1964; *The Social History of a Javanese Town*, 1965.

Editor of *Old Societies and New States*, 1963.

GLUCKMAN, MAX. Born 1911, South Africa; studied at The University of Witwatersrand, B.A.; Oxford, D.Phil.

Anthropologist, Rhodes-Livingstone Institute, 1939-42; Director, 1942-7; Lecturer in Social Anthropology, Oxford, 1947-9; Prefessor of Social Anthropology, Manchester, 1949.

Author of *The Judicial Process among the Barotse of N.*

Notes on Contributors

Rhodesia, 1954; *Custom and Conflict in Africa*, 1955; *Order and Rebellion in Tribal Africa*, 1963; *Politics, Law and Ritual in Tribal Societies*, 1965; *The Ideas in Barotse Jurisprudence*, 1965. Editor of *Seven Tribes of British Central Africa*, 1951; *Closed Systems and Open Minds*, 1964.

SPIRO, MELFORD E. Born 1920, Cleveland, Ohio; studied at University of Minnesota, A.B.; Northwestern University, Ph.D.

Instructor and Assistant Professor of Anthropology, Washington University (St Louis), 1948-52; Assistant and Associate Professor of Anthropology, University of Connecticut, 1952-7; Professor of Anthropology, University of Washington, 1957-64; Professor of Anthropology, University of Chicago, 1964 to date; Fellow, Center for Advanced Study in the Behavioral Sciences, 1958-9.

Author of *An Atoll Culture* (with E. G. Burrows), 1953; *Kibbutz: Venture in Utopia*, 1956; *Children of the Kibbutz*, 1958.

Editor of *Context and Meaning in Cultural Anthropology: Essays in Honor of A. Irving Hallowell*, in press.

TURNER, VICTOR WITTER. Born 1920, Scotland; educated at University College, London, B.A.; Manchester, Ph.D.

Research Officer, Rhodes-Livingstone Institute, Northern Rhodesia, 1950; Research assistant in Social Anthropology, Manchester University, 1955; Simon Fellow, 1956; Lecturer, 1958; Senior Lecturer, 1960; Fellow, Center for Advanced Study in the Behavioral Sciences, 1961; Professor of Anthropology, Cornell University New York, 1963.

Author of *Schism and Continuity in an African Society*, 1957; *Ndembu Divination*, 1961; *Chihamba the White Spirit*, 1962; *Lunda Medicine and the Treatment of Disease*, 1963; and a co-author of *Essays on the Ritual of Social Relations*, 1962.

WINTER, EDWARD HENRY. Born 1923, U.S.A.; educated at Harvard University, B.A.; Oxford University; London School of Economics; Harvard University, Ph.D.

Colonial Jocial Science Research Fellow, 1949-52; Senior Research Fellow, East African Institute of Social Research, 1952-5; Assistant Professor of Anthropology, University of Illinois, 1955-7; Associate Professor, 1957-9; Professor of Anthropology and Chairman of the Department of Sociology and Anthropology, University of Virginia, 1959.

Author of *Bwamba Economy*, 1955; *Bwamba*, 1956; *Beyond the Mountains of the Moon*, 1959.

Co-editor (with J. Middleton) of *Witchcraft and Sorcery in East Africa*, 1953.